EARLY MODERN EUROPE 1500/1789

By JOHN B. WOLF

University of Illinois at Circle Campus

WILLIAM H. McNEILL, *Editor*

World Civilization Series

SCOTT, FORESMAN AND COMPANY
Glenview, Illinois   *London*

Foreword

Two assumptions underlie the Scott, Foresman World Civilization series: first, that there is such a thing as world history and not merely the history of separate civilizations and barbarisms coexisting in different parts of the world without important relations one with another; and second, that people learn more easily and with greater satisfaction if information is organized into a more complex intellectual framework than the bald matrix of a catalogue arranged according to proximity in time and space. Interpretation, then, with all the risks of omission and individual idiosyncrasy on the part of the authors; and synthesis, with whatever risks of error on the part of the editor, are the goals for which we have striven.

In any collaborative work, a key problem is how to reconcile expertise in detail with cohesion overall. In this series each author was invited to say whatever he thought ought to be said, but only within rather narrowly defined limits of space. The overall apportionment of space was regulated by a preliminary plan for which the undersigned was responsible. The basic architecture of that plan will be apparent from the titles of successive volumes; but choice of themes and apportionment of space within each volume were left to the discretion of the various authors.

The series itself has been organized to permit its use in a number of different ways. Books two through five, along with the first and last titles, make up a course in Western civilization; and books six through nine can also be used in the same way with the first and last titles to form a course in non-Western civilization. Taken together, all ten titles constitute the basic reading for a course in world civilization, while each individual book can be used either on its own or as a supplement to a conventional world history text.

How well this procedure permitted us to achieve our goals will be for each reader to decide.

William H. McNeill

EARLY MODERN EUROPE 1500/1789

ACKNOWLEDGMENTS

Cover: Siege of Magdeburg, by courtesy of the trustees of the British Museum, London.
Maps prepared by Cartographic Services Associates

FOR CAROLYN, CLARK, AND LAURA

SCOTT, FORESMAN
WORLD CIVILIZATION
SERIES

WILLIAM H. McNEILL
Editor

VOL. 1. ANCIENT TIMES, PREHISTORIC-500 B.C., GERALD KADISH

VOL. 2. GREECE AND ROME
750 B.C.-565 A.D.
A. R. BURN WITH J. M. B. Edwards

VOL. 3. EUROPE'S MIDDLE AGES
565-1500 A.D.
KARL F. MORRISON

VOL. 4. EARLY MODERN EUROPE
1500-1789 A.D.
JOHN B. WOLF

VOL. 5. MODERN EUROPE
1789-1914 A.D.
PETER N. STEARNS

VOL. 6. CLASSICAL EMPIRES OF ASIA
TO 630 A.D.
JAMES T. C. LIU AND J. A. B. VAN BUITENEN

VOL. 7. ISLAM AND THE MOSLEM IMPACT ON ASIA
SOUTHEAST EUROPE, AND AFRICA, TO 1500 A.D.
REUBEN SMITH

VOL. 8. THE NON-EUROPEAN WORLD, 1500-1850 A.D.
JOHANNA M. MESKILL, JOHN MESKILL,
AINSLIE T. EMBREE

VOL. 9. EMERGENCE OF WORLD COSMOPOLITANISM
1850-1950 A.D.
D. ANTHONY LOW, ALBERT H. HOURANI,
JOHN R. W. SMAIL, RALPH A. AUSTEN

VOL. 10. THE CONTEMPORARY WORLD, 1914-PRESENT, WILLIAM H. McNEILL

Preface

Until 1945, American texts customarily presented the history of early modern Europe as a dismal era of absolutism, marked by tyranny, social injustice, and senseless wars fought for the personal glory or dynastic interests of princes. This was in nice contrast to the Renaissance, presented as a period of individualism, or the French Revolution, seen as the opening of modern times. Even the experience of the Great War of 1914–1918 did not bring textbook writers to consider war as a process in society, and therefore to study the earlier ones carefully. Had not the war of 1914–1918 been been fought to "end all wars" and "to make the world safe for democracy"? In such a climate of opinion, it is not surprising that historians concentrated on the fortunate development of individualism, liberalism, popular sovereignty, and the other social dogmas of the nineteenth century which were believed to characterize the United States and which would be adopted everywhere on the globe as soon as other peoples were sufficiently developed.

In the period before and after the Second World War, this optimism suffered rude shocks: the rise of totalitarian regimes in Europe, the catastrophe of the Second World War and the Cold War, the emergence of dictatorial regimes out of the ruins of colonial empires, the threat of atomic war—all these developments threaten our liberal democratic ideals. In the new intellectual climate that resulted, we gain a changed appreciation of the early modern European scene. Once we see war as a process in our civilization rather than simply as an evil, the earlier experience may illuminate our own problems. We can see the state-building efforts of princes in a light other than selfish tyranny: in terms of the realities they faced rather than in terms of our own assumptions.

There is another aspect of early modern European history that has been neglected. Until recently, intellectual history tended to jump from a discussion of Renaissance humanism to the eighteenth-century *philosophes.* Since the Second World War, however, scholars have been focusing on the history of science. Western men imposed themselves upon other peoples around the globe by virtue of their military, economic, and political power, and fundamental to all of these was the epistemology of science and the emergence of the scientific-technological structures of the modern era. To understand this development, one must look into the processes that were responsible for the scientific revolution of the seventeenth century.

This text is intended as an introduction to the three centuries after 1500, a period vital in the formation of the institutions of Western society. Hopefully, it will provide insight into the complex development of the bureaucratic police state and the international institution of the balance of power that are characteristic of Western society. It should also help to explain the processes in Western civilization that allowed European men to dominate the globe and impose their political and economic institutions upon other peoples.

Like the others in this series, this book is intended to be a reliable frame of reference as well as an interpretative essay. At the end of each chapter there is a short bibliography of additional reading available in paperback editions; if the student wishes to go beyond these, he should consult John Roach, ed., *A Bibliography of Modern History* (New York and Cambridge, Cambridge University Press, 1968). There are also available a number of useful collections of readings. These are of two kinds; the first presents excerpts from historical sources to give the student a glimpse into the minds and assumptions of the men whose society he is studying. Andrew Lossky, ed., *The Seventeenth Century* (New York, The Free Press, 1967) and Herbert H. Rowen, *From Absolutism to Revolution: 1648–1848,* rev. ed. (New York, The Macmillan Company, 1968) are good examples of this type. The second presents excerpts from the works of distinguished historians to provide interpretation. Orest Ranum, *Searching for Modern Times,* 2 vols. (New York, Dodd Mead & Company, 1969), Brison D. Gooch, *Interpreting European History,* 2 vols. (Homewood, Ill., Dorsey Press, 1967), Norman Cantor and Samuel Bernstein, eds., *Problems in European History, Vol. 2: Early Modern Europe, 1500–1815.* (New York, T. Y. Crowell, 1970), and John Rule, ed., *Critical Issues in History,* 5 vols. [vol 4: *The Early Modern Era, 1648–1770*] (Lexington, Mass., D. C. Heath & Company, 1966)—each has certain advantages and special features.

Like any writer, I owe many debts to other scholars for ideas and interpretations, and to institutions for the use of books and manuscripts that have contributed to my picture of early modern Europe. At this time, I can only thank them without mentioning their names and hope that I have properly used the understandings that they have given me.

John B. Wolf

Contents

Chapter 1

Europe in the Early Sixteenth Century

At the opening of the sixteenth century there were six relatively advanced civilizations, or complexes of civilized communities, scattered over the globe. Two of these (India and China) were in Asia, a third (the Turco-Arabic society) occupied the Middle East, a fourth consisted of the Christian civilizations in Europe, the fifth covered sub-Sahara Africa, and the sixth was in the Americas. No one of these groups could be described as a homogeneous community, since in each there were differences of language, racial stock, economy, social and religious forms; however, much greater differences existed among the major complexes, thus marking them as separate societies. Indeed, even though the peoples of the various civilizations were all principally concerned with agriculture, animal husbandry, and, perhaps, fishing, their religious beliefs, social and political organizations, and modes of life were evidence of great variety in their historical evolution. There had long been some contact and a measure of cultural diffusion among them, at least among the four societies that occupied the Eurasian continent, but the enormous distances—measured in terms of time as well as the dangers that faced the traveler—placed limitations upon movements between and among the several complexes. In general, it might be said that in 1500 the four cultures occupying the Eurasian continent were more or less at the same stage of technological development and social stability. The Islamic societies of the Middle East and India may have had a slight advantage in military and political organization, and the Chinese may have had a more stable social structure, but the Christian Europeans seem to have been the more adventurous, for they made the first meaningful contacts with Asia, Africa, and the Americas. In 1500, however, it would have been a bold, perhaps even a rash man who would have predicted that the peoples of western Europe, whose political order could only be described as a melee of confusion and conflict, would actually establish a hegemony over all the other societies of the globe; indeed, that they would practically force the others to adapt themselves to the social, economic, and political patterns that were emerging in the West.

This fact seems to represent one of the most important questions to which the historian can address himself: How did it happen that these Western Christian societies achieved this hegemony? In the twentieth century, most of the problems of the entire world seem to flow from the impact of European ideas and institutions upon other peoples of the earth, or from the non-European world's efforts to adjust to those ideas and institutions. The processes by which this interesting situation developed are obviously complex, and understanding them must include consideration of the historical evolution of both European and non-European peoples. So pretentious a study is clearly beyond the limits of this short text, and yet the European story of the years between 1500 and 1789 obviously must throw much light upon the question since it was in these years that the European peoples first emerged with the power to assume their self-appointed place as masters of the destinies of the earth.

EUROPE, 1500

Political Characteristics. What do we mean by the terms "Europe" and "European Christian Society" in 1500? The concept "Christian Europe" has had many interpretations. It once meant only the area included in the Gallo-Roman West in contrast with the Byzantine-Oriental East; in the twentieth century, it surely includes everything west of the Urals, perhaps both North and South America, and maybe even South Africa, Australia, and New Zealand. In 1500 there were Christian European peoples living in Poland, Hungary, Scandinavia, Russia, and on the Baltic coast, but they were unquestionably on the frontier of Christian Europe which should largely be defined as the territory covered by the Holy Roman Empire, Italy, and the kingdoms of England, France, and the Iberian peninsula.

In a sense, at the opening of the sixteenth century we find European society delineated by the same political power complexes that loom large in the twentieth century: Germany, England, France, Spain, and Italy. But there are enormous differences between the sixteenth-century kingdoms of those areas and their twentieth-century successors. The sixteenth-century political congeries may have had names that can be confused with modern states, but they were not at all the same sort of political entities.

These sixteenth-century "states" had emerged from an ancient past and bore witness to their history in their political institutions. Their rulers governed a complex of estates, quasi-independent towns, feudal vassals, and corporate institutions sometimes largely independent of the crown. Rebellion was endemic and in some cases even recognized as a legal right. There were many contests for the control of the crown. In 1500 the Tudor dynasty had been on the throne of England for some fifteen years, having won it after a long and bloody civil war; the kings of Aragon and Castile confronted rebellion by their Moorish subjects, Aragonese separatism, and immensely rich and powerful grandees whose wealth allowed them to regard themselves as peers of the kings. The French Valois family had only recently secured its throne against powerful vassals—who happened also to be kings of England (Hundred Years' War)—and had still to face possible rebellion by dukes, peers, and princes who resented the centralizing policies of the royal government. In Germany, the situation was even more complex. France was a "federal" kingdom, but the Holy Roman Empire of the German nation was at best a "confederation" of principalities, clerical lands, free cities, monastic foundations, and other quasi-independent estates loosely bound together under the emperor and the Diet. All clamored for recognition of "German liberties," i.e., their rights to govern themselves, and, on another level, the vassals insisted upon their "liberties" vis-à-vis their overlords. The emperor's power to act as emperor was limited by lack of money and soldiers, his coronation oath, traditions, and the "constitution" of the empire. Obviously, then, none of these sixteenth-century rulers had the power to control his subjects, regulate public life, or mobilize military potentials in the manner of a modern state.

Since in most of these kingdoms and principalities the right to rule—that is, the succession to the crown—was regulated by heredity (as was the succession to property or fiefs), dynastic politics played an important role in the internal as well as the external affairs of these states. On the internal level, when a vassal died without heirs, his fief reverted to the crown. In the same vein, two French kings in succession found it expedient to marry a princess of Brittany to be sure that that province should not escape the French crown. In the area of external politics, the problem was even more complex. Practically all the crowns of Europe had enlarged the areas under their control by inheriting provinces or kingdoms as the result of planned and/or lucky marriages. Thus, princesses were pawns in the game of diplomacy, and family agreements were the basis for the erection of sovereign authority. As we shall see, early in the sixteenth century the Austrian Hapsburg family came close to inheriting all the crowns of Europe as a result of successful marriage alliances.

However, the mere fact that the same man might wear the crowns of many separate provinces did not necessarily unite those provinces in any but a personal union. Indeed, the constitutional structures of these sixteenth-century political entities were so varied as to defy description. Most kingdoms, principalities, and provinces within the realms still retained some form of parliament (Estates in France, Diet in Central Europe, Cortez in Spain, Landtag in Germany) in which the politically important *estates,* or classes, usually clergy, nobility, and wealthy townsmen, met to present grievances or requests and to vote subsidies for the prince. But there was no common pattern. In England, with its "unitary" constitution, Parliament was drawn from the lords, temporal and spiritual, and from the country gentlemen and important townsmen of the entire realm. Under the Tudor kings, who proved astute parliamentarians, it enjoyed great powers over political and religious affairs. In contrast to England's rulers, the kings of France, Aragon, Bohemia, and the Burgundian complex each ruled over a "federation" of provinces or kingdoms that may or may not have had their own parliamentary bodies; in some cases, there would also be a General Estates, or Diet, that would bring together representatives from all the provinces or principalities in a particular realm. The Holy Roman Empire, as a confederation, presented the most complex situation. Nearly all of its principalities had a *Landtag;* the so-called Burgundian inheritance had a General Estates, as well as provincial ones; the free towns were joined in the Hansa league; and the Empire as a whole had a Diet of three houses—electors, princes, and towns.

This mélange of institutions reflects the basic fact that the society of Europe, from which these states emerged, was not the same from place to place; there had been feudal *laws* and feudal *estates*, but no single feudal *law* or feudal *estate*. These differences had not been resolved by the sixteenth century.

Princes and kings also played varying roles in the context of their political traditions. The king originally was a soldier who led his vassals to war to defend the kingdom. Medieval kings had been expected to care for their governmental expenses out of the income from their domain lands, and the costs of their military actions were borne by the military services due them from their vassals. By the end of the thirteenth century, however, more money was needed to carry on the activities that had become necessary to govern a kingdom. The king's normal income was not enough. The need for "subsidies" had been the first reason for assembling the Estates or *Stände* to advise the king; along with advice, they were asked to give money. As long as the requests were modest, these subsidies could be granted after some recognition of grievances. But there was a serious limitation on the amount of money that any prince could hope to raise. In the first place, Europe did not produce great surpluses that could easily be drained off for the needs of state; secondly, the very people who did have surplus money, or who were at least able to live comfortably on their incomes, were the privileged classes, who could refuse to pay taxes. Their personal or corporate privileges and liberties protected them from paying taxes. The result was that new revenues had to come either from the slender flow of trade that could be taxed by tariffs or excise dues, or from impositions on the peasants and poor, who could not defend themselves except by the endemic rebellions that marked the incursions of the tax collectors. Thus, the executive powers of the kings of Europe were severely limited by the narrow base for their revenue collections.

Some princes were better off than others. By 1500 the king of France had the right to collect a war tax, the *taille,* from his richest provinces, without further authorization from the Estates of the realm. In other of his provinces (*pays d'état*), he had to bargain with the provincial parliaments. The king of England was usually given a "subsidy" for life at the opening of his reign; if he needed more money, he had to go to Parliament for it. Most

4

German princes could not hope for anything from their *Landtage* beyond the right to collect an excise tax. And in all cases, even if taxes were granted, it was not always easy to collect them; princes lacked administrative personnel, and their subjects often either refused to pay or rebelled.

As we have said, the king was a soldier. He was also a judge. But there were considerable variations in the exercise of these roles. By 1500, mercenary companies had largely taken the place of the feudal array, but they were expensive. The king hired troops for garrison duty in his fortifications and to act as guards in his court. In event of war, he would expand the army for a campaign, but at the end of the campaign the soldiers were dismissed. The soldiers were usually hired by a captain or general commissioned to recruit his company or army; the government paid the officer a lump sum, and he took care of all details. The war ministry did not emerge until the seventeenth century as the directing agent for the army.

The judicial functions were even more varied. There were seignorial courts, towns courts, church courts, and royal courts. The latter tended to gain ascendency because they provided an opportunity for appeal. In addition to the regular courts, subjects could direct appeals, petitions, protests, and the like directly to the king. Some of them would be handled by the king, his chancellor, or his privy council; others would be referred to regular courts of justice. But there was no standard practice for all of Europe, and in most of Europe in 1500 justice was a matter of favoritism, bribes, or chance. It was not until the late seventeenth and eighteenth centuries that even the advanced countries provided proper justice for most of their subjects.

The complexity of the political situation was enhanced by the fact that provinces, lands, even kingdoms that came under the rule of a family, usually retained their unique institutions. This is so true that it can be said that the chief political problem in France from 1500 to the present has been the unification of the kingdom. The Revolution of 1789 only continued the work of Richelieu and Louis XIV, and they in turn were expanding the programs of Louis XI and Francis I. An example of this problem of political unification that did not have the "happy solution" provided by the French Revolution and the empire is the so-called Burgundian inheritance. This was a complex of provinces and cities on the estuaries of the Rhine, the Maas, and the Scheldt rivers and in the border areas between the kingdom of France and the Holy Roman Empire. Before the death of Charles the Rash in the late fifteenth century, it also included the French duchy of Burgundy. Each of these twenty-some political entities had a separate constitution with estates, town councils, and seignorial regimes; by 1500 all had become accustomed to sending deputies to a General Estates to discuss the problems of their common ruler, the duke of Burgundy, but this should not be mistaken for unity. The city of Antwerp or the city of Ghent under certain conditions could block any measure to be taken by the whole. Moreover, these provinces, while part of the Holy Roman Empire and represented in its Diet, were situated in several different circles of that empire and therefore under different imperial orders. We should note that in the sixteenth century, the problems of this political complex were grossly enlarged when its ruler, Charles von Hapsburg, inherited the crowns of Spain and the Hapsburg crowns on the Danube. He was elected emperor of the Holy Roman Empire and thus became a universal emperor.

Along with the variety of customs and laws that separated them, the peoples of Europe spoke different languages, knew different folk tales, ate different food, and wore different styles of clothing. We usually believe, however, that they worshipped the same God at the same altars; or at least that most of Europe that lived under the rule of the Roman Catholic church did so. Even this belief is probably faulty. The intellectuals of Europe understood their theology and their church rituals more or less under a common pattern, but the peoples of Europe worshipped God quite differently. There were great variations between the religious patterns of Spain and Italy, where Mediterranean Roman culture had firm roots, and the patterns of northern Europe, where Wotan and Thor had once held sway. The religious rebellions of the sixteenth century were to show that religious Christendom was not a single entity any more than was political Christendom.

Economic and Social Aspects. Sixteenth-century princes were often tempted to formulate great plans requiring military operations by land or sea in order to strengthen their dynasties or to extend their sway, but these plans were usually jettisoned because there was seldom enough money to support them. Charles v, whose lands were scattered from the Danube to the Atlantic, quickly exhausted the treasury of his Burgundian lands and discovered that none of his other territories except Castile was able or willing to provide him with more money. Castile, because its constitution had been altered to give the crown power over taxation, and because its mariners and adventurers had discovered and exploited the riches of the Americas, could be required to shoulder most of the expenses of a universal empire, but its resources really were not equal to the task. Thus, both Charles v and his son Philip ii often found their plans thwarted by bankruptcy. Lesser princes suffered the same fate, but more quickly. Henry viii learned that it was easy to spend the treasure that his father's parsimony had accumulated, but difficult to get more. Even the kings of France, whose tax base was probably the best in all Europe, were always in need of money, always near financial ruin. The simple fact was that no prince had resources for sustained ambitious military projects. The great mass of the people lived at a sustenance level and produced little surplus that could be drained off for their king's use.

Agriculture was the principal economic activity of the people of Europe. Depending upon the section of the continent, between 85 and 95 percent of the population lived in villages and tilled the soil. In other words, about nine rural workers were required to provide enough surplus food for one urban dweller or soldier. Most of the peasants barely produced enough to support themselves. Their gardens supplied them with roots such as beets, turnips, carrots and the like, and with the leafy vegetables like cabbage, lettuce, and greens. In their fields they raised the important crops: wheat,

6

rye, oats, barley, and buckwheat, and perhaps peas or beans. These provided their basic foods: bread and porridge. The yields were pitifully small. Grain culture quickly exhausts the fertility of the soil, and since there were too few animals to provide fertilizer, each piece of land had to be left fallow every third or fourth year. If peasants in their need tried to work their lands more heavily, the price was reduced yield that they could ill afford. In the best circumstances, the yield was not more than six to eight fold, and five fold was more common. Even this required the hardest of labor that involved using all available men, women, and children in the fields. They got little help from their animals, which were too small and too easily fatigued to be of much use. In favored areas of Europe, men cultivated the vine or the olive, both of which provided exportable commodities, but most of Europe produced grain.

Even honest toil would not guarantee these people freedom from famine, which was endemic from the sixteenth through the eighteenth centuries. The primitive agriculture could not feed the population and at the same time provide surpluses for years of poor harvest. Crop failures seem to have been less frequent in the sixteenth than in the seventeenth century, when the "little ice age" descended upon the world, but they came often enough to hinder any important population growth. Famine was usually followed by the other Horseman: plague. Smallpox, typhoid, measles, and scarlet fever were also common complaints. The incidence of death from disease seems to have increased in famine years, perhaps because of malnutrition. In any case, famine and disease were the iron brooms that put limits on population and, in the seventeenth century, may actually have brought about a reduction in the total population of Europe.

Studies of the problems of demography during these centuries, when governments kept no statistical records to aid our researchers, are as yet sparse, but the work that has been done indicates broad outlines of the processes at work. For example, available evidence shows that for every hundred children born during these years only about forty-eight reached the age of twenty. In the next ten years, females tended to die more rapidly than males because of the hazards of childbirth; during their thirties, the males died more frequently. By the age of forty not more than 20 percent of the hundred still survived. Wealthy noblemen and townsmen, whose diet was somewhat better and whose way of life less hazardous, tended to live longer than peasants and lower-class townsmen, but even so very few of them reached the age of fifty-five. The occasional oldster who reached eighty was an anomaly. It will be readily seen that this population process produced a surplus of males in the twenty-to-thirty age bracket. Older men with either property or personal charm whose wives had died in childbirth might marry two or more young women, thereby preventing less desirable men from finding mates. These "surplus males" became beggars, thieves, or soldiers.

Overall, there was apparently a slight increase in the total population in Europe in the sixteenth century, but toward the end of the century the Spanish population seriously declined as a result of migration, war, high taxes, and economic crisis. In the seventeenth century, the trend for Europe as a whole was definitely downward largely because, although most areas remained quite stationary, both Spain and Germany suffered considerable losses in population. It was not until after the 1730's that the birth curve in most of Europe began to show measurable advances over the death curve, and that the population, consequently, began to grow.

The social structure of the various European societies provided unequal protection against the evils of the world. The central social cell for all Europe, after the family, was the parish, which, with its church, was the center for social and political activity. The parish provided important protection for the individual as well as direction and meaning for his life. In the countryside, the whole rhythm of agricultural life revolved around the parish activities: the fields were blessed in the spring; there were prayers for rain, thanksgiving prayers for good harvests; prayers for protection against brigands, and even against plans for peasant revolts. This pattern was less true in the towns where the wealthy worshipped in the same church as the artisans, the poor, or the beggars but did not share patterns of life with the lower classes. The rich in the towns had their own private sources for food and drink and the other necessities of life, and their social activities centered in the corporation or in their profession. Their poorer neighbors found company in men of their own order. In a way, the whole city with its walls, rather than the parish, was the basis for security against brigands and an oasis of peace. And yet the "quarter" and the parish were important; the church bells called men to help put out fires, to consider problems common to all, or, importantly, to pray.

Life in the towns was unquestionably less severe and more varied than in the country. City men ate better, slept more comfortably, dressed better, and lived more securely. But there also were drawbacks to city life. The problems of sewage and garbage disposal were never solved; the streets were incredibly filthy and quite unsafe after dark; the rich lived secure behind their walled enclosures, but the poor were terribly crowded in dirty, badly cared-for sections where public services were nonexistent. These urban complexes were smelly and prone to plagues and epidemics; when the wind was right, a voyager could smell Paris five miles away.

We formerly believed that most European men lived and died within a few miles of their birthplaces. This may have been true for the majority, but recent studies have shown that there was considerable movement from place to place. Surplus young males often had to leave their villages; they became vagabonds, beggars, and soldiers, or somehow found a place in urban life as hewers of wood, carriers of burdens, servants, or perhaps thieves. Moreover, the guild journeymen who made hats, barrels, shoes, or other such things, often moved from place to place after they had completed their apprenticeships; the hardening of the lines in the guilds made it difficult for them to become masters unless they could marry a master's daughter or widow, or were themselves the sons of masters. Other guilds were by nature migratory; the stonemasons, thatchers, carpenters, and others who followed the building trades wandered from one construction job to another. When to these people are added the merchants, diplomats, clerics, pilgrims, soldiers, and royal officials with their retainers, all of whom also took to the highway, we discover that there was a goodly company of men who moved from here to there carrying news and ideas, goods and royal commands, and, sometimes, disorder with them.

By the sixteenth century, the seas and rivers of Europe carried as large a flow of commercial activity as had ever been seen, even in the most prosperous years of the Roman Empire. This commerce was in the hands of merchant guilds, merchant companies, and chartered companies in various stages of capitalistic development. The entrepreneurs were taking risks by sending goods to market, but they modified those risks by joint ventures, royal support, and even a primitive form of insurance. Thus, goods from all of Europe, the Near East, the Baltic, and—via Venice, Spain, and Portugal—from Africa, Asia, and the New World of the Americas were made available to the inhabitants of the larger cities. In the course of the sixteenth century, merchant houses from Flanders, Germany, Italy, France, and England made great progress toward the creation of a capitalist structure.

There were two axes for the commerce of Europe. The older one centered in the Mediterranean: Venice was the most important point of entry for Levantine and oriental goods, but cities like Genoa, Barcelona, and Palermo shared in this trade whereby African or oriental goods were exchanged for European products and grain. The merchants of the Mediterranean basin sent their goods overland to Germany or France or, via a trading fleet, to the Atlantic and North Sea ports. The other axis joined the Atlantic with the North Sea and the Baltic with the hinterlands of the great rivers that flowed into those seas. The Spanish and Portuguese, after 1500, sent their ships around Africa to Asia and across the Atlantic to the New World, but they acted as wholesalers of colonial goods; the Dutch and to a lesser degree the merchants of England, France, and the Baltic cities thus became retailers for the Iberian commerce. Dutch or Flemish merchants found it easy to enter this trade because they had long since been the most important purchasers of the huge Spanish wool crop, and also because they were subjects of Emperor Charles v, who was also king of the Spains. On the basis of their trade in fish, woolen goods, and colonial wares, the Dutch and Flemish merchants gained a pre-eminent position in the commercial life of Europe. When they revolted against their king in the late sixteenth century, they continued to expand their economic position by trade or by war with the enemy; at the end of the century they were strong enough to round Africa on their own and invade the Iberian monopoly of the New World and Asia.

By the sixteenth century, European men understood banking procedures that allowed them to transfer large sums of money from one end of Europe to another without shipping coin or metal. The Italians were still important as bankers, but by 1500 south German and Flemish banking houses had made Augsburg and Antwerp into financial centers of Europe. These bankers loaned money to princes, operated mining concessions, transferred funds, acted as deposit banks, and even carried on a primitive casualty insurance business. Their operations were sometimes extremely hazardous for they loaned money to kings and princes whose fiscal irresponsibility often made them bad risks.

Historians have long been interested in the price structure that existed in the sixteenth century. Even before the flow of silver from the New World created rising prices, precious metals mined in central Europe had begun to flow and to generate a rise in prices. After the first quarter of the sixteenth century this process accelerated rapidly with the influx, into Spain primarily, of metal from Mexico and Peru. Little of the metal remained in Spain, for it was exchanged for goods or shipped out to pay for soldiers fighting in Italy, Germany, and Flanders. Thus, prices all over Europe responded to the influx of precious metals; by 1600, prices had risen nearly threefold in less than a century; and they were to continue to rise until about 1630 or 1640, when the mines of the New World no longer proved so productive. While this influx of precious metal tended to give buoyance to the economy, another tendency of the century had a deleterious effect on trade. Princes, confronted with war costs far beyond their means, turned to the expedient of debasing their coinage. But mixing tin or lead with silver only gave them a momentary escape from their problems, for the debased coins quickly lost value and created great difficulties in all commercial transactions. The money changer had always been an important agent; he became even more important as commerce grew and the values of money became more uncertain.

The commerce of Europe was largely in raw materials or semi-finished goods. Even traffic in cloth involved mostly pieces that had yet to be dyed, shrunk, sized, and filled. In other words, most items of intercity trade were not ready for the consumer when they arrived at their destinations. These items were worked up for use in the towns and cities of Europe by craft artisans, who practiced their trades in small shops where they made hats, shoes, barrels, clocks, guns, and the like; or by merchant manufacturers, who hired laborers to manufacture soap, mirrors, tapestry, starch, cannons, bells, books and many other items on a scale larger than could be done in the artisan shops. The artisan workers were organized into guilds that controlled the manufacturing processes and regulated the training of apprentices. By the sixteenth century, the democracy that had characterized the guilds in earlier centuries was in full decay. The master craftsmen who owned the shops were in the process of becoming capitalist entrepreneurs, and many of the guildsmen thus found their only possible livelihood in working for the merchant manufacturers.

Perhaps the most interesting development was the beginning of a method of manufacturing usually called the "putting out" system. This procedure utilized peasant labor that was free from guild controls. A merchant manufacturer would contract with some peasants to produce woolen or linen yarn; then others wove it into cloth, others dyed or bleached or shrunk the cloth, and finally, after several such "divisions of labor," the merchant put the cloth on the market. This system could be extended to other items besides cloth, provided the manufacturing process could be broken down into a number of comparatively simple tasks not requiring a large expenditure of capital for tools. Whenever larger capital outlays were necessary, the shop system with a merchant manufacturer or entrepreneur as director and with artisans or laborers doing the work was the usual solution.

It should be noted that much of the "manufacturing" in this era can best be described as *usefacture,* that is, the making at home of products for the use of the household. Both in the villages and in the towns the women spun thread, wove cloth, and made clothes for the family and servants; much of the furniture was made at home, and many, if not most, of the tools were also made there. Wandering craftsmen sometimes assisted in this work for board and lodging and a little money; most of the people of Europe could not afford to buy or order goods that were in the great commercial marts or manufactured in the shops. The economy was largely a subsistence economy which required men to "do it themselves."

Indeed, the overriding fact about the economy of sixteenth-century Europe was the relatively low productivity of its people. The great mass of agricultural workers often could not support themselves by labor in their own fields (if they had any) and had to hire themselves out to their wealthy noble or clerical neighbors or to urban merchant manufacturers, simply to make ends meet. The dues that they owed to the landlords, to the prince, and to the church were so great that there often was not enough left to keep them alive in years of crop failure. The towns and cities, too, were crowded with poor who made their living carrying burdens, cutting wood, drawing water, or playing out the roles of robber, cutpurse, or beggar. Even many skilled artisans lived on a slim margin, so that a rapid rise in the price of bread meant starvation for them, too. The ships that plied the oceans and rivers and the pack trains of goods that followed the roads served the princes of church and state, the noble landlords, and the wealthy town patricians; the mass of men had little or nothing to do with such things; they lived in rural or urban poverty and had no reason to expect any betterment in their lot. Drought or famine might increase their misery, but there was little that could transform their poverty into prosperity.

THE CHURCH IN TROUBLE

In 1500 European men were more or less united under the religious leadership of the Roman Catholic church, but there was much dissatisfaction with many aspects of that institution. Indeed, by the opening years of the sixteenth century, demands for the reform of the Church in "head and members" had reached a mighty chorus. Demagogs like Savonarola, gentle scholars like Erasmus, and statesmen like Sir Thomas More were only the more important names of the small army of pious, thoughtful persons who demanded reform. The anticlericalism and the demands for reform that had surfaced a century or more before in the conciliar movement, the Lollard and Hussite heresies, and at the Council of Constance had not been stilled by the Renaissance papacy. Indeed, the Church's history seemed to cry aloud for some reforming action: the Babylonian Captivity, the fourteenth-century schism, the conflicts between advocates of papal and conciliar authority, the failure of the Council of Constance to effect real reforms, the scandal of the fifteenth-century Renaissance papacy that encouraged corruption at all levels of the Church and brought unworthy men to high ecclesiastical positions—all were crying for change. To these voices were added others that drew inspiration from Renaissance scholarship which purified texts, prepared new editions of the Holy Scriptures, and introduced Platonic ideas into Christian theology.

Unhappily for the Church, reform was not easy. The papal curia was deeply involved in Italian politics both to maintain its government over the Papal States and to ward off the efforts of those who would place the pope under the councils. For at least a half century the popes had needed politicians, diplomats, statesmen, and soldiers rather than moralists, saints, or theologians to maintain themselves. As a result, appointments to the College of Cardinals, as well as elections to the papacy, had brought men into the Church government whose worldly lives ill-fitted the teachings of Christ. They could maintain the Papal States in the complex setting of fifteenth-century Italy, they could beautify the city of Rome with its churches and papal palaces, they could patronize poets, sculptors, and humanist scholars, but too often these men who decorated the cultural life of Rome and governed the Church gave it a pagan tone rather than a Christian one. The men in control were satisfied that they were doing the right thing, so the moralists and reformers could beg, thunder, or pray for change with slim chance that the arrogant men in power would listen. It required a revolution to break the latter's hold on the Church.

Not the least of the Church's troubles stemmed from the great expense of its government. All over Europe, bishops' correspondence dealt more with money than with God's mercy or His intentions; and in Rome the cost of maintaining the political and military position of the Papal States, of rebuilding the city in Renaissance splendor, and of sustaining the European prestige of the papacy, required huge sums of money. Without a broad tax base from which to draw revenue, the papal curia continued and extended the unfortunate fiscal policies that had already aroused antagonism in Europe. Church offices, exemptions, indulgences, papal writs—indeed all such things were for sale. Some of these practices, such as the sale of indulgences, were to be repudiated by the Council of Trent, but in 1500 there was no way to check scandalous misuses of power. Pious Christians became anticlericals because of the spectacle of the men who occupied clerical positions; as that anticlericalism grew it created a climate of opinion dangerous to the unity of the Church.

There was still another level at which the papacy and the unity of the Church itself were in trouble. For over two and a half centuries, the papacy had been forced to give ground before both the demands of temporal rulers who insisted upon their divine right and the encroachments of national assemblies of the clergy. Princes wished to control revenue and appointments to Church offices within their territories; and bishops insisted upon the right to control their own sees, upon equality with the bishop of Rome, who was only first among equals, and upon assemblies to govern the Gallican, Anglican, Spanish, and other churches. All this meant that powers such as Innocent III (1178–1216) had exercised could never be regained. Indeed, the best that the papacy could hope for was an agreement with a prince or king over the constitution of the Church in his territories. The Concordat that Pope Leo x made with Francis I (1517) at the expense of Gallican pretentions was an answer to this problem. It left the appointment of bishops in the hands of the king; the pope only installed them in office. Indeed this Concordat virtually made the Church into an agency of royal government. The Spanish kings had long since established similar controls over the Spanish Church, but it was not so easy to find such a solution for the Holy Roman Empire, where the emperor depended upon the clergy in the principalities to help him control the local princes. The constitution of the Holy Roman Empire was too complex to allow for a simple solution to the problem of Church government.

In 1500 the various princely governments of Europe were in quite different stages and lines of development, but everywhere the Church provided the value system that cemented the population into communities. There were no secular "isms" in the sixteenth century, only spiritual ones. And yet no prince was willing to allow Rome to exercise control over his territory even though the mystique of the era assumed that the Church was a single institution under the papal monarchy. Princes, therefore, strove to limit papal power on many levels. In France the *Parlement* assumed the right to decide what was heresy; in Spain the Inquisition (under the control of the kings) had even more extensive powers. All princes contested the right of the popes to domicile a tribunal in their lands, and yet the papacy did pretend to that right. It was at this level that the papacy was most exposed, for sixteenth-century princes were in the process of extending their control over all corporate interests and institutions within their territories. Princes could not tolerate a situation that would leave the control over the institution that gave unity to their subjects in the hands of a power beyond their control. The Church was too important to be independent of the prince; it was an instrument of the prince's power necessary to his government.

The event that resulted in a severe crisis for Western Christendom was Luther's challenge of the sale of indulgences. Martin Luther, monk and professor of theology, had no intention of disrupting the Christian community when he nailed the Ninety-five Theses to the door of the church. He was simply acting as a Christian theologian hoping to purify the doctrine of his church. He saw the sale of indulgences as an evil for his country and a scandalous departure from the true teaching of Christ. However, in protesting the sale of indulgences, he opened a Pandora's box of questions about grace, papal power, and Church practices. Soon he was on the defensive; his opponents were armed with the whole corpus of Church doctrine and practices, while he was armed with his interpretation of the Holy Scriptures, which he regarded as the sole source of truth. As the argument developed, Luther was driven from one position to another; an honest, if somewhat emotional, man, he stubbornly defended his beliefs even when they led him to challenge the papacy itself. As Luther read the Scriptures, he came to believe in a conception of God that dwarfed man so completely that man could not save himself from God's wrath. Only through faith in God's mercy could man hope to be saved. But this belief placed him in direct opposition to the teachings of the Church, which provided the sacraments for man's salvation; by questioning the effectiveness of the sacramental system, Luther also denied the assumption that the Church could provide salvation, and with this he denied the efficacy of relics, masses for the dead, and most of the other practices of the Church. Furthermore, since he believed the Holy Scriptures to be the sole source of truth, he translated the Bible into German and gave his version to the people. Proclaiming the priesthood of all believers, he thus opened wide the gates of heresy. At the same time, in his conflict with the pope, Luther appealed to the princes as the true protectors of the Church. He endowed princes with divine right not only to govern the temporal affairs of men but also to protect and regulate God's church on earth. It mattered little that his opponents insisted that his teachings were contaminated with Hussite doctrines; Luther's protests found a ready audience in Germany and, indeed, throughout much of Europe, where dissatisfaction with the corrupt clergy and papal government made men ready for new ideas.

Luther's protests spawned a pamphlet war that took the papal court at Rome by surprise but succeeded in converting clergymen, princes, and scholars to his cause. In an effort to silence him, Luther was brought before the emperor and the Diet. He was a brave man; he refused to recant: "Here I stand," he exclaimed; "I neither can nor will recant since it is neither safe nor right to act against conscience." These were dramatic events that often obscure the fact that there probably would have been a Reformation even had Luther never lived. It was no accident that the elector of Saxony would not send his subject to Rome for judgment before a papal court, or that there were German princes willing to risk the wrath of pope and emperor to protest their faith in Luther's ideas. All over Europe there were thoughtful men who had read the caustic sarcasm of humanist critics of clerical misbehavior and stupidity, and who had themselves become convinced that the Church needed reform in head and members. Even deeper than this, there was a philosophical level that brought men into conflict with the Church's teachings. The realist philosopher had no trouble with Church doctrines, for he believed in the reality of ideas; he could accept the transformation of bread and wine into the body and blood of Christ without question. But the nominalist could not. For him, no matter what was said the bread and wine remained bread and wine; indeed, the Trinity was three Gods, not one person. Thus, for the nominalist there was left only faith; he could believe but he could not accept all the trappings of mysticism that had been attached to the Church. On another level, perhaps more broadly based than that of either the humanist critic or the nominalist philosopher, was the fifteenth- and sixteenth-century man's preoccupation with death, hell, and salvation. The popular woodcuts were those depicting the "dance of death"; the interest of the people was centered on the fear of hell and the hope for salvation. As a wise scholar of the period remarked, a best seller would not have been entitled *How to See Rome,* but *How to Avoid Hell.* Luther and the reformers who followed him had no trouble finding an audience.

Actually, in the first two decades following Luther's assault on Rome, four more or less distinct types of reform developed in competition with each other. They were: Luther's Protestant church, the Swiss Reformed church, the Anabaptists, and reform within the Roman Catholic church.

Of those groups that broke with Rome, Luther's was the most conservative. Luther based his doctrine upon the proposition that man is saved by faith alone. Therefore, he rejected most of the sacramental system of the medieval Church, excepting only baptism, holy orders, and the Eucharist. Since salvation was the free gift of God, the whole system of relics, masses for the dead, requests for intercession of saints, veneration of the virgin, pilgrimages to famous shrines, and other such colorful actions were jettisoned. The mass was simplified and read in the vernacular; scripture reading, hymn singing, and sermons became important parts of the service.

Luther was also a political conservative. He placed faith in that rare monster, the good prince, to whom he entrusted control over his church; at the same time, he simplified the structure of church government. His faith was placed in the upper levels of society; when the peasants revolted against oppression and asked for his support, he urged the princes to treat them severely.

At the other end of the scale, the Anabaptists were the most radical group to emerge as reformers of the Church. They advocated a return to primitive Christianity, to the time when Christians could not live in the world. Indeed, the Anabaptist communities resembled societies of married monks who hoped to find salvation by refusing contact with the sinful world. They read the Scriptures and took seriously the commandments of God—even the one that forbade men to kill. But who would halt the invasion of the Ottoman Turks if men refused to fight or to pay taxes to support fighting men? Every indication is that the Anabaptists were pious, godfearing men who actually tried to imitate Christ and achieve salvation by eschewing the evil actions of man. They were nonetheless treated by their Lutheran and Catholic neighbors just as the primitive Christians had been treated by the Roman society: their leaders were killed, their meetings were broken up, they were driven from the land. The world had as little use for them as they had for the world, but the latter was armed with the power to destroy those who affronted its values.

The Swiss reformers presented a third face of the Reformation. The movement started with a humanist priest, Ulrich Zwingli, who simplified the services of the Roman church, insisted that salvation was the work of

God's grace and not obtainable through sacraments, ended celibacy for the clergy, and introduced a more democratically organized church government. This "reformed" church, however, did not find a great leader until the mid-sixteenth century when John Calvin emerged as both high priest and theologian. With legal training in France, Calvin centered his attention on the Old Testament where he found an all-powerful, all-knowing God whose grace is predetermined and therefore not open to discussion. Prayers could be said to thank Him for his graces but not to ask for favors. Every man's destiny was fixed before he was born, and there could be no altering it. Calvin's teachings on morals and behavior were puritanical and austere. The elect of God had the right to be free from scandalous behavior by other men, and, therefore, what we call "blue laws" were the order of the day. The Calvinists gloried in their pale cheeks, their spare bodies, their plain dress; they worshipped God with hymn and psalm singing and sermons on theology; their lives reflected the fact that they knew of their own salvation. Since their government was centered in the congregation and the assembly of laymen and ministers, the Calvinists did not need to ask the princes of this world for recognition; indeed, their missionaries converted men and then taught them that they had the right to resist rulers who harmed God's church. In the second half of the sixteenth century, Calvinist radicals actually broke into churches to destroy "idols" and "icons," and they raised the flag of revolt against rulers in many parts of Europe.

A somewhat different strain of the Reformation developed in England. Many English divines had been influenced by the reformers of the Continent, but the Anglican break with Rome came after the English king, Henry VIII, learned that his intended queen, Anne Boleyn, was pregnant but that Rome refused to grant him a divorce from his current wife. Henry had no intention of reforming the doctrines of the Church, but he did ask Parliament to sever the lines with Rome and establish the crown as supreme over the religious establishment in England. Another series of acts confiscated for the crown the property of the monastic foundations in England, thereby making it difficult to return to the previous Church constitution. During Henry's life the Church provided a battlefield for men who wished to retain the religious services and beliefs of the medieval Church and those who wanted to simplify and reform both. At his death, the English Church began to move toward a Calvinist position under Edward VI, but when Edward also died, Mary Tudor, Henry's daughter by his first, Spanish-born wife, tried to return it to Rome. She, too, died before her ambition could be accomplished, and Elizabeth I managed to strike a tenuous balance between the conflicting tendencies within the Anglican church. But the crisis was only postponed until after her death, when the whole problem of the role of the crown, of bishops, of congregations, of synods flared up to plague the seventeenth-century English kings.

The Roman Catholic church also had a "reformation." By the time Paul III was elected pope (1534), it was evident even in Rome that the Church was in serious trouble and that reform was imperative. The new pope's first appointments to the College of Cardinals were an indication of his intention to give a new orientation to the Curia, and in the following years one measure after another was adopted to end the scandals in the Catholic community. Even before the election of Paul III to the triple crown, Emperor Charles also recognized the need for reform; his solution was to call a council on the model of the Council of Constance in which both the reformers as well as men who held to the old Church, could be represented. This did not suit the Curia. Paul III and his successors were as insistent upon the monarchical constitution of the Church as the Renaissance popes had been, and they wanted the reform to come from the pope, not from a council. The reformers in northern Europe were scarcely more cooperative, and so, even though the Council of Trent did finally meet in 1545, and again in 1551 for sessions that were quickly adjourned, it was not until 1562–1564 that the Trentine decrees were finally formulated to define the reforms of the Church and affirm its doctrines. By that time, most of the reforming decrees had already been proclaimed by the papacy so that the Council merely ratified the reform. The doctrinal statements of the Council of Trent, however, did give new form to Catholic orthodoxy by specifically anathematizing the doctrines of the other reformed churches, and sharpening, perhaps hardening, certain doctrines of the medieval Church. This so-called Counter Reformation by popes and council gave the old Church both a firmer statement of its teachings and new institutions to revivify its constitution. The Roman Inquisition, the Congregation of the Index, the Jesuit order, and other reformed religious communities put real power into the hands of the men who believed that God had placed upon them the obligation to reunify Christian Europe under the Roman Catholic church.

HIGH POLITICS: THE ERA OF CHARLES V

A mapmaker of Europe in the early sixteenth century, reversing the pattern to which twentieth-century men are accustomed, placed the south at the top of the page rather than at the bottom. The result was an interesting projection that showed Europe faced with a huge semicircle of Mohammedan states. From the Black Sea to Morocco men followed the banners of Islam. This preoccupation with the Moslem world fitted the realities of the period; for the first time since the high tide of the Mohammedan conquest hundreds of years before, Europe again seemed really to be threatened from the East. From the time of the Crusades, Christians had encroached upon Moslem territory: Southern Italy, Sicily, the other islands in the western Mediterranean, and the whole of the Iberian peninsula had been reconquered for the Christian community, and the Islamic states on the North African coast of the western Mediterranean were so weak that they invited invasion. At the end of the fifteenth century, however, in the Levant and in the Balkans a new Moslem power, the Ottoman Turkish Empire, was consolidating the whole of the Near East into a powerful force that could

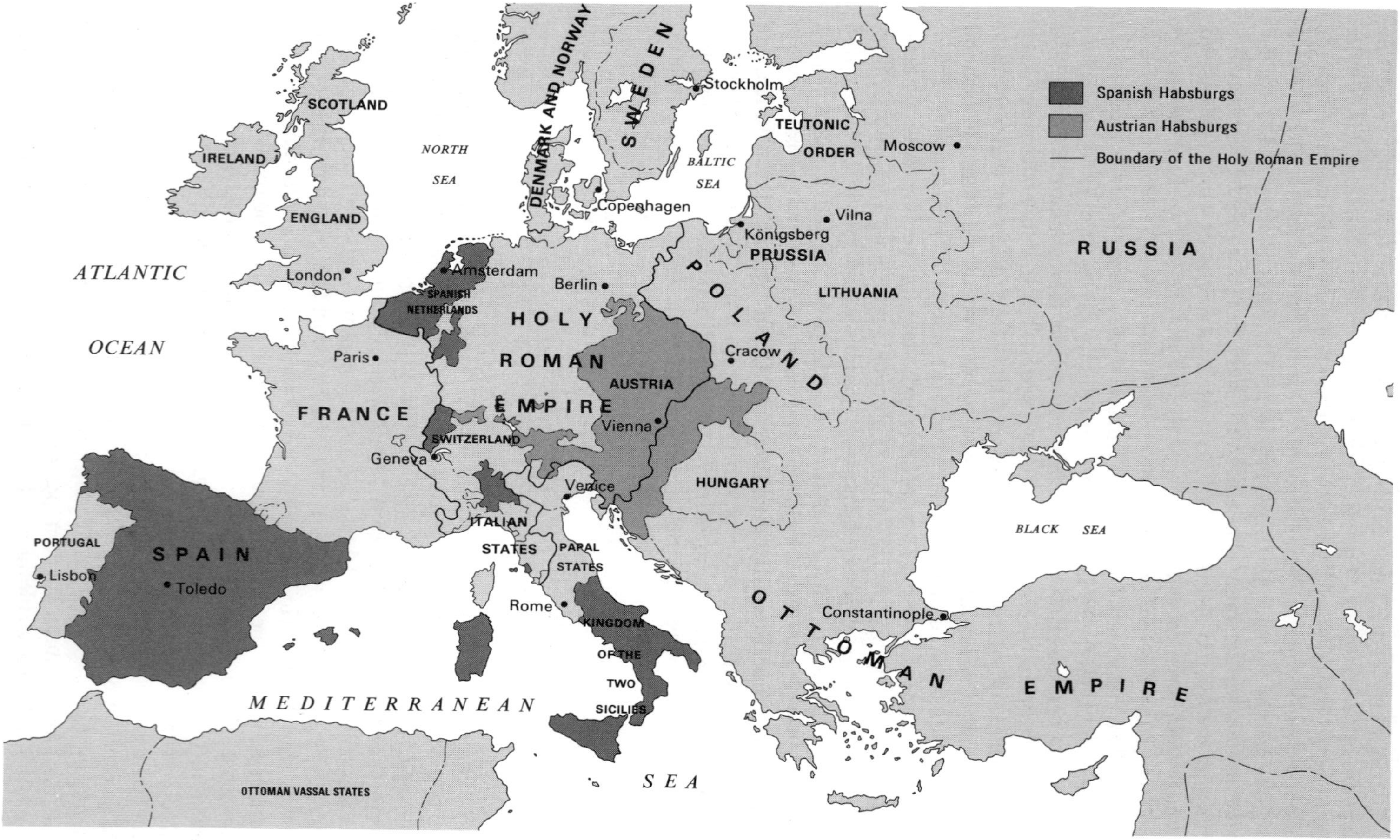
Spanish Habsburgs
Austrian Habsburgs
Boundary of the Holy Roman Empire
SCOTLAND
IRELAND
ENGLAND
London
ATLANTIC
OCEAN
NORTH
SEA
DENMARK AND NORWAY
SWEDEN
Stockholm
BALTIC
SEA
Copenhagen
TEUTONIC
ORDER
Moscow
Vilna
Königsberg
PRUSSIA
LITHUANIA
RUSSIA
Amsterdam
SPANISH
NETHERLANDS
Berlin
HOLY
ROMAN
EMPIRE
POLAND
Cracow
AUSTRIA
Paris
FRANCE
Vienna
SWITZERLAND
Geneva
Venice
HUNGARY
ITALIAN
STATES
PAPAL
STATES
PORTUGAL
Lisbon
SPAIN
Toledo
Rome
KINGDOM
OF THE
TWO
SICILIES
BLACK SEA
OTTOMAN EMPIRE
Constantinople
MEDITERRANEAN
SEA
OTTOMAN VASSAL STATES

EUROPE IN THE MIDDLE OF THE 16TH CENTURY

exert strong pressure on Christendom. In the early sixteenth century when the North African Barbary communities recognized Turkish overlordship, Europeans from the Danube to the tip of the Iberian peninsula felt the threat of Islam under Ottoman leadership. The aforementioned mapmaker only reflected the fears that this new "scourge of God" aroused in the hearts of European men. The Turks and the Islamic raiders, rather than Luther's heresy or Columbus' America, were the subjects of conversation when thoughtful men came together. When members of the Spanish Cortez or the German Diet spoke of "defending Christendom," they meant defending it against the Ottoman Turks, not against the German heretics.

Most sixteenth-century Europeans did not realize that the Ottoman Empire was a political congeries almost as diverse and confusing as the political structures in the West. The Ottoman Empire began its expansion from Anatolia in the fourteenth century, and in a little over two hundred years its sultans had been able to conquer the confusing complex of sheikdoms, emirates, and principalities, in Mesopotamia, Syria, and Anatolia; they had also crossed the straits to conquer Greece, Bulgaria, and the great city, "guarded by God," Constantinople (1453). In 1525, from Egypt to the estuary of the Tigris-Euphrates on one end, and to the Danube on the other, the writ of the Sultan was law; at least that is the way it seemed to the men who watched this onward march of Ottoman power. This Ottoman Empire was formidable indeed, but it was also subject to many problems of organization and control. The conquest of lands ruled by Mohammedans proved easy to accomplish; often it was enough for the sultan's army merely to enter the land to secure capitulation. But it was not so easy to organize the conquered area. The sultans usually did not try to alter the traditional governments of their new provinces; in both the cities and the countryside they retained the former rulers under the supervision of a Turkish garrison, with a pasha or beylerbey to collect the taxes and represent the Ottoman presence. Almost the same pattern was followed when Christians came under the sultan's rule. The Turks were tolerant of their subjects' beliefs so long as the taxes were paid and order respected. The noblemen in the country and the town governments were allowed to continue to govern; the Turkish pasha and his soldiers only supervised their activities. The Christians were encouraged, but not forced, to turn Turk, that is, to convert to Islam; they were required only to pay taxes and respect the orders of the sultan's representatives. Thus, throughout much of its empire, the government of the Ottoman Turks more resembled an army of occupation than a political state. The system had both strengths and weaknesses, but as long as the sultan's army remained powerful and continued to make conquests, he could command both money and men on a scale that made him dangerous to his neighbors.

The real strength of the Ottoman Empire depended upon the succession of strong men to the crown. When a weakling appeared, the empire quickly fell into decay. It had been the fortune of the empire to have had a long line of strong and imaginative men inherit the throne from the fourteenth until the mid-sixteenth century. Since they regularly murdered their brothers upon reaching the throne, no serious contests for the crown, and few civil wars, disturbed the Ottoman community.

The sultan had at his disposal an institution that, in strong hands, was a formidable instrument of power: a system for recruiting a corps of military and political personnel completely dependent upon the will of the ruler. From time to time, each subject Christian population paid a "boy tax"; youths aged twelve to twenty were taken from their homes, converted to Islam, and enrolled in the famous janissary corps. The most intelligent of them became agas (generals), viziers, begs, or pashas to administer the government and command the armies; the rest became an elite corps of infantrymen, the hard core of the Turkish army. These janissaries were pampered but disciplined slaves; they were not allowed to marry and their lives belonged to the sultan. As long as the ruling sultan knew how to manage this formidable instrument, it was a significant force to be contended with by non-Ottoman peoples, but as soon as a weakling appeared the janissary corps became dangerous to the Turkish state. The sultan could also depend upon the saphis (Moslem cavalry), irregular troops from his conquered provinces, and many Christian renegades to support the janissaries in the field. In 1500 this Turkish army was undoubtedly one of the best, if not the best, in the entire world.

Until the sixteenth century, Ottoman power was essentially a land animal, but after the conquest of Egypt (1517) it became important to establish sea communications between Alexandria, Greece, and Constantinople. The Knights of St. John on the island of Rhodes, warlike monks who carried on a continuous sea war against Islam, stood in the way. After initial failures to crush the knights and the pirates who joined forces with them, the Turks finally were successful in 1522 and expelled them from Rhodes. From that time onward, Ottoman sea power was a factor to be contended with in the eastern Mediterranean, and a decade later, when joined with naval armament from Tunis and Algiers, it was able to reach into the central and western Mediterranean as well.

Happily for the Christian West, the Ottoman Empire faced Persia and upper Egypt as well as Europe, and its military institutions were so organized that they could be directed against only one foe at a time, since the sultan's presence was necessary for any success. Thus, in the first years of the sixteenth century, Ottoman power was pitted against Persia and Egypt. Selim I, surnamed The Grim, first destroyed his brothers, then attacked Persia and established control over the entire Euphrates valley and Kurdistan (1514–1516). He next turned southward, captured Cairo (1517) and made himself master of all Egypt. Selim I was succeeded by his son Suleiman, surnamed The Magnificent (1520), who turned the empire's forces toward Europe. It was he who captured Belgrade and gained control over Serbia (1521) and, the following year, over Rhodes. In 1526 his armies defeated the Hungarians at Mohaċs, where Louis, king of Hungary, was killed; by 1529 Suleiman's forces had reached Vienna but failed to capture the city. It is small wonder that both Lutheran and Catholic sixteenth-century divines, watching the seemingly inevitable onrush of the Ottoman arms, concluded that God had created the military power of the Turkish empire to punish Europe for its sins.

At almost the same time that the Ottoman Turks were attempting to re-create the great Islamic empire that had rolled over so much of the world, a new arrangement in the political structure of western Europe seemed about to recreate the empire of Charlemagne. In 1500 there were four powers in western Europe more or less equal in strength: the kingdom of France, of England, the crowns of the Spanish Catholic kings of Castile and Aragon, and the Holy Roman Empire, including the Burgundian inheritance. By 1520 an almost incredible series of events had placed the crowns of the Catholic kings of Spain, of the Burgundian inheritance, and of the Empire all on the head of Charles von Hapsburg. Even more important were the facts that by 1520 the crown of Castile included dominion over the Spanish New World, from which a flow of precious metals had begun to pour into Europe, and that the crown of Aragon included Naples and Milan. Nor was this all that came to Charles v. His sisters and aunts were married to the kings of England, Hungary, and Portugal, his brother was married to the heiress of the throne of Bohemia, and within a few years another sister married the king of France. At first glance, it seemed that the Western Christian empire of Charlemagne was about to be reconstituted in time to block the assaults of Islam. Small wonder that true believers saw the rise of the house of Hapsburg as the work of God.

However, the solution was not so simple. With these crowns came problems as dangerous to Charles' government as the Ottoman Turks. The king of France, Francis I, regarded the rise of Hapsburg power as a mortal threat to his kingdom: Charles' crowns not only bordered France on every side but also brought with them conflicts that could not easily be resolved. The Hapsburg family had never surrendered its claim to the duchy of Burgundy, which the French crown had occupied at the death of Charles the Rash (1477), and the French Valois house had not given up its pretentions to Milan, Naples, and Sicily. The result was that war between Hapsburg and Valois was endemic. Within the Holy Roman Empire, too, the Ottoman Turks were not the only threat to the imperial authority. The problems raised by Luther's rebellion broke out almost simultaneously with the death of Charles' grandfather, Emperor Maximilian, and they were allowed to develop in the period when the princes of Germany and Europe bargained over the succession to the imperial crown. By the time Charles was able to go to Germany, the Lutheran rebellion had become a political as well as a religious problem. Luther could not be sent to Rome for trial nor even silenced in Germany because his religious convictions suited both the consciences and the political aspirations of many of the German princes. Germany was threatened with civil war if the emperor attempted to force the princes to obey his will.

If the king of France was unquestionably Charles' enemy and the Lutheran princes vassals of doubtful loyalty, the king of England was a friend and relative of questionable political value. Henry VIII had little of his father's judgment and much ambition to play a great role in the world.

In a reckless continental war, he quickly ran through the treasure that Henry VII had left him, and there was little chance for him to find enough money to support other large military operations. Nonetheless, his friendship was important for the Hapsburgs, in part because English seamen, with their traditions of piracy, could so easily endanger the lines of communication between Spain and the Netherlands and even between Spain and the New World. Henry more or less supported the Hapsburgs against the Valois as long as Charles' aunt, Catherine, remained Henry's queen, but when Henry broke with Rome and divorced his wife, England also became a potential foe. There was another possible enemy, the papacy. The emperor's reaction to Luther had not been satisfactory to many important figures in Rome, for Charles had agreed that there were problems in the papal curia that needed reform and, even as early as his first encounter with heresy in Germany, he had talked of a Church council to solve the problems, a solution unacceptable in Rome. Then, when Pope Leo X died (1522), Charles secured the election of his tutor and friend, Adrian IV, who immediately began to talk about reform in a way embarrassing and distasteful to the Italian cardinals. Adrian died within a year, and the next pope, Clement VII, was a Medici, quite unwilling to become a tool of the Hapsburgs. On the contrary, he allied the papacy with France. Clearly, the supposed unity of Western Christendom that had been characteristic of Charlemagne's empire was not to be easily recaptured even though the Turks were pounding at the gates of Europe.

Perhaps Charles' most serious problem was the fact that, for all the crowns he wore, he could not depend on most of them for any sort of financial or military assistance. He did not rule over an organic state; his crowns were not even a loose confederation. Each province assumed that its local autonomy, liberties, and customs would be respected by the prince who happened to be its ruler; each insisted that its revenues and soldiers should be used only for its interests. But if Charles were to organize Christendom he had to find money and troops that could be used on the Danube, in Italy, or wherever he needed them. He could draw a little money from his Flemish, Dutch, and Walloon subjects in the Netherlands; but the townsmen and nobles of those provinces were more interested in exploiting the Spanish crowns than in supplying the emperor with money to fight the Turks. The constitution of the Aragonese kingdom strictly limited the powers of its ruler and provided Charles with very limited financial resources. From Germany and the Hapsburg provinces on the Danube he could find some money for defense against the Turks, but even this was largely insufficient and rigidly controlled. Only the kingdom of Castile had a constitution that allowed its king to tax, and, luckily for Charles, Castile also controlled the Spanish New World that was about to pour silver into Europe. This, however, proved to be too narrow a base to support the obligations that his crowns imposed upon the emperor.

One of the first tasks facing Emperor Charles was to establish control over the western Mediterranean. His grandparents, Ferdinand and Isabella, had driven the Moors from the Iberian peninsula and begun the conquest of the important harbors on the North African coast. They had also released a hornet's nest against their people, for the expelled Moors took to the sea and joined raiders from the Barbary as corsairs. Their raids on the coasts of Spain for slaves and loot were facilitated by the fact that other Moorish people (Moriscoes) who had chosen to remain in the lands of their ancestors gladly cooperated with the raiders. At the same time, the corsair assaults on all Christian shipping endangered the lifelines between Spain and Italy. When the Spanish began to make headway against the Barbary cities, the most daring, and undoubtedly the most able, of the corsair chiefs, Kheir-ed-din Barbarossa, evoked the aid of the sultan of Turkey by placing his fleet and the city state of Algiers under Turkish control, thus making the Turks a power in the western Mediterranean.

Perhaps Charles could have driven the Moslem fleet from the western end of the sea if he had not also become involved in a series of wars with Francis I, wars that he could not conclude. In these conflicts, Charles managed at one point to make Francis I his prisoner; at another he found himself at war with the pope as well as with the king of France, and he suffered the humiliation of seeing his forces sack the city of Rome itself (1527). Later Francis I, as an ally of the Ottoman Empire, allowed the Turkish Barbary admiral, Kheir-ed-din, to use Toulon as a base for the latter's fleet. An ally of the Protestant princes, too, Francis was also able to secure control over the important bishoprics of Metz, Toul, and Verdun in spite of anything Charles could do. These conflicts coincided with the high point of the Turkish advance; the sultan's armies reached Vienna, but the Turks failed to take the city. Charles, for his part, had equally frustrating military experiences. In 1541, for example, he planned a great expedition to capture Algiers. He landed and prepared to besiege the city; then a great storm arose that wrecked his ships, spoiled his supplies, and spread disaster throughout his armies. Later, in Germany, after he had had a respite from the Valois wars, his armies seemed about to be completely victorious against the Schmalkaldic League of the Lutheran princes, but the extent of his victory disturbed his German allies enough to cause important elements to change sides and evoke the aid of the French king. Charles was forced to withdraw from Germany and allow his brother, Ferdinand, to make peace (Augsburg, 1555).

There were a number of reasons behind the frustrations of sixteenth-century war and politics. In the first place, no prince, not even the king of France, whose taxes were worth the mines of Peru, or the king of Castile, with the revenues of the New World and the Castilian taxes, had sufficient money to mount a military force large enough to effect a decisive victory. The tax structures were too primitive, the credit structure available to princes too weak, and the problems of warfare too great for a striking military success. The costs of military adventures were mounting fast in the early sixteenth century. European cannon manufacturers had learned to cast guns of bronze that were more flexible and more useful than the forged weapons of the preceding century, but they were expensive. Henry VIII, for example, nearly bankrupted his treasury with the purchase of the "twelve apostles" (cannons were still given names—as we name ships) from a Walloon forge. These guns were becoming necessary for any siege operation, and they were fast being fitted into the naval armaments of the era. On land, however, they created major problems. Iron balls and powder needed to serve the weapons were costly to purchase and even more costly to transport any great distances. The roads of Europe were not metalled, so, unless water transportation was available, the movement of a siege train was fantastically expensive. Charles experienced this problem of logistics when he attempted to invade France from Italy; the whole enterprise broke down because of transportation costs. The cannon also made possible a revolution in naval warfare. Oar-powered galleys, similar to those of the Greeks and Romans, that depended upon the ram and the launching of missiles (arrows mostly) for offensive powers, were still the chief naval weapons in the Mediterranean, but in the Atlantic the Portuguese and Spanish, and, soon after, the peoples on the Channel and the North Sea, were learning to power warships with sails and to use the cannon in place of the ram as the primary offensive weapon. The new ships were more effective than the galleys for long voyages in stormy waters, and eventually they were to become almost as maneuverable. By the end of the sixteenth century, ships powered by sails and outfitted with cannon invaded the Mediterranean and made the galleys obsolete—even huge galleys like those of the Venetian Republic could not compete with the sailing vessels. But these new ships were terribly expensive to build and to operate.

To increased costs for weapons and logistics were added other problems harassing military efforts of the period. In the first half of the sixteenth century, the art of war had developed rapidly; while bows and arrows were still used, the basic weapons of the infantry were becoming the pike and the arquebus. The pikemen could stand off a cavalry charge or push home an assault while the arquebus was more effective than the long- or crossbow had ever been as a missile launcher. Cavalry practices, too, were changing; in place of the disorderly charge of the feudal cavalry, the horsemen were learning to maneuver in unison, using pistols and sabers as their weapons. But these soldiers, too, were expensive. They were mustered in companies by captains, who, as military entrepreneurs, "sold" their services to the princes. They had no particular loyalty to anyone except for money. The most famous of these sixteenth-century soldiers were the Swiss mercenaries who would insist upon being paid before a battle, and, if they were not, they would simply march off the field. Like his fellow monarchs, Henry VIII found that these mercenary soldiers could quickly "eat up" money such as that which his father had left him; Charles V discovered that they could bankrupt a rich prince.

The commanders of these soldiers also created a problem. Princes had traditionally relied upon themselves or members of their families to command their armies. The mercenary condottieri (leaders) were dangerous to trust; in Italy in the preceding century, one after another of them had usurped power to make themselves rulers of the Italian principalities, and even as late as the mid-sixteenth century such soldiers were more interested in their own advancement than that of their prince. However, members of the prince's family were not always satisfactory commanders either. For example, the duke of Bourbon, constable of France, did not hesitate to desert his cousin Francis I and join Emperor Charles' armies when he feared that Francis would not do as he (the duke) wished. For this reason it was common for the king to march with his armies. Like Charlemagne seven hundred years before, Charles V spent most of his life in the saddle, for only by being present in person could he be sure that his orders would be carried out. This was as true for the sultan of Turkey as it was for the Christian emperor.

When we consider the obstacles that space, lack of money, and inadequate and often untrustworthy subordinates placed in the way of statesmen wishing to organize universal political programs for Europe, it is not difficult to understand why Charles V was unable to accomplish most of his objectives. Europe was still too large in terms of moving men and supplies from place to place, and its economy was too weak to produce surpluses that would be available for princes. Charles, discouraged and ill, found it best to turn over to his brother, Ferdinand, the crown of the empire and the Hapsburg holdings on the Danube (the *Erbländer*) and to his son Philip the crowns of Spain, the Netherlands, Italy, and the New World. He retired to a monastery to prepare himself for his departure to the next world, where he undoubtedly hoped that frustrations would be fewer and chances for success greater.

CIVILIZATION: HIGH CULTURE

In 1500, western Europeans still looked to Italy and the Mediterranean basin as the most important cultural as well as economic axis for their world. Rome was the spiritual capital of Western Christendom, and Italy the schoolmaster for men from all Europe. Italian artists, engineers, physicians, architects, lawyers, musicians, and scholars were invited north to practice their professions and to teach, and northerners went to Italy to finish their educations. There were other cultural centers: the Burgundian court in the Netherlands; the Valois court in France; the circles of artists and scholars associated with German and Netherland cities such as Nürnberg, Antwerp, Rotterdam, or Augsburg. But even these were more or less dependent upon Italy for inspiration and ideas. It is not an accident that Leonardo died in France, that Erasmus went to Venice to study and to work, that Van der Goes' most important painting was done in Florence, or, later in the century, that Shakespeare gave Italian settings and plots to his best-known plays. After 1500, the Italians lost political and military control over their own destiny, but for more than two centuries Italy maintained its cultural hegemony. The burst of cultural energy that gave Italy this hegemony had already run for more than a hundred years before 1500.

Historians, fascinated by the problems of genius and creativity, have called the movement the Italian Renaissance.

The word "Renaissance" is probably a misnomer. It implies the "rediscovery" of classical civilization as a *Zeitgeist* that somehow endowed men with a special *vertù* and an urge to individuality. This conception had much to recommend it to men in the late nineteenth century, who believed that they were witnessing the triumph of individualism in their own time and therefore looked to an earlier period to discover the origins of their world. However, these notions of rebirth and rediscovery must be modified and redefined in light of recent scholarship. In doing this, though, we must not miss the fact that in Florence, Venice, Rome, and other Italian cities men emerged whose labors in the fields of art, engineering, and scholarship profoundly affected the course of European civilization over the following three centuries.

The process of recovering the ideas and works of classical civilization was already hundreds of years old by 1500. From the tenth century on, men had been "recovering" classical culture. The writings of the Church fathers, the law codes, some of the works on medicine—these were needed to understand the Christian religion, to practice the methods of dealing with the more complex economic and personal problems that developed after the eleventh century, and, of course, to help men stave off the evils of ill health. By the twelfth and thirteenth centuries, isolated scholars were interested in Greek and Roman literature, mathematics, and "natural philosophy." Aristotle was accommodated into Christian theology, and the natural philosophers were already discussing problems of light, motion, and mechanics. The most important efforts to recover the literature and philosophy of the ancients, however, came after the fourteenth century when men began to realize the probable extent of the corpus of classical literature and to learn to edit the documents that they had "found." The discovery that the Latin language had a history, that it changed from century to century, provided a tool for understanding the classical cultures. The process continued into the seventeenth century: The writings of classical historians, poets, philosophers, essayists, dramatists, soldiers, merchants were "recovered," edited, and published. By the seventeenth century, Roman inscriptions, even the Bible, became objects of these editorial efforts. The men who found and edited these texts have been called humanists; the Greek and Latin literature has been called "the humanities."

By the opening of the sixteenth century, the work of recovering and publishing the writings of the ancients was enormously facilitated by the development of the printing press. Movable type and new presses were invented in the fifteenth century, and within a hundred years the printers had significantly changed the patterns of scholarly activity. At first, scholars scorned the printed page as a poor substitute for the elegance of the handwritten manuscript, but soon they recognized the great advantages that the printer had to offer them: Books could be produced more cheaply, and more important, once the text was properly established, each copy would be without the errors that inevitably crept into the manuscript copies. As we look back, the emergence of the printed book becomes the most important single fact in the intellectual history of Western man, indeed, of world civilization. It made possible our "book and reading culture" based upon universal literacy. In the sixteenth century, books were still reserved for the elite of the society, but the time would come when the presses would produce books for everyone.

It has often been assumed that the more or less pagan Renaissance culture of the sixteenth century dominated the intellectual world of that era, but a glance at the books that came off the presses will quickly dispel this idea. It is true that the works of Seneca, Marcus Aurelius, Cicero, and other luminaries of the pagan world became more readily available with the development of the art of printing, but it is also true that the bulk of the paper that was stamped with the printed word bore witness to the Christian civilization of the era. Books of the Old and New Testaments, edited by humanist scholars like Erasmus as well as by more traditional savants such as the authors of the Spanish Complutensian Polyglot Bible in which the Old and New Testaments were printed in parallel columns in the original languages, were offered to the public. Even more numerous were the books of prayers and devotions, books of Christian meditation, that helped men to accept the difficulties of everyday life. Added to these were the works of the theologians, which included Pico Mirandola's efforts to integrate Plato into the Christian theology as well as the massive writings of the men who were making the Reformation. The presses carried polemical effusions filled with down-to-earth, scurrilous language as well as historical arguments proving that Luther or Calvin or the propagandists for Rome were either right or wrong, depending upon the author. Humanist scholars unquestionably played a role in the advances of the printing presses. They were editors and translators of the classical authors; they wrote tracts of criticism on manners and morals; they used their learning in the service of both church and state. But they were not the only ones to prepare manuscripts for the printers of books and pamphlets.

One consequence of the humanist movement in Europe was the extension of the number of schools where young men were taught to read and speak Latin. The reform in the Church, both from within the old Church and in the new religious communities, also produced new schools, most of them oriented toward a humanist education modified by Christian thought. Calvinist academies, Jesuit colleges, royal and municipal schools of one kind or another turned out an ever-growing army of young men armed with intellectual equipment that made them good servants for princes, advocates before the law courts, and propagandists for religious or political causes. By the end of the sixteenth century, some regretted that there were so many scholars who could read Latin, for there often was not enough employment for all of them. The process, however, was destined to continue and the schools to expand, for the printing press invited the rise of a literate community of men, and man's desire to know urged the development of more sources of information and knowledge.

The humanist movement was the intellectual side of the so-called Italian

Renaissance; the development of painters, sculptors, and architects was its artistic counterpart. (See the pictorial essay on pp. 80–85.) Like the interest in classical literature, the sixteenth-century styles of art were the outgrowth of a combination of classical artistic understanding and indigenous Italian developments of the preceding two hundred years. Italian painters had learned to present three-dimensional tableaux on two-dimensional surfaces and to convey solid qualities of weight, the illusion of motion, accurate perspectives, and harmonious colors. The sculptors had solved the problems of casting large bronze pieces and of "liberating" their subjects from marble. The architects, using classical models but going beyond them, had achieved such structures as St. Peter's at Rome. The prestige that Italian art had achieved by the opening of the sixteenth century was so great that it tended to blight promising indigenous styles (French sculpture, for example) elsewhere in Europe. In the Flemish and Dutch Netherlands and in southern Germany, indigenous styles did manage somewhat to resist Italian pressure.

In other areas of human endeavor, Italy was a center for the emerging thought of the European society. By the first half of the sixteenth century, the humanist scholars had managed to edit the complete works of Ptolemy and Galen as well as most of the Latin mathematical treatises. These texts had a profound effect upon the thinking of the natural philosophers who were in the process of becoming physicists, anatomists, and astronomers. As we shall see in Chapter Four, the important impact of Greek, Roman, and Arabic astronomy, physics, and mathematics had to wait until Europeans knew the full texts of the great practitioners of these sciences. All of this effort, of course, was not concentrated in Italy, although in Florence, Padua, and Rome there was a climate favorable to the development of new ideas and new approaches to the world that even the vigors of the Counter-Reformation Church did not destroy.

SUGGESTED READING

Myron Gilmore's volume in *The Rise of Modern Europe* series, *The World of Humanism, 1453–1517* (1962) provides a provocative introduction to Europe at the opening of the sixteenth century. Karl Brandi, one of the most respected German historians of the last generation, has a superb biography of *Emperor Charles V: The Growth and Destiny of a Man and of a World Empire* (1965), while H. G. Koenigsberger's *The Hapsburgs and Europe, 1516–1660* (1971) places the emperor in a larger perspective. Two books by Roland Bainton will introduce the student to the Reformation: *The Reformations of the Sixteenth Century* (1956), and *Here I Stand: A Life of Martin Luther* (1954). In addition there is a nicely illustrated volume by A. G. Dickens, *The Reformation and Society in Sixteenth-Century Europe* (1966), and one by G. R. Elton, *Reformation Europe 1517–1555* (1966). Henri Daniel-Rops, *The Protestant Reformation,*

2 vols. (1961); Karl Holl, *The Cultural Significance of the Reformation* (1966); and George L. Mosse, *The Reformation* (1965) provide alternate interpretations. R. H. Tawney, *Religion and the Rise of Capitalism* (1948) and L. W. Spitz, *The Reformation—Material or Spiritual* (1962), provide an introduction to the controversy over religion and economics. There are a number of interesting biographies: See Johan Huizinga, *Erasmus and the Age of Reformation;* Erik Erikson, *Young Man Luther* (1958); R. W. Chambers, *Thomas More* (1958); Francis Hackett, *Henry Eighth* (1970); Garret Mattingly, *Catherine of Aragon* (1960); and Jaques Courvoisier, *Zwingli: A Reformed Theologian* (1963).

PHILIP VILLIERS DE L'ISLE-ADAM (1464–1534)

After Egypt was added to the Ottoman Empire, the sultan could no longer tolerate the "pirate nest" of the Knights of Saint John on the island of Rhodes; they cut communications between Egypt and Constantinople and harassed Moslem commerce in the waters of the Levant. Since the end of the eleventh century, the Order of the Knights of Saint John of Jerusalem had been a factor in the Near East, first as hospitalers aiding Christian pilgrims, and later as corsairs fighting the Holy War, the Crusade against the Moslem infidels. The knights, mostly younger sons of noble families who had to make their own way in the world and preferred to be soldiers rather than monks, came from all over Europe. The order was rich in lands, its holdings extending from Germany to England and from Spain and France to Italy. Its galleys constituted a powerful naval force in an era before temporal rulers maintained fleets "in being." In 1521, Turkish Sultan Suleiman II decided that these dangerous neighbors must be driven from their island stronghold of Rhodes. It was no simple decision, for the Turkish divan well remembered that some thirty years before the knights had successfully resisted another sultan's efforts to dislodge them.

This decision came at exactly the time when the order elected a new grand master. The knights chose Philip Villiers de l'Isle-Adam, a member of a French noble family of Beauvais. His career as a sailor, councillor, and diplomat, as well as his reputation for valor and military skill, made him a natural choice. At the time of his election he was serving as the order's ambassador and agent at the court of Francis I of France. He had hardly reached Rhodes when it became evident that a storm was about to break over the island, and he knew full well that the princes of Europe were so deeply involved in wars with each other, in contests over religious reformation, and in efforts to consolidate their power at home that he could expect no help against his dangerous foes.

The Turks landed on the island in June 1522. By August, Suleiman himself had to come to bolster the courage of his soldiers, for the knights drove off every assault with great slaughter, even when the wall of their fortification was in ruins. The battle went on until December, when the sultan proposed a capitulation treaty that would permit the knights to leave the island with the honors of war. Suleiman's respect for Villiers de l'Isle-Adam caused him to recognize the grand master as an equal. Since his supplies were low and his soldiers wearied, wounded, and few in number, the grand master accepted, and, with his knights, his archives, his servants, his mercenary soldiers, and nearly 5000 inhabitants of Rhodes, he withdrew to Crete and thence to Italy. In the treaty of capitulation, the knights agreed to end their war with the Ottoman Empire, but Villiers de l'Isle-Adam did not recognize an end to his crusade against Islam. He was determined to find another island home where the Knights of Saint John could establish a base for their corsair raids.

The pope installed Villiers de l'Isle-Adam in the town of Viterbo, but a landlocked site was of no use to the sea raiders. The old grand master thus began to travel around the courts of Europe seeking a suitable home. He was in Madrid when Francis I was prisoner of Emperor Charles; he was in London before Henry VIII rebelled against the papacy; he followed Charles V from Spain to Italy to Germany. He asked for Majorca, for Elba, for the Hyères Islands off southern France, but kings were slow to give up territory that might be useful to them. Finally, Charles V offered him the islands of Malta, Gozo, Comino, and Cominoto and the city of Tripoli as a fief of the crown of Aragon-Sicily in return for the gift of a falcon on every All Saints' Day. The old man was not fooled about the emperor's generosity; he knew that of these islands only Malta was really habitable, and even it was little more than a rocky point of land in the sea south of Sicily. The emperor's gift had been made primarily to secure the services of the knights in the defense of Tripoli, which was almost constantly under siege, from the land by Mohammedan tribesmen and from the sea by the Turkish and Barbary navies. But there were also advantages; even though there would be a problem feeding the people on Malta, the island did have an excellent harbor, rock with which to build fortifications, and a location in the central Mediterranean that would make the knights a thorn in the side of Islam. The grand master's ambassador took the oath holding the hands of the viceroy of Sicily on May 29, 1530, and shortly after, Villiers de l'Isle-Adam and his knights landed on Malta and began the building of their fortified position. The work proceeded apace with the labor of Moslem slaves captured in sea raids and landings on the Smyrna coasts. By 1534 when Villiers de l'Isle-Adam died, the double harbor of Malta was already beginning to take on formidable proportions and the several "*langues*"[1] had already started their palaces.

Thirty-one years after Villiers de l'Isle-Adam's death, his fortified city was the target of a massive Turkish assault, and again European princes were unable or unwilling to send aid to the besieged. This "great siege," however, unlike the one at Rhodes, ended in a Christian victory that brought Malta and its knights fame and glory that lasted for centuries. The grand master had done his work well. ■

---

[1] The Order was divided into "*langues*" or languages of Provence, Auvergne, France, Italy, Aragon, England, Castile, and Germany, but well over half of the knights usually came from France.

KHEIR-ED-DIN BARBAROSSA (1485?–1546)

Four sons were born to a humble Moslem potter on the island of Metelin (Lesbos) in the eastern Mediterranean. The eldest, Aroudj, went to sea as a corsair against Christian shipping, was captured and enslaved by the Knights of Saint John on the island of Rhodes, was ransomed by a pious Moslem prince, and finally secured a ship of his own to cruise against the Christian unbelievers. He and his brothers sailed for the western Mediterranean, one of the first Ottoman corsairs to invade those seas, and soon, establishing for themselves a reputation as their "holy war" (Djehad) spread terror along the coasts and shipping routes from Italy to Spain. By the time he was thirty-five years old, Aroudj had become a legend both in Christian and Moslem lands. His red beard gave him the name Barbarossa, his courage and impetuosity made him feared and/or revered by young and old throughout the Mediterranean world. Other Turkish corsairs came to him and accepted his leadership so that he soon commanded a fleet and could muster hundreds of soldiers to carry out his will. By treachery and audacious courage he managed to install himself as "king" in Algiers and a number of small cities on the northern coast of Africa; he found allies among the Moorish people driven from Spain and the tribesmen in the hinterland who had a strong taste for plunder, as well as among Turkish adventurers and Christian renegades who flocked to his banners. But Aroudj's career was abruptly ended when he came to grips with the Spanish commander at Oran.[1] He was killed in a skirmish in 1518, and most of his army was captured and beheaded. Fortunately for his brother Kheir-ed-din, the Spanish did not follow up their victory with an assault on Algiers.

The motley crew of sailors, adventurers, pirates and holy men who had rallied to Aroudj accepted Kheir-ed-din Barbarossa as their new chief, but even with their support his hold on Algiers was precarious, for the native Algerians, as well as the Moors and Arabs in the back country, hated the Turkish corsairs who ruled them as conquered peoples. Kheir-ed-din managed to mollify the Algerians long enough for one of his captains to sail to Constantinople with an offer to the sultan to accept Turkish overlordship in return for military assistance. This seemed to be the only way to fill the gaps in his army left by Aroudj's ill-fated expedition. The emissary

---

[1] His brother Isach was also killed in the campaign.

31

reached Constantinople just when the Turkish divan was coming to realize that its greatest foe was the military power of Charles v and his Spanish kingdoms. The sultan accepted the offer, sent 2000 janissary soldiers and some 4000 Levantine volunteers to firm up Turkish power, and named Kheir-ed-din a pasha and the beylerbey of North Africa.

In the next decade and a half, Kheir-ed-din created an empire on the North African coast. His military forces were composed of Moors from Spain, Christian renegades, and Levantine adventurers who were anxious to fight a holy war that would also be profitable. His ships were built and powered by Christian slaves captured by raids deep into Spain and Italy. His rule extended from Spanish-held Oran to Tunis, from the Mediterranean Sea to the Sahara, and he governed these lands by a combination of force, violence, intrigue, treachery, and peaceful persuasion. At no time was his hold secure, yet he showed his subjects that it was unwise to resist him. The real strength of this empire, however, was in the corsair fleet that was a scourge for all the Christian coasts of the Mediterranean basin. These ships brought in slaves, freed Spanish Moors from their "cruel masters," and grew rich capturing Christian ships. Kheir-ed-din, as ruler of Algiers, took his share of all this booty. There were thousands of Christian slaves in Algiers, and its wharves and warehouses were filled with wheat, oil, wine, wax, leather, cloth, hardware, and other commodities taken from Christian ships. By 1534, Kheir-ed-din was strong enough to drive the king of Tunis from his throne and add that rich land to the Turkish North African empire.

These triumphs, however, finally aroused the wrath of Christian Europe. Charles v prepared a mighty armada (1535) to attack Tunis and return it to its rightful ruler as a vassal of Spain. Kheir-ed-din did not have forces equal to Charles' army, and when the Arabs and Moors who should have been his allies showed signs of treason, Kheir-ed-din and his "Turks" slipped out of Tunis and made their way to ports on the north where he had hidden part of his navy. While Charles was establishing his Arab puppet as ruler of Tunis, Kheir-ed-din and his fleet attacked Majorca and sailed away with thousands of Christian men, women, and children and large quantities of merchandise. In Algiers, where gloom had spread with the news of the fall of Tunis, there was much rejoicing when the corsair fleet anchored in the harbor loaded with booty.

In the years that followed, Suleiman called Kheir-ed-din to Constantinople and entrusted him with the control over the building and equipping of a mighty Ottoman fleet that soon became the most powerful navy in the world. As admiral-captain-pasha, Kheir-ed-din subjected the islands at the entrance to the Adriatic Sea to Turkish control, then ravaged the coasts of Italy. When Suleiman and Francis I made an alliance against Charles v, Kheir-ed-din led the Turkish Navy to the western Mediterranean and established a naval base at Toulon. This show of Ottoman power—almost a hundred fifty galleys and hundreds of smaller ships— terrorized the Spanish-Italian states but did not greatly alter the course of the war against Charles v. When Kheir-ed-din returned to the eastern waters, both the king of France, who was paying him a huge monthly subsidy, and the Christian population of Spain, Italy and the Islands, breathed a sigh of relief.

Kheir-ed-din's last years were spent in Constantinople, where he was the trusted advisor of the sultan and the hero of Ottoman sailors. He built a beautiful palace for himself and his wife (an ex-Christian noblewoman) and a magnificent mosque that became his place of burial. He died in 1546, an example of the fact that the son of a potter could rise to command the sultan's fleet and carry the title of beylerbey of North Africa. ■

Chapter 2

Dynamics of Political Change:
An Era of Civil and Religious Wars

It is very difficult to be precise about the forces at work at a given time in any society, and it is even more difficult to write with assurance about a society as pluralistic as that of the sixteenth and early seventeenth century. However, a careful review of the problems then facing European leaders will reveal that between 1550 and 1650 civil warfare was rampant everywhere. Indeed, practically no section of European society escaped civil rebellion in those years. Careful students have tried to give the civil wars a common denominator, but it has always been evident that, even though there were problems common to most of the uprisings, unique local conditions were always present. Three things emerge. First, the economy of all Europe was undergoing difficult problems of adjustment as the agricultural and rural communities and the commercial societies of the ocean and river lines of communication were forced to adjust both to the price changes that came with the flow of gold and silver from the New World and to the climatic changes that brought distress to European agriculture and famine to both rural and urban communities. These economic problems also coincided with the first great push of European men for the domination of the non-European world in America and Asia.

Of equal importance with the economic forces that lay behind the process of European development was the enormous effort on the part of princes to create absolute political power that would modify the pluralistic political organization of Europe. "Absolute power" did not mean that a prince could do what he wished; it meant that he did not share the powers available in the context of rights, customs, charters, and laws with other corporative powers in the kingdom. But absolute power was not all that they wished. European politicians and statesmen were also seeking new formulas for the mobilization of the potential power of the community for common purposes, and this inevitably evoked opposition from men defending the "liberties" that their fathers had enjoyed, liberties that often merely meant the right of landlords to control local communities.

Lastly, but probably not least in importance, was the crisis that developed when the Counter-Reformation forces of the church of Rome locked in combat with the expanding force of revolutionary Calvinism. Ideology in this era did not concern the fate of man on earth as much as it did the fate of man as a creature seeking salvation in the next world. But ideology was important; late sixteenth-century and early seventeenth-century men were as scandalized to see their fellow subjects worship at "strange altars" as twentieth-century men are to see their fellow citizens seek economic salvation in communistic or bourgeois imperialistic ideologies. These sixteenth- and seventeenth-century ideologies were often little more than flags to give legitimacy to rebellion; yet for many men they were the vital stuff that led to civil strife and even to massacres.

No matter which one believes to be most important—economic forces, political ambitions, or religious prejudices—the fact remains that these forces acted differently from one community to another because in each there were indigenous problems that modified and directed the flow of events.

ECONOMIC REALITIES

By the middle of the seventeenth century, European men had no more sources of power for their economy than those also available to earlier societies. Nor did they possess any metals that the societies of the ancient world did not also have, and their agricultural techniques were not appreciably more advanced than those of classical times. Nonetheless, the men who lived at the turn of the seventeenth century had learned to manufacture cannon and muskets that extended their military power beyond that of any people heretofore seen on the earth; and they had learned to build ships, powered by sails, that were larger and more manageable than any ever before constructed. Thus, their military power, once they managed to bring soldiers under the control of the state, was greater than that of the ancients and of other societies on the globe at the time.

Furthermore, seventeenth-century men learned to forge iron and to construct machines that aided them in the manufacture of everything from books to silk thread. This gave them a technical ability unknown to other peoples, so that even though they were still dependent upon a primitive agriculture and their industry relied upon wind, water, and the backs of men and animals for power, their furnaces, shipyards, and shops were portents of the civilization that was to come.

We must not, however, be dazzled by the powerful warships that gave European men hegemony over the rest of the globe. They undoubtedly represented the highest technical achievement of the contemporary European society, but the vast majority of European men had no part in the processes that created them. Most of them were still tied to the soil, and for most of them, because they were threatened with periodic crop failures that brought famine and death, farming was at best a hazardous occupation. Studies in demography clearly indicate that the population of seventeenth-century Europe either remained stationary or actually declined.

The proprietorship of the land differed from place to place, but in general it can be said that nowhere in Europe did any considerable number of the peasants who worked the land own or control enough acres to support themselves and their families. They were forced to work for their wealthier neighbors. Thus, when the price of bread mounted to three or four times its normal figure, the peasants suffered just as much as the poor in the towns for they, too, had to buy bread. There were a few rich peasants in the villages, men with large numbers of oxen or horses who could plow their own and their neighbors' lands (for a fee); there were also landless men in the countryside who often wandered from place to place as beggars or seasonal workers, but the majority of the peasants had some marginal connection with the land, and remained more or less fixed in their villages living in poverty that, in years of bad harvest, threatened their lives with famine.

Agricultural methods of the period were much the same as those of the high middle ages. In the north of Europe, the three-field system was usual, and the plots were long and narrow to allow the heavy plows to work the fields. In the south where the plowing was less effective, the plots were odd-shaped and were often left fallow every other year. The grain was harvested by hand with a sort of sickle and thrashed on a "floor" with flails. All villages were not able to allow one third of their fields to lie fallow each year, but failure to do so often had to be paid for in reduced yields. Most of the peasants could not survive without the opportunity to work on the lands of their more prosperous neighbors (wealthy peasants, lords, and the Church) and the right to pasture their animals on the common fields and cut wood in the common forests.

While those in the countryside continued their traditional ways of life, the cities and towns of the Europe that bordered the oceans or the larger navigable rivers had already begun to stir with the new spirit that later generations would call "capitalist." Most Europeans in the late sixteenth and seventeenth centuries still lived and died in an economy that provided only sustenance and most of them possessed very few things that were not made at home, a usefacture production, but there were some who produced for profit, who sold for profit, who organized the market, floated loans, discounted papers, bought and sold insurance—in short, who were creating the market economy that was to dominate the future. These people may have been relatively few in number, but their importance for the emergence of the characteristic forms of European society was disproportionately great.

The Amsterdam market dominated much of European commerce by the mid-seventeenth century, for the Dutch had a near monopoly of the carrying trade of northern and eastern Europe from the ports of Spain and Portugal to the Baltic and White seas. The goods of all Europe and of the Americas and Asia flowed into Amsterdam and the other Dutch harbors. There these commodities were processed, graded, sometimes adulterated, and then reshipped to other ports of Europe. Englishmen did not trade directly with Swedes or Danzigers or Frenchmen; all of these people sent their goods to the Netherlands and bought what they needed from other lands in the Amsterdam market. This situation was a source of much concern for many non-Dutchmen. Both Cromwell and Charles II attempted to cut the Dutch out of the carrying trade between English ports as well as between England and European ports other than those of the Netherlands. They were especially anxious to exclude the Dutch from trade in fish because the fishing fleet was the source of seamen for the merchant fleet. On the French scene, Colbert tried to build a French merchant fleet and exclude the Dutch from that nation's market. The Anglo-Dutch and the Franco-Dutch wars of the years 1650–1672 had roots in the commercial organization that made the United Netherlands the center for so much of the commerce of Europe.

The other axis for European trade was in the Mediterranean basin. Barcelona, Cadiz, Seville, Marseilles, Genoa, Leghorn, Naples, Venice, the Sicilian harbors, and the Levantine ports of the Ottoman Empire in Asia Minor, Egypt, and on the Black Sea were the important centers of this trade. The fact that the flow of silver from the New World declined rapidly after 1640 meant that the Seville and Cadiz harbors were less important than they had been earlier, but there was a lively commerce between southern France and Italy and the ports of Spain and Portugal. The trade with the Ottoman ports was still significant since those cities were also in contact with the Arab merchants in the Persian Gulf, the Red Sea, and the Indian Ocean. This trade was largely divided between the English Levant Company operating on the basis of a treaty that went back to Elizabeth's time, the French merchants of Marseilles and Toulon who profited from the capitulations in Francis I's treaties with the sultan, and the Venetians whose trading interests went back to the medieval era when Venetian ships dominated the commercial picture in the eastern Mediterranean.

If we look at the lists of commodities offered for sale in Amsterdam, Barcelona, Venice, or any of the other ports of entry in Europe, we can learn much about the structure of European economy. There were first of all items of food and drink: dried fruits, wine, "colonial goods" (tea, cocoa, coffee, and spices), dried and pickled fish, wheat, and a variety of other grains. The cloth trade had long been important, and we find Indian cottons and woolens and linen from all parts of Europe, some highly finished, others still requiring shrinking, fulling, and dyeing before the cloth could be used. The fine cloth came from the Flemish and Italian cities; the linens from Silesia, Ireland, and elsewhere; and the tweeds from England and Scotland. Most of these cloths were for the luxury market or for processors who would prepare them for that market; the poor of Europe usually wore cloth made at home or in their own villages. There were also many other commodities for sale:

hardware—hammers, saws, sickles, muskets, cannon, bullets, and blades; jewelry—pins, beads, broaches, rings; soap; beer; starch; and books. But those items that we would list under "manufactured" or "finished" commodities did not bulk in the market as the most important commodities of trade. There were piles of raw materials to be sold to craftsmen or merchant manufacturers for further processing: iron, tin, copper, lead, hemp, tar, pitch, coal, furs, and timber—to mention a few. Most of these commodities could be "graded"; indeed, there were three grades of Swedish iron on the Dutch market, five or six grades of leather. The fact that one could buy standard "graded" goods in Amsterdam was one of the important reasons for the Dutch commercial hegemony.

Commerce was controlled by merchant families or companies of merchants who established "factories," or warehouses, in the trading centers of Europe. The great trading companies like the Dutch East and West India companies, the English Levant, Muscovy, Plymouth, and India companies, and the French companies founded later by Colbert bulked large in the overseas trade, but the inter-European trade was largely in the hands of merchant families with connections in several cities. Many of the "factories" in Spain, Portugal, France, Germany, and the Baltic were only thinly disguised Dutch enterprises that took on the protective coloring of the host countries to preserve the right to trade in time of peace as well as in time of war. All of them, Dutch or otherwise, were controlled by men whose motives were to make profits and to extend their empires of activities. In the latter part of the seventeenth century, the urge for profits led to the creation of many speculative ventures that were set up to attract the purchase of shares. The most amusing may have been an English joint stock company for "a purpose yet to be announced," but such stock jobbing should not hide the fact that the merchants of Europe had laid the foundation for the great expansion of commerce that occurred in the early eighteenth century when European merchant ships plied the seas of the world and gave notice of the world hegemony of European civilization.

Some of the creative effort of these businessmen was devoted to manufacturing as well as to commerce. In general, two types of capitalist enterprises emerged for the manufacture of commodities. There were some items, like soap, beer, starch, books, tapestry, chinaware, guns, and glass, for which there was a relatively constant demand and which required a rather large capital investment for manufacture. In general, these items tended to be made in shops owned by merchant-manufacturers who employed craftsmen or laborers on a day or piece basis. The owner or owners had to know the markets for both the raw materials and the finished products and to take the chance of the entrepreneur. In some cases, these men could secure from the king or some wealthy nobleman or clergyman a charter or other assurance which would guarantee for their products a relatively stable market; in England there are still shops "by the appointment of the duke of this or that" which testify to that practice.

The other form of manufacturing enterprise is generally known as the "putting out" system. (See Chapter One.) This was most common in the cloth trade where peasants or rural workers could be hired to spin and dye thread and weave cloth in their own homes. The entrepreneur might supply the raw materials and even the tools, but the worker would do his task at home. There were many forms of the "putting out" system fitted to the local needs or customs, but in each the key figure was a businessman who understood the market and took the risks. Historians interested in social justice or conditions of labor have variously described this system as one which allowed the worker to live at home with his family under healthful conditions in a bucolic situation that contrasted with the ugly condition of the factory, or as a system of sweatshop labor in which the worker was exploited by the entrepreneur who virtually made him a peon or slave as soon as he fell into debt. Whichever it was, the fact remains that this system allowed for a division of labor and for relatively effective production of goods, perhaps the most effective possible in the era before the development of steam power.

The early seventeenth century witnessed a crisis in several parts of Europe resulting from the extended use of iron. The iron industry was a "forest" enterprise, for iron was made with charcoal and the forges had to move to find fuel supplies. The industry was also in competition for wood with other industrial activities. The tanners used oak bark for their leather processing; most of the things that men made, from windmills to tables, were made of wood; the shipbuilders, too, needed wood. But it was the forge that really ate up the forests, so much so that before the seventeenth century was over, the English iron industry had been severely crippled by a shortage of wood. Coal could be used, and was, for the manufacture of soap, beer, and other such things, but there were "humors" in the coal that, when used in the forge, "corrupted the iron." This was an era that knew no chemistry; it was not until the eighteenth century that an English iron-master learned by accident that coke and limestone could be used in the forge to produce usable iron. Many seventeenth-century writers who saw the forests being devoured by the forges were fearful that the whole European economy would be crippled by the lack of wood, and their dire predictions might have come true had not the new process been discovered in time.

To facilitate the distribution of trade goods and provide markets for shares of the joint stock companies, silver-gold ratios, and many bulk commodities, men developed banks and exchanges that could transfer large sums of money by bills of exchange, provide insurance for ships and cargos, serve as a stock market for shares, and carry out other banking and financial services. These were not new; thirteenth- and fourteenth-century Italian and Antwerp banking houses had long before pioneered in these services, but by the early seventeenth century the Bank of Amsterdam, as well as the exchange in that city, had become all-European institutions. Anyone who was an important trader had to have an account in Amsterdam. There were also banks in Genoa, Stockholm, Hamburg, and other cities; at the end of the century the Bank of England was born to finance a war and continued its existence to assist commerce. In addition to these more or less public banks, in most of the important cities of Europe there were banking families, some of them ex-goldsmiths, others ex-merchants, whose bills of exchange almost passed as legal tender. In other words, by the second half of the seventeenth century, the institutions of the market economy, motivated by the urge for profit and power, were well established in the more advanced centers of Europe even though most of the people still lived outside that economy.

The economy of Europe in the period 1550–1700 was only slightly modified by the wars that raged from one part of the continent to the other. The armies were not large by standards of the following centuries, and their weaponry was simpler than what was to come in the next two hundred years. The same was true of the navies; before 1600, warships were not much different from commercial vessels, and their firepower was relatively weak. Soldiers and sailors did encourage the growth of the cannon industry, gunsmiths, and other weapons manufacturers, but they did not yet call for standardized equipment, nor did they require large numbers of uniforms. The soldiers' need for bread, forage, cheese, and meat did encourage the growth of capitalist entrepreneurial activity; but the greatest impact of war on the economy was not to come until the following centuries. Perhaps, the rise in taxes, the rebellions against these tax increases, and the undisciplined pillaging of the soldiers as they passed through a community were more significant impacts of the wars on the economy of Europe.

THE REFORMED CHURCH AND THE COUNTER-REFORMATION

The Diet of Augsburg (1555) gave to the German princes the right to govern the Church within their lands. This agreement practically ended the revolutionary phase of the Lutheran movement, for Lutheran political philosophy bowed completely before the power of the prince, whose divine right to rule was unquestioned. The Lutheran clergy thus became agents of princely power and lost the revolutionary and missionary fervor that had once characterized their movement. But this did not bring peace to Christendom nor did it end the conflict for the religious soul of Europe, for within and without the church of Rome vigorous new religious movements emerged to join battle. The Reformed church of Switzerland and the Rhine, that had very early shown important divergences from Luther's theological and political doctrines, found in John Calvin a theologian and a leader who inspired a band of pastors, preachers, and politicians to work for the "cause" and make it into a real revolutionary movement. At the same time, the reform of the Roman Catholic church moved forward with precision and excited its devotees to attempt to recover the lost unity of the European religious community. (See Chapter One.) In particular, the Jesuit order, founded on militant religious principles and organized as an army, provided personnel to preach, teach, and conspire in the interests of the Roman Catholic religion. In the hundred years after 1550, a dominant motif in

European affairs was the conflict between Calvinism and the Counter-Reformation. Inevitably, this religious confrontation became involved with the political issues raised by the efforts of the princes to establish absolute power and with the ambitions of Hapsburg Spain to achieve hegemony in Europe.

Calvin's Reformed church was made of sterner stuff than that of the Lutherans. John Calvin had found in the Old Testament, with its legalist forms and its conception of God as protector of his elected people, an inspiration that greatly influenced his teachings. With rigorous logic he pursued Saint Augustine's doctrine of grace and predestination. All the trappings of the medieval Church had to go: sacraments, church decorations, prayers for the living as well as the dead. The altar disappeared and the pulpit, moved to the middle of the church, became the center of interest. In place of begging God for the favor of salvation, the congregation sang psalms praising His glory, while the preacher became a theologian instructing his flock in the mysteries of the Christian religion. No one could really know that God had destined him for salvation, but the Calvinists found it easy to assume that they were the elite, the elected, who would join Him in heaven.

The political teachings of the Reformed church fitted the needs of people faced with the encroachments of princely power. Unlike the Lutherans, the Calvinist Reformed church did not rely upon the prince either to reform the church or to govern it. The Reformed church had started with popular reforms in the towns that eventually captured both the cathedral and the town government; it had not depended upon government to deliver the power to reform the church into the hands of the faithful. Congregational or presbyterian organization of the parish and a system of representation in regional or national synods allowed laymen and clergy to share in church government even without the cooperation of the princely power. Calvinists did accept the idea of divine right, but they defined it quite differently than either Lutheran or Roman Catholic theologians did. Not only the prince, but each level of the social hierarchy obtained divine right from God. Thus, the nobleman in his manor, the town council in the city, the great lord over his fief, and the king in the kingdom exercised power through a right given by God. Furthermore, Calvinist divines also taught that men on the lower levels of the political hierarchy had both the right and the obligation to resist a prince who oppressed God's church. This, in effect, provided a religious flag for rebellion, a justification for an appeal to God (i.e., to the sword) against an "unjust" prince. In many parts of Europe where townsmen or noblemen found themselves in conflict with the expanding and encroaching power of their prince, Calvinism provided the cloak for revolt.

Missionaries trained in Calvinist Geneva and other Swiss cities were soon joined by others from cities on the Rhine and the Rhone, from Navarre, and from Scotland. They spread out in all directions, so that by the end of the sixteenth century the Reformed religion had become well established in southern France, the Rhineland, the Netherlands, northern Germany, and as far east as Poland, Hungary, and Transylvania. Geneva was still the spiritual capital, a city in which refugees from persecution had crowded out those citizens who wished to remain Roman Catholic, and from which plans, propaganda, and missionaries of the "cause" flowed into the Reformed community. By the end of the sixteenth century, this Calvinist cause had about the same connotation to Roman Catholic rulers that the Communist party program had to Western democratic statesmen in the years following the Russian Revolution. Perhaps rightly so, for Calvinism was an aggressive power in a world that did not hesitate to use military force to achieve its ambitions.

By the time the third session of the Council of Trent took place, hopes for recovering the heretics into the church of Rome had faded almost completely. In the first two sessions, there had been efforts to find formulas that might bridge the differences; at the session of 1562–1563, the mood was defiant rather than conciliatory. The Trentine decrees specifically anathematized the teachings of both the Lutheran and the Reformed communities and hardened and narrowed the doctrines that had emerged in the medieval Church. Trent, like the reforming papacy, also passed specific acts of reformation with the intention of ending the scandals that abuses of Church government, of exemptions, and of ignorant and untrained as well as immoral clergymen had brought into the Church.

The Trentine decrees, however, were only a "charter" for the reformed Roman Catholic church; the so-called Counter-Reformation was already proceeding on a broad front before these decrees were promulgated. Indeed, the picture of the Church reformed in the late sixteenth century clearly shows how pluralistic and diverse were the efforts to rebuild the Roman Catholic community. In France, the Trentine decrees were never published because the *parlements* of that kingdom regarded them as an invasion of both the Gallican liberties and the prerogatives of the court; yet, in France there emerged a Catholic League to defend the Church as well as new religious orders to propagandize the faith and minister to the evils that beset mankind. In Italy, the Roman Inquisition, and in Spain and Portugal inquisitions indigenous to those kingdoms sought to impose conformity. The Congregation of the Index set up censorship controls to protect the faithful from the contamination of heretical literature. The Jesuits sent forth into Europe bands of teachers, preachers, and confessors to kings and princes as well as missionaries who won for the Church converts all the way from India to Japan. Once Latin Europe realized the seriousness of the threat to the Church, a mighty force was released to defend it.

Of all the forces at the disposal of the Roman Church, the Jesuit order achieved the most important successes—as well as the worst reputation among its foes. Working on the assumption that the leaders are important in forming the manners, morals, and direction of society, the Jesuits made every effort to convert and educate the men who would be rulers, statesmen, soldiers, as well as the sons of important noblemen and patricians. Their schools soon became famous both for their excellence of education and for the fervor which they instilled in the hearts of the young. In these schools young men aged ten to fourteen were separated from family and the world

RELIGION IN EUROPE DURING THE MID-17TH CENTURY

Catholic
Lutheran
Reformed
Greek Orthodox
Boundary of the Holy Roman Empire
* Huguenot Centers

RUSSIA

POLAND

Mixed Catholic and Lutheran

SWEDEN

BALTIC SEA

DENMARK AND NORWAY

NORTH SEA

SCOTLAND

Mixed Catholic and Reformed

IRELAND

ENGLAND

Mainly Anglican with Dissenting Sects

NETHERLANDS

ATLANTIC OCEAN

HOLY ROMAN EMPIRE

AUSTRIA

SWITZERLAND

ITALIAN STATES

PAPAL STATES

FRANCE

SPAIN

PORTUGAL

SARDINIA

KINGDOM OF THE TWO SICILIES

MEDITERRANEAN SEA

TRANSYLVANIA

HUNGARY

Mixed Catholic, Reformed, Unitarian, Anabaptist, etc.

Mixed Catholic and Reformed

Some Moslem Groups

OTTOMAN EMPIRE

BLACK SEA

for four to eight years and carefully taught Latin, classical literature, and the fundamentals of Catholic theology (Saint Thomas). On another level, the Jesuits provided kings and princes with confessors who "understood" that a prince must have more moral freedom than a private person. As spiritual mentors, these Jesuit priests were in a position to influence the direction of policy as well as to keep the Jesuit general in Rome informed about the politics and political personalities of Europe. Finally, Jesuit teachers also emerged as political philosophers. Like the Calvinists, they were quite unwilling to tolerate diversity of belief in territories they controlled; but demanded freedom of the individual conscience and the right of the individual to practice his religion in those lands where Catholics were in a minority. A surprising outcome of the Reformation era was the fact that both Calvinist teachers and Jesuit philosophers were champions of liberty—at least in lands where they could not control the government. The Jesuit teachers also stood for two doctrines that appeared both dangerous and repugnant in many parts of Europe. The first was the ultramontane doctrine that not only vested control of the Church in the papal monarchy at Rome but also proclaimed that the pope had the right to dethrone, and release subjects from their obedience to, kings who did not abide by God's will. The second was a doctrine of tyrannicide which insisted that a tyrannical king—one who did not do God's will—could be assassinated by the first man who came upon him. These were strong words in the Europe of the late sixteenth century; they implied a supremacy of papal power over the secular rulers that shocked many men in Catholic as well as in Protestant or Reformed countries.

By producing two militant religious forces, the Reformation intruded upon the conflict between princes, who were trying to make their power absolute, and noblemen and townsmen, who were trying to preserve their "liberties." Thus, in the century 1550–1650 religious flags covered rebellion against political power as well as resistance to religious tyranny.

THE DYNAMICS OF CHANGE: PRINCELY POWER

Men around Holy Roman Emperor Charles v often wrote and talked about the empire in terms that went back to Dante's *De Monarchia.* They painted a world in which a universal empire could be revived and the peace and prosperity of Europe assured. When one and only one emperor rules, the age of peace is possible: one shepherd, one flock. Charles saw himself as the ruler who could, if Europe would allow it, establish a harmony among the many crowns; but a lifetime of frustrating warfare left that dream in shreds. At the end of his political career, he had to watch Germany accept the division of the Church as a political fact. His brother at the Diet of Augsburg (see p. 39) recognized the formula *cujus regio, ejus religio,* which left to the prince the decision about what religion his subjects would practice. Instead of pursuing the ideal of a universal empire, Charles' son, as his successor in Spain, Italy, and the Netherlands, believed God intended him to give efficient government to his lands, to defend the integrity of the Church, and to check the spread of heresy everywhere.

Philip II assumed the most important of his father's crowns; but he did not have the responsibility for all Christendom upon his shoulders. Since his inheritance included both Italy and Spain, and hence the necessity for maintaining communications in the western Mediterranean, he did have to confront the Islamic raiders of North Africa. But he felt no responsibility for clearing the entire Mediterranean basin of Turkish naval power. In the Netherlands and Spain, he was confronted with different problems. The governments of both were anarchic and cumbersome. His aims were to make a government for Spain as a whole out of the crowns of Aragon and Castile and to make a government for the Netherlands out of the disorderly complex of seventeen provinces of the Burgundian inheritance. In both lands, he found serious religious problems. In Spain the Moriscos, descendants of the Moors who had superficially adopted the Christian religion, were a constant threat to the security of the land. They gave aid and comfort to raiders from the Barbary coast; they were a potential "fifth column" ready to aid a Moslem attempt to reconquer the Iberian peninsula. In the Netherlands the spread of heretical ideas was almost equally disturbing, for Philip II and the men of his time regarded religious unity as the cement of society. The Church was the custodian of the beliefs, aspirations, and loyalties of the community; divergence from the Church was a public scandal that could not be tolerated.

Thus, from the moment (1556) he accepted the scepters from his father, Philip II imposed upon himself the tasks of bringing order to the governments of his lands, creating unity among his peoples, and establishing Spanish control over the western Mediterranean Sea. His hand was made strong by the facts that treasure was flowing from the New World and that Castile was still reasonably prosperous and thus able to support these limited objectives.

Philip II had his father's experience behind him. He had seen Charles' projects blighted because there was not enough money to carry them to a conclusion or because the men upon whom he had depended failed in their mission or their duty. Thus, Philip understood that if he were to achieve the objectives that God had placed upon his shoulders, he must give his realms efficient and effective government. The ramshackle political structures in both Spain and the Netherlands cried out for reorganization along more rational lines. In the Netherlands, for example, many of the bishops governing the Church in provinces under Philip's rule were suffragan (subordinate) to archbishops whose sees were outside of the Hapsburg Netherlands. In Spain, Charles had not been able to consolidate the government of his kingdoms under a single council; it was Philip's aim to make the Council for Spain a governing body that would give a common rule to Castile, Aragon, Granada, and Navarre and act as a coordinating agency for the Indies, Italy, and the Netherlands. Only thus could the thirty-odd crowns of the Hapsburg empire have a common direction. In his ambition to bring order out of the chaotic political structures that he inherited from the past, Philip was only acting in the spirit of his age.

Philip's program was revolutionary in that it aimed at the rationalization of the pluralistic political order. Other sixteenth-century princes had also seen the need for such reforms. The Catholic kings of Castile had established their right to tax even before Charles v came to the throne. Charles had to face rebellions by his grandees, but they were unable to halt the centralizing process. In France, Francis I, continuing the work of his Valois predecessors, had given his kingdom a new provincial government and, by a concordat with Rome, had secured control over the Catholic church in his kingdom. In England, the reformation of the Church allowed the Tudor monarchs to extend both their economic and political power by the confiscation of Church lands and the establishment of royal supremacy over the Church organization. The same had happened in Germany where princes, after a civil war, were assured the right to control the religious behavior of their subjects and the machinery of Church government. In the administration of justice, royal absolute power also continued to expand. Royal courts were supplanting seignorial and town courts, thereby depriving lords and town governments of this essential instrument of control. The advisors of princes were not slow to see that what was necessary to make all this more effective was to supplant the anarchic political and religious organization that had been inherited from earlier eras with a more rationalized structure.

But revolutionary movements usually evoke opposition on the part of those whose powers and liberties are endangered. Princes could not expect to encroach upon the traditional positions of their great vassals and towns without meeting opposition. The great lords—whether grandees in Spain, *Les Grands* in France, magnates in Poland, Hungary, and Bohemia, princes in Germany—well remembered that kings were once only first among equals, or, as the coronation oath of Aragon put it, "no better than we are." These men were ready to defend their liberties against the encroachment of the king. The town governments, too, remembered their past struggles to achieve control over their own affairs. They wanted the king to provide protection on the highways and security from invasion, but they did not want him to tax their business activities or extend his powers over their communities without their consent. Towns like La Rochelle, Antwerp, London, Frankfurt, and others had charters wrested from feudal lords that made them into quasi-independent politico-economic entities, and they were unwilling to give up these "liberties." It should be noted that the rebellion in the Netherlands against Philip II was sparked by two measures, one an effort to give a rational episcopal organization to the Church, the second a tax upon commerce. Both were aimed at enlarging the power of the prince; both encroached upon the traditional liberties of important people in the land.

In spite of the opposition that was bound to develop, princes like Philip II had to try to consolidate their power in order to obtain more revenue. The ambitions for imperium arose from the example of Charles v; from the rising costs of cannon, warships, and soldiers; from the imperious demands of their servants for a more rational order in the kingdom; from the will to power that seems to excite men called to the throne. All these factors conspired to urge princes to seek absolute power. But this drive for extension of royal authority also created a reaction that easily led to civil war. In the hundred years following 1559, civil wars, under flags of religion and "liberties," raged in nearly every kingdom of Europe. The course and the outcome of these civil wars were always conditioned by the traditions as well as the political realities of the country involved in the struggle.

PHILIP II AND THE MEDITERRANEAN

In the first years after Philip II ascended his father's thrones, the political situation in Europe seemed most favorable for the young ruler. His wife, Mary Tudor, was queen of England, and even though she could not produce a child, she did make secure his northern flank. The pope at Rome, Paul IV, was his enemy, but in the Spanish Inquisition as well as in the newly formed Jesuit order and other elements of the Church, Philip had friends and influence throughout the Roman Catholic community. And perhaps most important of all, his arch enemy, King Henry II of France, was anxious for peace. Henry II was much concerned about the spread of heresy in his kingdom, but he was limited by the disorders in his treasury. The treaty of Cateau-Cambrésis (1559) between Henry II and Philip II marked the end of the Hapsburg-Valois wars and prepared the way for the era that gave new form to European political society.

Unlike his father who spent so much of his life on horseback, Philip II was a man of ink and paper, an administrator who attempted to rule the vast enterprise of his empire from his palace office. Unfortunately for him, he assumed that all important decisions must be made in his court and council; in an era when communications were slow and transportation difficult, this conception of his role created problems for his soldiers and governors. Indeed, it often made nearly impossible the execution of any policy at all.

One of Philip's most pressing problems concerned the sea lanes that united his Mediterranean empire. The communications between Naples, Sicily, Milan, and the Tuscan ports and the Spanish peninsula were endangered by the Turkish-Barbary naval forces. In the 1550's a new Moslem admiral, Dragut, commanded the sultan's western navy; after Dragut had established a firm base on the Tunisian coast, the Moslem forays made the coasts of Spain, Italy, and the islands unsafe. But the Ottomans also found their lines of communication endangered. Charles V had established the Knights of St. John on the island of Malta, from which they and other Spanish-Italian pirates preyed upon Moslem shipping. Malta was as important to Christian control of the western Mediterranean as it was dangerous to the Ottoman-Barbary naval forces. The conflict between the contending powers however, was inconclusive until 1565, when the sultan decided to try to wipe out the nest of Christian "pirates." The siege of the fortifications of Malta was one of the great military epics of the century. A handful of Christian soldiers stood off a powerful thrust for months; the Turks took three of the four forts, but when a small relief force from Sicily finally arrived, Ottoman losses had been so great that they were forced to lift the siege. Dragut was killed in this conflict.

Suleiman the Magnificent died the next year. However, his successor's government still had enough force to inaugurate a new attack, this time against the Venetian installations on Cyprus (1570). That island was too deep in Ottoman waters for effective relief, but in 1571 a Holy League, inspired by the pope and consisting of the Spanish and Italian naval powers, assembled a great armada to attack the Turkish fleet in the mid-Mediterranean. The battle was joined at Lepanto on October 7, 1571. The Christian soldiers, armed with arquebuses and cannon and protected by metal breastplates and helmets, overpowered their Turkish counterparts, who were largely armed with bows and arrows and lacked personal armor. The rams of the Christian galleys finished the conflict: Eighty of the opposing ships were sunk, one hundred and thirty captured; less than forty escaped. Don Juan, an illegitimate son of Charles v and commander of the Christian forces, became the hero of every young nobleman in Europe.

Lepanto, of course, was a Spanish victory even more than an Italian one because after that battle the Spanish navy had only to deal with the raids of the Barbary corsairs; the Turkish navy kept to the eastern Mediterranean. However, it was not only the victory of Lepanto that checked Ottoman power. Suleiman's successor, Selim ii, surnamed "the Sot," was not a ruler to extend the conquests of the two great sultans who had preceded him. Under his rule, the Ottoman Empire sank into a lethargic slump; the janissaries ceased to threaten Christian Europe either on the Danube or in the western Mediterranean. It would be another hundred years before a Turkish army again appeared as a menace to Christian Europe.

CIVIL WARS IN FRANCE

When Henry ii and Philip ii ended the Hapsburg-Valois wars at Cateau-Cambrésis (1559), both rulers expected to turn their attention to the problems created by the conversion of a minority of their subjects to the reformed religion. Henry ii, however, was almost immediately killed in a tournament accident, leaving his young son a kingdom with a treasury made empty by a half century of war. Francis ii, too inexperienced and too weak to govern, gave the management of his affairs over to his wife's uncles, the duke of Guise and the cardinal of Lorraine. Within a few months, a conspiracy to kidnap the young king and control his government became the first act of an intermittent civil war that ravaged the kingdom of France for the next forty years.

The stakes in this conflict were both religious and political. For the preceding hundred years, the Valois kings had done much to centralize the government of the kingdom. The semi-autonomous dukes, who had been, in fact, peers of the king, had disappeared; the crown had absorbed their lands and titles. Thus, the kingdom of France had changed from a confederation of more or less autonomous provinces under the ducal families into a federation of provinces all under the king. Under Francis I and Henry II, the process of consolidating royal control had continued apace. The king of France had advantages that other contemporary rulers lacked; he could collect a war tax, the *taille,* in most of his provinces (*pays d'élection*) without consultation of the Estates. However, as the king strengthened his judicial and administrative powers, he inevitably encroached upon the authority of the towns and of the great nobles. When a weak king appeared, those men who objected to the rise of royal authority saw an opportunity to restore feudal relations and decentralize power in the kingdom.

The ambitions of the "great ones of the land" were confused by the additional fact that a large number of the urban communities in the south and west of France had been converted to the Reformed religion (Huguenots). There were many factors involved in these conversions. Some have pointed out that the Huguenot strongholds were the same as the Albigensian (Catharist) ones of the thirteenth century; others, that this was the revolt of the south against the rule of the north. Since the Huguenot missionaries made progress primarily in the urban centers, their movement can also be seen as similar to the Calvinist conversions elsewhere. In addition to the urban converts, however, the new religion found support among part of the high nobility of the realm. The Bourbon-Condé family, next in line to the throne after the Valois family, could trace its adherence to the new faith back to Margaret of Navarre whose humanist leanings had led her to join the reform a half century earlier. (The Bourbons became kings of Navarre when Anthony married her daughter, Jeanne.) Thus, the duke of Bourbon and his cousin, the prince of Condé, were natural leaders for a reformed party. They found important followers among the members of the Montmorency family (Coligny, d'Andelot, Châtillon), one of the oldest in the kingdom, as well as among a considerable body of noblemen of lesser importance who for reasons of their salvation or their personal interest joined the Huguenot religion.

Nor were the Protestant nobility the only ones interested in power. In the north and east of France, the nobility tended to remain faithful to the old religion and hostile to innovation, and yet these Catholic noblemen proved to be as avid as the Huguenots in their quest for power in the kingdom. The leadership of the Catholic party fell to the house of Guise, a cadet branch of the ducal family of Lorraine that had established itself in France early in the century and, with its members serving as soldiers and advisors of the Valois kings, had become rich and powerful. The family was related to many of the more important French noble houses as well as to foreign dynasties. For example, the young queen of Francis II, Marie Stuart of Scotland, was a niece of the duke of Guise. Perhaps because of its power and influence, the Guise family was not universally loved; the Huguenot noblemen of the south usually referred to the family as a "foreign" house, not completely welcome in France.

Francis II died (1560) before the prince of Condé could be executed for his part in the conspiracy to kidnap the young king. The Huguenots were sure that God had acted to save their leader, for Francis' death ended the government of the family Guise and introduced into French politics another figure, the queen-mother Catherine de Medicis, who became regent for her ten-year-old son, Charles IX. A regency government in France was bound to be weak, for the regent could not act like a major king. Catherine de Medicis and her two sons occupied the throne until the murder of Henry III in 1589. Their interests were served by neither the Bourbon nor the Guise. Catherine and her children, Charles IX and Henry III, were not strong rulers, and yet they did have political ambitions and an interest in preserving the throne and the authority of the king's government. Confronted with powerful ambitions of great nobles, Huguenots, and Catholics, they tried to govern by compromise, conspiracy, and cajolery. It was Catherine who first proposed the policy of religious toleration that Henry IV adopted almost forty years later; it was she who assembled a "flying squadron of beauties" to keep the young men of the court interested in sex rather than in politics; it also was Catherine who forced her son Charles IX to agree to the massacre of the Huguenots on the feast of St. Bartholomew in 1572. None of her children was able to sire an heir; this fact added to the confusion and the problems of the civil wars that followed 1561.

The civil-religious wars in France were characterized by assassination, massacre, and conflict that pitted townsmen against their neighbors, relatives against each other, and province against province. Historians count eight of these wars in less than forty years; each of them was relatively brief, but brief also were the periods of truce between them. The religious side of the conflicts aroused strong emotions. The psalm-singing Huguenot communities were a public scandal in Catholic eyes, while the Mass was idolatry and superstition in the eyes of its opponents. Each group hated the other violently. In the early stages of the wars, the Huguenots insisted upon their right to defy the king because, since the crown gained many advantages from its association with the Catholic church, the Valois kings usually came down on the side of the Huguenot enemies. But in the latter stages of the wars, it was the Catholics who assumed the right to defy the king, perhaps even to dethrone him. The factors that brought about this shift in attitude also induced Philip II of Spain to concern himself with the problems of France. It was simple enough. Neither Charles IX nor Henry III could produce an heir; the Valois line was obviously coming to an end, and a new dynasty would soon occupy the throne. Under the Salic law, which regulated succession in France, the throne could only be inherited through the male line. In that case, the next in line was Henry of Bourbon, king of Navarre, who also was the leader of the Huguenot party. The St. Bartholomew's Day massacre had come on the occasion of Henry's marriage to Catherine's daughter Margaret; he had escaped death by becoming a

Catholic, but shortly afterward he rejoined the Huguenots. With the prospect that he would become king, the Huguenots also became royalist, but the Catholics were determined that no heretic would be their king.

By the time this problem emerged as the central focus of the French civil wars, Philip II was deeply engaged in a conflict with the northern provinces of the Netherlands. Since the rebels in that civil war also carried the flag of the Reformed religion, Philip did not want to see a Huguenot on the throne of France who might aid the Dutch rebels. Moreover, the situation also offered to Philip the possible opportunity to place a family favorable to Spain on the French throne.

By the 1580's the political situation in France was shaping up for the War of the Three Henrys. The Catholic towns and noblemen had organized themselves into a Catholic League under the leadership of Henry, duke of Guise. As a member of the house of Lorraine, the duke could trace his line back to Charlemagne, who had ruled France as king long before Hugh Capet, the ancestor of both the Valois and Bourbon families, was elected to the throne. The League proposed to use the Estates General as the instrument to place Henry of Guise on the throne; some even suggested that Henry III should be deposed. Henry de Bourbon, as leader of the Huguenots and heir in the male line, led the other protagonists in the conflict; they had the Salic law on their side, but probably not more than one-fourth of the important people of the kingdom. Henry III was caught in the middle. He was not a strong man, nor did he understand how to win loyalty to his person, but he did have a strong sense of his position as king. When an uprising in Paris proved that the duke of Guise, rather than the king of France, controlled that city, Henry III plotted and executed the murder of this rival, thus depriving the League of its best candidate for the throne.

Henry III, fleeing the wrath of the League, joined Henry de Bourbon in hopes of implementing a compromise that was being suggested by a "middle party," the so-called *politiques,* who argued that religious toleration was essential to the community and that the Salic law was fundamental to the kingdom. Henry III did not solve the question; he was murdered by a monk who believed that he was doing God's will. Henry de Bourbon then claimed the throne, but he did not really occupy it until after years of civil war, conversion to Catholicism (1593) required even by the *politiques,* and extensive gifts of hereditary offices, money, and privileges to his opponents. Paris and the kingdom were not "won by a Mass"; Henry was forced to buy the loyalty of his Catholic subjects in a way that could create a new "feudality" in the kingdom.

Henry's conversion appalled the Huguenots, who began to look about for a new champion to take his place. To keep their loyalty, Henry negotiated the charter of Huguenot rights and liberties known as the Edict of Nantes (1598). This famous document in effect created a Huguenot republic within the kingdom of France. The Huguenots were allowed control over soldiers and fortified towns, regular assemblies, the right to serve in the king's government, and, of course, the right to practice their religion. If the crown surrendered privileges and wealth to the great Catholic noblemen, it gave the Huguenots a position in the kingdom of a quasi-independent power. For the next fifty years, France was troubled by the efforts of the royal government to recoup the power that had been lost in the civil wars and to rebuild a strong central authority.

SPAIN, THE NETHERLANDS, AND ENGLAND

The kingdoms of Spain were bound to the Netherlands both by ties of dynasty and long commercial relations. For centuries, the Netherlands was the most important market for the huge Spanish wool clip, and in turn Spain purchased the manufactures of Flanders and the "northern commodities" that Dutch merchants brought from Germany and the Baltic. When Spanish and Portuguese ships imported goods from Asia and the New World, commerce between the Netherlands and the Iberian peninsula expanded rapidly as the Netherland merchants took over the role of middleman between Iberia and northern Europe. This traffic, however, had to pass the southern coast of England, a fact that made Anglo-Spanish friendship most important, for English seamen had a long tradition of piracy, and shipping in the Channel was a natural target unless the English king discouraged the practice. In the mid-sixteenth century when Philip II mounted his father's thrones in Spain, the Netherlands, and Italy, his wife was Mary Tudor, queen of England. Thus, it seemed that his hold upon the complex of crowns that Charles V gave him was reasonably secure. Even the fact that he answered his Netherlands-Flemish subjects with a speech from the throne in Spanish did not necessarily mean that he would have trouble with them.

Charles V had been born in Ghent, spoke Flemish fluently, and understood the traditions of the people of the so-called Burgundian inheritance. Philip II, however, was appalled at the disorder in the political and ecclesiastical constitutions of these provinces. The administration was a hodgepodge of rights, customs, special privileges, charters, and practices that almost defied understanding. Philip II was a "modern prince"; he saw the necessity for bringing order out of the chaotic structures inherited from the past to provide uniformity and to assure princely power. The absolute state that he wished to establish was a state in which the power to govern would be lodged in the hands of the prince and not shared with the other competing authorities that made up the political pluralism of the era. The Netherlands presented a particularly thorny problem because its cities and noblemen had a long tradition of rebellion against rulers who tried to impose their will at the expense of these rights, charters, and customs that appeared so chaotic by the mid-sixteenth century.

The religious problem in the Netherlands was one that had to occupy Philip's attention. Reformed clergymen had made some inroads in the cities among the ignorant in the streets as well as among the noble and patrician families who had read Erasmus and the Christian humanists. The regent at

Brussels forbade the introduction of bizarre religious cults (Lutheranism, Anabaptism, Calvinism), but this did not stop the spread of the new doctrines. Philip decided that his first act should be to bring order into the religious make-up of these provinces by erecting three archbishoprics under a primate to control all the bishops and clergy of the area; he also started the process of inquisition to seek out and punish heretics. These acts caused considerable unrest; the people opposed the new constitution and resented the Inquisition. In 1566 a delegation of some 250 to 300 young noblemen appeared before the regent, Margaret of Parma, to request the government to modify its program against heresy. One of her counselors gave the protesting party a name by urging her "to pay no attention to 'these beggars'" (*ces gueux*). A few weeks later, people in the streets sought to make an impression by breaking into the churches in cities and towns and smashing the statues, rending the pictures, breaking the church windows and altars, and burning books in an iconoclastic fury resembling that of the early Christians who smashed the temples and idols of the Roman world. Lutheran and Calvinist nobles and patricians disavowed the violence, but the regent was unable to restore her authority.

Philip II was outraged; his response was to send soldiers and a new governor, the duke of Alva, to punish the perpetrators of violence and to restore princely power. In the terror that followed, a number of important noblemen were executed; William of Orange, the first nobleman of the land, quietly left the country. It was not long before members of both the Catholic and Reformed churches resented the brutal repressions. Furthermore, Alva had to find money to support his troops, so he forced the General Estates to impose a heavy sales tax upon the provinces. This tax on business and Alva's repression of the non-Catholic religions changed the riots in the streets into a civil war in which "sea beggars" with letters from William of Orange seized the islands off the coast, harassed Spanish commerce, and defied Alva's authority. Alva's reaction was prompt but not entirely effective. Unhappily for him, it aroused anti-Spanish sentiments in the Catholic as well as the Reformed sections of the population. By 1572 the northern provinces of Holland, Zeeland, Utrecht, and West Friesland had elected William of Orange commander in chief of their armies, and they were looking to England and France for support against their Hapsburg ruler.

Philip II was unfortunate in many ways. When he replaced Alva with the more reasonable Requesens, the latter died before he could accomplish his mission and was not replaced for over a year. Spanish troops, unpaid and out of control, mutinied and sacked Antwerp, murdering some 6000 of its inhabitants (1576). As a result, in 1576 thirteen of the provinces gave William of Orange virtually sovereign power for the duration of the conflict (Pacification of Ghent) and the next year a General Estates of all the provinces confirmed the choice. Philip appointed his half-brother, Don Juan, the hero of Lepanto, to be governor, but it was too late. The only decision possible was a military one. Don Juan and Alessandro Farnese of Parma did succeed in driving William out of the Walloon part of the Flemish provinces before Don Juan's death (1578), and Parma, who became regent, managed to draw the predominantly Catholic provinces into a political union (The Union of Arras, 1579). This, however, only consolidated the rebellion in the northern provinces by evoking the Union of Utrecht a few weeks later. By 1580 the Netherlands was in fact divided between the provinces of the rebellious north under William of Orange and the provinces of the south under Parma and the Spanish. Catholics in the north began to migrate southward while Protestants in the south moved north; the result was that the cities, at least, tended to be either predominantly Protestant or Catholic, and religion became a cementing agent for each of the two regimes. In July 1581 this situation was formalized when the meeting of the General Estates of the northern provinces declared independence from Philip II and chose William of Orange to head the new government until a sovereign could be selected. William was murdered three years later.

Naturally, the civil war in the Netherlands soon involved neighboring kingdoms. The rebels appealed to the queen of England and to the king of France for help. Both rulers had reasons for caution, as well as reasons for aiding the rebellion. Elizabeth I had come to the throne in 1558 when Mary died; Philip II proposed that she, his sister-in-law, should become his wife. This solution would have satisfied Spanish policy, and it might have erased the stain of illegitimacy from Elizabeth's birth, but she knew well that it would have been very unpopular in England. When Philip finally realized that she was simply putting him off, he married the French princess, Elizabeth of Valois. Both Philip and Elizabeth I had good reasons for not allowing England and Spain to drift into war, and yet both also had reasons for conflict. Elizabeth gave niggardly aid to the Dutch, but she sent her "sea dogs" to harass the Spanish sea-lanes both in the Atlantic and in the Channel. Philip tolerated this activity to avoid the greater evil of outright conflict, but he also conspired against Elizabeth I with Catholics in England and others interested in placing Mary Stuart on Elizabeth's throne. As the situation of the rebellion in the Netherlands became more and more tense and the depredation of English corsairs more damaging, Philip decided that the only way to win in the Netherlands was to break the power of England. This required him to prepare a huge naval expedition, the so-called Armada, for an attack on England.

There were military, political, and logistical problems to be considered before such a plan could be effected. Even when the Armada was finally assembled, some of these problems were still not solved. The Armada was made up of ships of many different types, armed with different equipment, and manned by men from all over the Mediterranean basin who had not acted together before. The movement of the entire Armada was limited by the speed of the slowest ship, a fact that also limited its maneuverability. An additional problem of great moment emerged from the fact that Parma's army in the Netherlands would be needed for a successful invasion of England. But the Armada could not put into the Netherlands harbors because of the shallow bars that guarded them, and Parma could not send out his troops in small ships because the Dutch navy, with shallow draft ships, would interdict any such maneuver. Perhaps the Armada was doomed before it left the Iberian ports, but its doom was completed when the Spanish admiral failed to bring his fleet into one of the English harbors where its superior firepower might well have allowed him to land marines and other soldiers. Instead, he proceeded up the Channel, herded by the faster, more maneuverable English warships, and then encountered the storm in the North Sea that scattered his ships, wrecked many of them, and drove the rest around the English islands in great confusion. The result was plain: England was safe from Spanish invasion, and the Spanish could no longer hope to use the sea route from Spain to the Netherlands to supply their forces. It was a disaster for Philip's program.

Parma might nonetheless have been able to impose some sort of military decision upon the northern provinces had not the situation in France distracted his army. As we have seen, the death of Henry III (1589) brought the throne of France into question: Henry IV, a Protestant, could claim it by virtue of the Salic law, but the Catholic League refused to accept a heretic king. However, the murder of Henry of Guise a short time before had deprived the League of a glamorous candidate. Philip hoped to supply France with a queen in the person of his daughter, whose mother was a French princess. She could marry a French nobleman and make him king. The prospect was enough to persuade Philip that Parma's army could best be used in France. It did occupy Paris for a time, but Parma died, and by the end of the 1590's, Henry IV had been able to rally most of the kingdom behind him so that there was nothing for the Spanish to do but make peace.

With the Spanish occupied in England and France, the men in the northern Netherlands were able to consolidate their position both politically and economically. Prince William I of Orange was assassinated in 1584 when his son, Prince Maurice, was only seventeen years old. In the following years, an important political confrontation emerged in the Netherlands. The patrician families who owned the ships, the commercial houses, and the banking and insurance interests came to have much influence in the General Estates. As the regents in their cities and provinces, they dominated large segments of the political power. On the other hand, the Orange family, represented at the moment in the person of Prince Maurice of Nassau, controlled the military forces of the provinces, and the princes of Orange aspired to become kings of the United Netherlands. The regents, however, resisted this action, and since they had the money and the votes in the Estates, they constituted a formidable force.

Equally as important as this political conflict was the fact that the Dutch merchants grew rich during these years. Their ships dominated the commerce of the Channel and the North Sea; they ranged into the Baltic, to the Sea of Azov, and finally they intruded into the Portuguese monopoly in Asia by sailing around Africa and establishing themselves in Ceylon, India, and the Islands of the East Indies. With this wealth at their disposal, they easily stood off the Spanish efforts to return them to Spanish rule. The line between the Spanish Netherlands and the United Netherlands became a military frontier that marked the limits of Spanish power. After the death of Philip II, the effort to reconquer the rebellious provinces was only half-hearted, and by 1609 the Spanish government was willing to sign a twelve-year truce recognizing the *de facto* independence of the United Netherlands. As we shall see, in the seventeenth century these northern provinces became a great power in Europe, capable of making war with the kingdoms of England and France on equal terms.

THE GREAT GERMAN WAR (THE THIRTY YEARS' WAR): FIRST PHASES 1618–1629

While civil rebellions in France and the Netherlands were moving toward solutions, events in Germany were creating a crisis that would provoke a religious confrontation and then develop into a civil conflict that would last thirty years. The problems of Germany were more difficult than those of either France or the Netherlands because of the complexities of the Holy Roman Empire. There was an emperor and the Diet, but the principalities, the episcopal establishments, the free cities, the monastic foundations, the petty sovereignties, the free knights—all the 2000 more or less overlapping jurisdictions made the empire a "political monster." The religious settlement of the Diet of Augsburg, which left to the local rulers the power to determine the religious practices of their subjects, had strengthened the princes vis-à-vis the emperor, but it had also created a Pandora's box for it assumed that the religious status quo of 1555 would remain forever. Moreover, since it was made before any extensive Calvinist missionary work in Germany, it included only Catholics and Lutherans in the settlement. By 1610 two of the four secular electors, those of the Rhine Palatinate and Brandenburg, were Calvinists, and, of course, the status quo of 1555 had not prevailed. What was more ominous, by 1610 a Catholic League and a Protestant Union had come into existence as the political and military agents of the opposing confessional factions. Both were probably illegal, but who in the empire could decide this point?

The emperors of the late sixteenth century had done little to improve the position that the first wave of the Reformation had left them. Indeed, the German branch of the house of Hapsburg became weakened with each decade because its territories had been divided among several heirs, and the *raison d'être* of the Hapsburgs as rulers of Bohemia, Hungary, and the Danubian provinces had ceased to exist when the Ottoman Empire no longer threatened to expand up the Danube. In both Bohemia and Hungary, many of the great magnates and lesser nobles had converted to Calvinism, perhaps as a way of defiance of their "foreign" king. Furthermore, in most of the Hapsburg lands the rulers had not insisted upon their right to require religious conformity; in the kingdom of Bohemia, a Diploma of Religious Liberties recognized the rights of dissenters from the Roman Catholic church. When the emperors were weak in their own lands, it was unreasonable to expect them to be strong in the politics of the empire.

However, in the second decade of the seventeenth century a Hapsburg prince emerged who was determined to alter this situation. Prince Ferdinand, duke of Styria, believed, like his relative Philip II, that God had placed an obligation on his shoulders. As one after another of the crowns of the German Hapsburgs (The Austrias, Styria and Carinthia, Hungary, Bohemia, Tyrol) fell on his head, he became more certain of his destiny. Ferdinand was a "modern prince"; that is to say, he was determined to exercise power unobstructed, as far as possible, by other institutions in his lands, In Styria, he bypassed the *Landtage,* introduced royal servants who were graduates of the university law schools, and organized an absolutist regime that tolerated no religious dissent of any kind. When he became king-designate of Bohemia, he introduced a strict interpretation of the Diploma of Religious Liberties that promised to undermine the intention of that decree. In appearance, Ferdinand was an easygoing man who enjoyed the hunt and the life at court, but he was also a serious person who scourged himself as punishment for his sins and who might change his ministers but not his policy. This was the prince who became king of Hungary, king of Bohemia and emperor of the Holy Roman Empire in 1618–1619; he also found himself on a collision course with another of his contemporaries, Frederick, count of Palatine of the Rhine, and with the Calvinist magnates of the kingdom of Bohemia.

Prince Frederick was not a talented man, but he occupied a critical position in Europe in 1618. His uncles were the prince of Orange, Stadtholder of the Netherlands, and the duke of Bouillon, military leader of the French Huguenots. His father-in-law was James I of England, and his wife's uncle was the king of Denmark; furthermore, he had a crafty advisor, the prince of Anhalt, who secured for him the presidency of the Protestant Union and an alliance with the Calvinist prince of Transylvania. When the Calvinist Bohemian magnates dethroned Ferdinand and elected Frederick to be their king, this young elector of the Palatine seemed to embody the Calvinist cause in Europe. That was what Anhalt wished—for he was one of a small clique of Calvinist politicians who plotted the overthrow of the Catholic Hapsburgs in central Europe and the triumph of Calvinism. However, Anhalt had not counted on the fact that Louis XIII of France, still an adolescent, was at war with his Calvinist subjects, and, when asked to support Frederick against Ferdinand, refused because he was sure that he saw a Europe-wide Calvinist plot. He not only refused, he also urged the Lutheran princes of Germany to stand aside in the conflict between Frederick and Ferdinand over the throne of Bohemia. The network of alliances that Anhalt had woven around his young prince fell apart. There was a battle at White Mountain (1621) outside of Prague; Frederick fled from Bohemia as its "Winter King," and Ferdinand, after taking revenge, changed Bohemia into a monarchy with the crown hereditary in the house of Hapsburg.

Ferdinand's victory at White Mountain had not been his own doing. He had called upon Maximilian, duke of Bavaria and head of the Catholic

League, to use the League army against Frederick. In return, he promised Maximilian that he would transfer the electoral crown of the Palatinate Wittelsbach family to the cadet line in Bavaria. This act bypassed the Diet of the empire and probably was illegal; nonetheless Tilly, commanding the League army, invaded the Palatinate to secure the electoral crown for Maximilian, causing a Spanish army also to enter that principality to be sure of the supply lines between Spain and the Netherlands. Thus a new phase of the war, the struggle for control of the Rhine, had begun.

The twelve-year truce in the Netherlands was over, and the war between the king of Spain and his erstwhile subjects in United Netherlands now became united with the war in Germany. This opened what is known as the Danish phase of the war, or the battle for the Rhine. Christian, king of Denmark intervened on the side of the Protestant princes, but the Protestant party soon found itself confronted with overpowering military force. The Spanish army under Spinola operated in the Netherlands; the Catholic League army under Tilly and a new imperial army under Wallenstein operated in Germany. The Dutch were contained; Frederick's mercenary, Count Mansfield, was driven from Germany and killed; and the king of Denmark suffered crushing defeat at Lutter-am-Barenberge.

Emperor Ferdinand II now seemed to have the power to impose his will on the empire without consulting the Diet. His first usurpation of power was a proclamation, the Edict of Restitution, by which he ordered all Church territories that had been secularized since 1552 returned to the Catholic church. In concrete terms, this meant two archbishoprics, twelve bishoprics, and hundreds of monastic institutions; Ferdinand's action also involved the fate of important towns like Augsburg, Magdeburg, Minden, and Bremen and other territories of several prestigious Protestant princes. Even more important, it was an assumption of power that could become a basis for extending the authority of the emperor over other aspects of German political life. Nor were the German princes the only ones to worry about their "liberties" in the face of Emperor Ferdinand II's soaring power and ambitions; in France the new imperial power, added to the strength of the Spanish armies in the Netherlands and the possibility of imperial-Spanish naval power in the Baltic and North seas, revived the fears of Hapsburg hegemony.

PROBLEMS OF FRENCH INVOLVEMENT 1610–1636

At the time when Louis XIII refused to support Frederick, count of Palatine of the Rhine, for the crown of Bohemia, the kingdom of France was in serious trouble; and a decade later when Ferdinand, victorious over the Danish king and the Protestant princes in the Rhineland, proclaimed the Edict of Restitution, the troubles that beset the French kingdom had not yet been cleared up. In spite of the obvious danger of Hapsburg encirclement and domination, the king and his minister, Cardinal Richelieu, were unable

57

to use French forces to check Ferdinand's progress. The problems of France stemmed from the unresolved issues of the civil wars and the cumbersome fiscal structure of the kingdom.

Henry IV had bought the loyalty of the great nobles and princes with hereditary offices, grants of money, privileges; he secured the submission of the Huguenots by allowing them to erect a Huguenot republic within the kingdom. During his lifetime, Henry did all that he could to erode these grants in favor of the crown, but after his murder in 1610 all the unresolved problems came to the surface. The regent, Marie de Medicis, was almost immediately confronted with great nobles who wanted to be "bought off" and with Huguenots who were suspicious of the Italian-born queen and her clerical friends. At first Marie tried to bribe her opponents, but her foreign policy only aroused more fears and hostility. Marie's mother was a Hapsburg princess; her advisors were men of the Counter-Reformation; and like the pope, she wanted to reconcile the Bourbon and Hapsburg dynasties. Her daughter, Elizabeth, became the wife of the heir to the Spanish throne; her son, Louis XIII, married Anne of Austria, daughter of Philip III. These Spanish marriages angered the great nobles who were excluded from power and frightened the Huguenots who saw in them a danger to their party.

Marie's regime solved none of the problems, but her calling of the Estates General in 1615 made it clear that the factions in France were so deep that only a strong government would be able to restore the prestige of the crown. In 1617 Marie's minister-favorite, Concini, was murdered, Marie was sent into exile, and the young king, assisted by Luynes, his confidant, attempted to rule. He had the same twin problems that had confronted the regency, except now his own mother became the center for the plots and rebellions of the great nobles who demanded recognition of "French liberties." Luynes, neither a good soldier nor a skillful politician, only succeeded in humiliating his master by maladroit negotiations with Richelieu, Marie's agent, and military failures against the Huguenot cities of the south. After Luynes' death, Louis found other ministers who also supported his policy of reducing Huguenot power, but they were not much more successful than Luynes had been. In the meantime, Cardinal Richelieu, advisor to Marie de Medicis, moved toward the center of power and in 1624 was invited to join the council.

Richelieu entered the king's government as a protégé of Marie de Medicis, but he quickly realized that both his own and Louis XIII's conception of the destiny of the kingdom required a shift away from the pro-Hapsburg, pro-Counter-Reformation conceptions of policy favored by the two queens and the so-called *devoté* party at the court and toward a policy based upon state interest that would place checks upon both the German and the Spanish Hapsburg rulers. It was not long before Marie broke with her erstwhile favorite.

Nor were his ideas about foreign policy the only point of conflict, for Richelieu was a man of vision—and his vision embodied a state in which the power of the king would not be curbed by the anarchic, feudal institutions of the past. This meant encroachment on French liberties as the royal power

58

pushed into the problems of the country by sending agents from the council to act in the king's name. Richelieu also sought to deprive the great nobles of their fortified castles by destroying all strong places except those on the frontiers. The elimination of dueling was another object of his program. Each French nobleman assumed that he wielded sovereign power and therefore had the right to settle disputes by the sword. The resulting fights in the streets created much disorder and bloodshed; on occasion, as many as twenty to forty of these noble-born ruffians fought pitched battles with each other to settle a quarrel between two of them. Louis XIII felt that if they wished to get themselves killed, it would be better to do it fighting the king's enemies rather than slaughtering each other. Attacks on this practice, and laws against it, however, were considered to be infringements upon the liberties of the nobles.

During the entire reign of Louis XIII, there were plots and actual rebellions on the parts of the *devoté* party and the great nobles, both of whom wished to be rid of Richelieu. In the first years after Richelieu joined the king, these plots were always centered around Gaston, duke of Orleans, the king's brother. Louis was sickly and he did not get on with his queen. The plotters envisaged his death and "Gaston I" marrying Louis' queen. The first of these plots gave indication of Louis XIII's and Richelieu's ruthless wills: Gaston was forced to marry a rich heiress on the same day that the more important members of the plot were beheaded. The next cabal was much more dangerous for Richelieu since Marie herself was its leader; she went directly to the king demanding Richelieu's dismissal. There was a terrible scene in which Richelieu also played his part. His enemies were celebrating his downfall when they learned that Louis XIII had called Richelieu to him and assured him of support. On this day heads fell, and Marie went into exile. Gaston then led an armed rebellion; the duke of Montmorency, first nobleman of the kingdom, brother-in-law of the prince of Condé, and godson of Henry IV was executed for his part in the uprising. Richelieu, secure in the support of the king, made it clear that rebellions patterned on the civil wars of the past would not go unpunished.

There were to be other plots in the future, but as long as Richelieu and Louis XIII governed the kingdom, none was successful. These two imposed the power of the king upon the disorderly elements that had learned rebellion in the preceding century.

The noble cabals were only part of the disorder that faced the crown and limited its power. By the Edict of Nantes, Henry IV had been forced to erect a Huguenot republic within the kingdom. His successor was convinced that the royal will could not prevail as long as the Huguenots could command armies and fortified cities, but before Richelieu joined Louis' government every effort to erode the Huguenot position had failed. Richelieu's first intervention in high politics, when he attempted to choke off the Spanish supply line into Germany by occupying the Val Telline, was negated by a Huguenot revolt. This experience convinced him that no policy could be successful until the Huguenots were deprived of their ability to rebel. He was more successful than his predecessors had been. By clever political action he maneuvered the city of La Rochelle, the most important Huguenot stronghold, into the position of rebelling against the rightful authority of the king and, worse, into inviting the English to intervene in French affairs. He assured the rest of the Huguenot community that his fight with La Rochelle was a political rather than a religious conflict. After the defeat of the city, he guaranteed the Huguenots the right to practice their religion, but he destroyed the fortifications of the city to such a degree that a plow would pass through the foundations. Within the next year, the other Huguenot strongholds suffered the same fate. The peace of Alais (1629) secured for the Reformed religion all the rights for the practice of religion that had been granted by the Edict of Nantes, but deprived the Huguenots of the military installations that had made rebellion possible.

Richelieu claims in his memoirs that he had assured the king that his policy would be to "destroy the military power of the Huguenots, to humble the great nobles, and to raise the prestige of the house of Bourbon in Europe." This assertion was probably made after the fact, but there is no question about Richelieu's vision as a statesman. He did succeed in intruding royal authority into the provinces more effectively than any of his predecessors by the use of royal officials—the intendants of police, taxation, and "justice." He and the king curbed the pretended rights of *parlement's* interference with the political and legislative powers of the royal council, and he succeeded in suppressing or absorbing the important military offices that had decentralized the effective power of the crown. The constable, the admiral, the lieutenants general of the infantry and the cavalry, and the grand master of the artillery had actually exercised the military power of the kingdom; Richelieu strove to bring these functions under the supervision of the council and a secretary of war.

But he was unable to do much to relieve the kingdom of its cumbersome fiscal institutions. The king of France had tax revenues superior to other princes in Europe, but they weighed almost entirely upon the people least able to pay. The wealthy nobles, magistrates, and clergymen managed to evade most of the taxes. As Richelieu's grants of subsidy to the Danish king and later to Gustavus Adolphus of Sweden, his wars against the Huguenots and nobles, and his intervention in Italy and later in the Netherlands demanded more and more money, the tax load became too great for many of the peasants to bear. Furthermore, these rising tax demands coincided with the harvest failures that several times drove the price of bread four times above the normal figure. Tax rebellions followed. There was hardly a year after 1624 that rebellion did not break out some place in the kingdom. In the 1630's, these rebellions multiplied rapidly. Some were isolated events, others were conflagrations that spread from village to village to encompass whole provinces. Some were the despairing efforts of a few peasants; some were inspired by clergymen or landowning bourgeoisie or noblemen; some were even led by noblemen, who saw the king's tax gatherer taking wealth from the peasants that they hoped to garner themselves. Richelieu never solved these problems, but he and Louis XIII responded to them with brutal repression.

With all these domestic problems to contend with, Louis XIII and Richelieu hesitated to act directly in the war in Germany. When Emperor Ferdinand's Edict of Restitution gave indication of the rising Hapsburg power as well as of the possibility that the imperial throne might actually become the power in Germany that the French throne was becoming in France, Richelieu worked in two directions. On the one side, he made a subsidy alliance with the king of Sweden who hoped to become champion of the liberties of Protestant Germany; on the other, he approached Maximilian of Bavaria with the suggestion of an alliance to protect German liberties. While Richelieu understood that French liberties could be a disadvantage to the king's government, German liberties had no such unfortunate connotation since they could be used to oppose the Hapsburgs. French statesmen later in the century were to show a similar regard for Hungarian liberties, which also were anti-Hapsburg. Richelieu hesitated to use French military power in Germany, partly because it was cheaper to subsidize allies who could achieve his aims, partly because he feared giving command of an army to a French nobleman who might not use it in the interests of the king.

THE GERMAN WAR, 1629–1635

The Edict of Restitution was a shock to both Catholic and Protestant princes. Even though the former approved of the idea of restoring the sequestered Church property, they did not like to see such an order proclaimed by an imperial fiat and executed by the imperial army. Further, this army and its commander were controversial. The fighting was over, and yet Wallenstein continued to recruit troops and billet them with the peasants all across north Germany without asking permission of the hosts. There was a strong demand for his dismissal—to which the Spanish ambassador added his voice for Wallenstein was quite uncooperative with the Spanish request for joint naval action against the United Netherlands. He was building a navy—but for his own purposes, not theirs. Wallenstein also offended the German princes by his rise to their rank; a simple Bohemian nobleman, he had rocketed himself to the rank of duke of Mecklenburg. Thus, after the defeat of Denmark, there was great pressure on the emperor for both the withdrawal of the Edict of Restitution and the dismissal of his commander. Ferdinand was resolved not to give up his edict, but he did have to mollify the princes for he was anxious to have his son named king of the Romans (that is, successor to the imperial throne); there would be little advantage to his family if he strengthened the monarchical powers of the throne but failed to see his son as his successor. He did dismiss Wallenstein, but the electors managed to avoid electing the young Ferdinand as king of the Romans.

This action came almost at the same time that Gustavus Adolphus, king of Sweden, landed on German soil (1630) with a little army of Swedish veterans. The more important Lutheran princes were not pleased to see him; they suspected his motives, and they feared that he would not be more successful or wise than had been the king of Denmark. Gustavus' position was ambiguous; he was in Pomerania for almost a year before any but a few unimportant princes joined him. The elector of Saxony, the real leader of the Protestants, would have preferred to reach a negotiated settlement with the imperials, but events took the matter out of his hands. Tilly, commanding the imperial army after Wallenstein's dismissal, was besieging Magdeburg to force the restoration of Catholic property. When the soldiers broke into the city, they got out of hand, and Magdeburg was sacked and burned with a great loss of life. This outrage forced the hands of both the Saxon and the Brandenburg electors, who now joined the Swedish king. Lutheran indignation over Magdeburg also added to Gustavus' war chest and allowed him to recruit more soldiers to fill out his ranks. The Swedish and Saxon armies moved against Tilly; at Breitenfeld (1631) they won a great victory. Tilly's army was in shreds, his artillery and his war chest captured, and the heart of Germany open to the Swedish-Saxon forces. Gustavus took charge; he sent the Saxon army into Bohemia to punish the emperor while he marched through middle Germany, the "priests' ally" levying contributions on a broad scale. Everyone, Catholic and Protestant princes, the emperor, the king of France who was paying him a subsidy, had now to ask: "What are the intentions of the king of Sweden?"

Had there been better agencies of information in seventeenth-century Europe, Gustavus Adolphus would not have been an enigma when he marched through central Germany to the Rhine. He had already been king of Sweden for 19 years, all of which had been years of war. He had fought the Russians and the Poles for control of the east coast of the Baltic Sea. Thanks to French intervention, he had disengaged his forces from the conflict with Poland by a truce so that he could enter the German war. His motives were probably mixed. Although he had been unwilling to enter the war earlier as an ally of the Danish king, he did pose as a defender of the Lutheran religion. He undoubtedly wanted to establish Swedish power over the German Baltic coast to ensure his absolute control of that sea. But as his power grew, Gustavus Adolphus had also developed a broader vision of his role. He was an excellent soldier, a good administrator, and he had at his side an advisor, Oxenstierna, who was one of the cleverest politicians of the era. The victory at Breitenfeld and the march across Germany could not but inspire such a man. Gustavus apparently conceived of a new German empire in which the kingdom of Sweden in the north would play the same role that the Hapsburg lands on the Danube had heretofore occupied. With this base of power, the Swedish-German empire could dominate Europe, or at least the Europe that Gustavus Adolphus knew.

However, much fighting would have to take place before such a vision could become a reality. Ferdinand, urged by some of the very people who had demanded that he dismiss Wallenstein, recalled his commander under conditions that practically gave Wallenstein a free hand for any course he might wish to take. Richelieu, too, had to take defensive measures; French troops occupied a number of points on the left bank of the Rhine, and the cardinal, perhaps surprised to find that the Swedish king was not just another condottiere general, unsuccessfully tried to keep the Swedish army from invading Catholic southern Germany. Richelieu hoped to save Bavaria as a French ally and Catholic counterpoise to the Hapsburgs. However, Gustavus Adolphus pushed into Bavaria and fought a battle with Tilly in which the latter lost his life. But Wallenstein invaded Saxony, thereby forcing the Swedish army to turn northward to defend that country. The two armies met at Lützen (November 16, 1632). When the battle was over, the Swedish army was in possession of the field, but Gustavus Adolphus was dead, and with him the dream of a Swedish-German empire.

The Swedes, however, did not leave. Oxenstierna took over the political direction of the army, and two of Gustavus' generals assumed command; in Sweden a regency government ruled for the child-queen, Christina. Even if a Swedish-German empire was impossible, the Swedish politicians and soldiers wanted to assure themselves of control over the southern coast of the Baltic Sea. This ambition was regarded with suspicion in Brandenburg, where the elector himself hoped to secure Pomerania on the death of its current duke who had no heirs. On the imperial side, there also was a problem. Wallenstein's behavior convinced Emperor Ferdinand that the commander planned treachery, and accordingly, the emperor ordered his murder (February 24, 1634). The young Ferdinand, who had only recently been elected king of Hungary, assumed command of the imperial army.

In 1635 the war again reached a crisis. A Spanish army under command of the Cardinal Infant, a brother of Philip IV, crossed the Alps to join Ferdinand. The combined imperial-Spanish forces met the Swedes at Nördlingen and decisively defeated them. More than half of the Swedish army was destroyed. The Cardinal Infant took his army on to the Netherlands while Ferdinand made a serious effort for peace in Germany. The Saxons and the imperials were able to reach a compromise that might have both ended the war and forced the Swedish armies to leave Germany. It was only a question of persuading the German princes to rally to this Peace of Prague which modified the Edict of Restitution, guaranteed the Lutherans their religious rights, and laid the basis for a military alliance of all German princes against the Swedes. The Calvinist elector of Brandenburg was shocked to find that Calvinism was not recognized, but the prospect of driving the Swedes from Pomerania outweighed his objections. Indeed, as the German princes rallied to the peace treaty, the Swedes also found themselves practically forced to sign the peace and prepare to withdraw from Germany. Had this happened, or had the Protestant and Catholic princes joined in an alliance to clear the empire of foreign troops, the German Hapsburgs would have been very strong indeed. This forced the French king to declare war on the Spanish Netherlands and actively intervene in Germany. Richelieu and Louis XIII held back from direct intervention as long as they could use subsidies to keep allies in the war to act as a check on the Hapsburgs. But when this was no longer possible, they entered the war themselves.

Almost simultaneously with the rise to power of Richelieu in France, the Conde Duque (Duke) de Olivares appeared in Spain as the minister-favorite of Philip IV. This flamboyant figure, painted so often by Velasquez in vigorous poses, deserves more attention from historians than he has received. Like Richelieu, he had a vision of monarchical power, but his was a more complex problem than the one in France. With a slogan "one king, one law, one coinage," he hoped to make the crowns of the Spanish Hapsburgs into an empire with true political unity. In this effort, Olivares was a statesman of his age in the mold of Richelieu, Ferdinand II, Charles I of England, and others who believed that only by use of monarchical power could the chaotic, disorganized political society inherited from the past be made into a viable institution. Like other men with this vision, he encountered demands for the recognition of "liberties." The Portuguese, the crowns of Aragon, the other provinces and principalities did not wish to be "Castilized," that is, brought under the real control of the king as was the kingdom of Castile. The Portuguese, for example, did not even pay the expenses of the expedition sent to expel the Dutch from the Portuguese colony of Brazil. And the crowns of Aragon stubbornly held to their special privileges and liberties that allowed them to avoid taxation. When it became obvious that his larger project of unification was destined to fail, Olivares strove to create a union of arms for all the territories under Philip IV. He wished to establish an army of 140,000 men drawn from the several crowns in accordance with their populations, with the understanding that one-seventh of this force would be at the disposal of any one of them that might be invaded. There were immediate objections; even though Spanish Italy was, in a sense, a dependency of the crowns of Aragon, the Cortez of that kingdom wanted nothing to do with the defense of Milan, which was always exposed to invasion. The Cortez of the crowns of Aragon also insisted upon strict constitutional rules about recruitment for foreign adventures. Olivares did finally persuade Aragon and Valencia to vote a subsidy for the king, the first since the days of Charles V, but Catalonia stubbornly refused.

Olivares' imperial policy led him deep into the war in the Netherlands and Germany and, as might be expected, increased the fiscal problems of the regime. He used every trick in the bag of seventeenth-century statesmen for finding new money: sale of offices, rents, titles, debasement of the coinage, deflation of the currency, new excise taxes, seizing of revenues belonging to the Church, and taking of silver from the New World belonging to private individuals (whom he compensated with unwanted paper); he found ways to wring money from both the grandees and the *hidalgos.* Most of the revenue, however, came from Castile where the royal authority was absolute. But by 1640 Castile was about to run dry. Its population was in serious decline, its industry and commerce in decay. Olivares' problems, however, did not decline; in 1637, for example, his budget was about twice his expected revenue, for the war had expanded into a conflict with Bourbon France as well as with the United Netherlands and Sweden.

When Louis XIII declared war on Spain in 1635, Olivares replied with an invasion of France that, for a moment, forced Richelieu to consider abandoning Paris. The Spanish-imperial troops, however, could not solve the problems of supply, and their invasion disintegrated into an unhappy pillaging expedition that left scars on the French for decades to come. In 1638–1639 the French invaded Catalonia; Olivares attempted to force the Catalans to pay for a part of their defense and supply troops to help the royal army drive out the invaders. The campaign, however, was badly organized; the Spanish armies robbed the peasants; a great number of casualties, both of noblemen and commoners, irked the population, and Olivares' continual demands and unconstitutional actions convinced the Catalans that the duke was about to overthrow their liberties. Olivares won his campaign in Russillon late in 1639, but he had created a situation that led to the rebellion of the Catalans in 1640.

The Catalan crisis was only the first explosion indicating the rapid decline of Spanish power. The invasion of France in 1636 had failed to achieve its aim; in 1637 the Dutch recaptured Breda; in 1638 Bernard von Saxe-Weimar, now in French pay, captured Breisach and closed the route down the Rhine for Spanish supplies from Milan; in October 1639, the Dutch navy defeated a Spanish armada in the Channel, and the attempt to reconquer Brazil failed. In 1640 no silver arrived from the New World. When the Catalan rebellion first started, Olivares did not believe that it could be dangerous; he was sure that the nobility of the province and the patricians in Barcelona would rally to the crown. When they joined the rebellion, the whole edifice of the Spanish monarchy began to shake. To shore up the situation, Olivares called upon the Portuguese nobles to assist in subduing the rebellion. This resulted in a revolt in Portugal that could not be suppressed since there were no loyal troops in the kingdom.

The Portuguese had long been restive under Spanish domination. Olivares tried to stifle the complaint that the king neglected their interests by appointing a member of the royal family, Princess Margaret of Savoy, as governor. This also allowed him to introduce a number of Castilians into the government of Portugal as Margaret's advisors. The rival for the throne was the house of Barganza, the richest and most influential noble family of the kingdom. As long as the duke of Barganza was loyal or under surveillance, Philip's government was relatively secure. Several plots to place the duke on the throne had failed, and Olivares believed that he had the situation under control. But when the Catalan revolt broke out, he decided to require Barganza and the other important Portuguese nobles to join the army as a measure that would take these potential Portuguese rebels out of that kingdom. Instead of obeying orders, they overpowered the palace guards, murdered Olivares' Spanish confidant, and escorted Princess Margaret to the frontier. The plot, of course, had French support, French money, and French arms just as did the rebellion in Catalonia.

Philip IV, confronted with two rebellions in Iberia, a dangerous foreign war in the Netherlands and Germany, and bankruptcy in his treasury, had to dismiss and exile his favorite. Olivares disappeared from the scene in

1641. He died a few years later after suffering bouts of insanity. The dismissal of Olivares was followed by the dismantling of his system of government, a return of control to the councils, and much greater decentralization. Indeed, there was not to be another servant of the Spanish Hapsburgs who would attempt to stem the tide of disintegration. From 1640 on, the Spanish crowns became more and more autonomous—now and then cajoled or bullied by the king to provide money for his projects, but hardly bases of royal power.

The Portuguese rebellion resulted in the separation of that kingdom from the Spanish crowns after nearly thirty years of intermittent war. Catalonia returned to the Hapsburg king a little over a decade after the rebellion. Catalan noblemen found that they preferred Philip IV to a regime dominated by the French government and Barcelona politicians, and after 1648, when the Frondes shook France, the rebels lost support from Paris. Furthermore, in these years of the mid-century, Mazarin was governing France, and his interests, more centered in Italy, left Catalonia to its own resources. By 1652 Catalonia was again loyal to Philip IV but under conditions that left the king little power to tax or control its affairs.

THE ENGLISH REVOLUTION

Almost at the same time that Catalonia and Portugal rebelled against Philip IV, a crisis in England unleashed a revolution that finally cost King Charles I his life. Like the civil war in Germany, the English civil war had both political and religious overtones. At the death of Elizabeth, James I of the house of Stuart ascended the throne in England. His reign was troubled because, unlike his predecessors, he did not have monastic lands to sell to support the expenses of the crown; therefore he had to go to Parliament for money. In Parliament, he found other problems: First of all, his peace with Spain and his friendly attitude toward the Spanish ambassador were unpopular. Moreover, his religious policy, which opposed the Puritan dissenters, caused much complaint, and his Scottish favorites, loaded with honors and riches in England, were a scandal. James, however, managed to live out his life without evoking too serious a crisis. He did become involved in the German war when his daughter, the wife of Frederick, count of Palatine of the Rhine, temporarily became queen of Bohemia, and later when his brother-in-law, the king of Denmark, entered the war. But James was essentially a man of peace. He supplied subsidies but resisted the demands for both troops in Germany and naval participation against Spain. He hoped to settle the whole conflict through diplomacy—perhaps by marrying his son to a Spanish princess.

Upon James' death (1625), Charles I came to the throne demanding war against Spain. The projected marriage had come to nothing more than a humiliation for the young prince; war was to be his revenge. The war went badly and in the next few years Charles' foreign policy was much confused, in part because he relied too much upon his favorite, the duke of Buckingham, whose political sagacity left much to be desired.

In the decade of the 1630's, Charles came into conflict with an important segment of English political opinion and power, and the crisis that developed was rooted in the internal politics of the kingdom rather than in its external affairs. Charles was resolved to be a "modern" prince. When Parliament refused to grant him subsidies, like Ferdinand in Austria or Olivares in Spain, he proceeded to collect them anyway. His most important advisors, Lord Stratford and Archbishop Laud, encouraged him in the use of strong methods to bring the Church as well as the rest of the kingdom under royal authority. James I had written a book to prove his divine right to rule; Charles needed only to be assured by his bishops before insisting that he, too, derived his power from God. But in exercising that power he stepped on the feet of men who believed that their liberties came from the same source. Actually, Charles' government was not harsh on the majority of the nation. The poor rates were levied more effectively than before or after his time; the rights of the landless and small peasants were protected against the enclosures of the common lands by the wealthy; and the court of the Star Chamber prevented illegal enclosures of arable land for sheep raising. Moreover, Charles initiated the construction of a modern navy for the protection of English commerce. But his reign did cost money, and when he could not get it from Parliament, he sought out forgotten taxes and invented new ones to provide for his needs.

Unfortunately for Charles, new and vigorous classes had arisen in England: the squires and country gentry, and the city moneymen. During the reigns of the Tudor monarchs following Henry VIII, as the crown disposed of the monastic lands that had been confiscated, a vigorous class of country gentlemen came into being. They were recruited from several sources. Some represented the cadet lines of the great lords of the land; others were the issue of wealthy peasant yeomen; many were the descendants of city merchants or professional people who moved to the country. These men knew how to make their lands pay: They introduced capitalist ideas to the problems of agriculture. Furthermore, their numbers and their wealth made them the most important class in the kingdom. These country gentlemen could count on the bourgeoisie of the cities, particularly London, as allies. In the late sixteenth century, England's trade in cloth, coal, iron, tin, and wool was expanded by the establishment of trading companies that sent English ships to the Levant, to Muscovy, to the New World, and, at the opening of the seventeenth century, to the Orient. At first much of the commerce was either in the hands of, or directed by, Flemish or Dutch businessmen and immigrants who had the experience of the Antwerp market and connections in the industrial and commercial cities of the Netherlands. But before the end of the sixteenth century, native Englishmen showed that they had learned the lessons well. Just as their thirteenth- and fourteenth-century predecessors had learned from the Hansa merchants who at first treated England as an underdeveloped country to be exploited, so sixteenth- and seventeenth-century English merchants learned the mechanics of the new commerce from the Netherlanders who had made Antwerp, Ghent, Brussels, and other Dutch and Flemish cities the centers of European commerce. By the first half of the seventeenth century, these English merchants were almost ready to contest with the Dutch for control of the European commerce, and in mid-century, they provoked the first purely commercial European war against the Netherlanders.

There were other sources for the wealth of English maritime ports. Even as late as the mid-seventeenth century, English seamen had a reputation for piracy in the waters of the North Sea, the Channel, and the Atlantic approaches to Europe; English pirates also operated in the Mediterranean from ports belonging to the dukes of Savoy and Tuscany and to lesser Italian princes as well as from Algiers and Moroccan Atlantic harbors. These men were the heirs to the traditions of freebooting and privateering of the sixteenth-century "sea dogs." They were an unruly lot on the sea, but once they had made their money, many of them settled down as respectable merchants or gentlemen.

While the country gentry and the city merchants and sea captains did not really constitute classes with common interests, they nonetheless found it easy to cooperate with each other. They were motivated by the economic drives and pressures that we call the capitalistic spirit. They were anxious to prevent the king from encroaching upon their "liberties" and "rights." The city of London stood to defend its charters and with them the right to govern the commerce in its harbor and the industrial and banking activities of its citizens. By the mid-seventeenth century, London's population was about one-tenth of that of the entire kingdom, and its merchant shipowners and moneymen commanded an even larger percentage of the wealth of the kingdom. When these people made common cause with the gentry, whose holdings were much greater than those of the high nobility, the combined group could speak for the important economic interests of the realm. The little people—peasants, artisans, laborers, beggars—may have constituted a majority of the population, but they did not count in the political processes of the kingdom. Thus, when Charles I antagonized both the city men and the gentry by collecting "illegal" taxes, utilizing royal courts to impose his regulations, and usurping authority that his opponents insisted encroached upon their traditional rights, the throne was in trouble.

Religious problems also plagued the first two Stuart kings. James I, as king of Scotland, had been forced to listen to Calvinist theologians and Calvinist political philosophy so long that he had acquired a great distaste for it. He found the Elizabethan religious compromise satisfactory and strongly opposed the Calvinists, who wanted to reorganize the Church by congregational control and to disestablish the episcopal structure. Charles I, even more than his father, wished to retain the traditional Catholic forms in the organizational structure of the Anglican church. Puritans, Presbyterians, and other sectarians were an anathema to him, and his ecclesiastical advisor, Archbishop Laud, brought all the pressure of the royal government to force the sectarians to conform to the established Anglican church. Unhappily for Charles, while the poor and the ignorant may have made up a majority of the sectarians, there were enough converts to Calvinistic ideas among the gentry and moneymen to make Laud's program dangerous to the king as soon as a crisis arose. Thus, religious issues were added to political ones in the arguments between Charles I and his subjects. When Charles' authoritarian religious policies in Scotland led to a rebellion in that poverty-stricken kingdom, the king's political difficulties in England also emerged. He had to call Parliament to ask for money to fight his civil war in Scotland, but the men elected to the English Parliament proved to be more interested in securing redress for their own grievances than in assisting their king.

The crisis in England broke the same year that Catalonia and Portugal exploded in revolt against Philip IV. Charles I called Parliament to secure money, but when the body wanted to talk about its grievances, the king immediately dismissed this "Short" Parliament. However, he could not find the money he needed without calling a second, or as it came to be known, "Long" Parliament. In the early days of the confrontation, Charles I was almost alone against a hostile Parliament that forced him to give up his favorites and began to strip him of his royal prerogatives. As the radicals enlarged their demands, however, there emerged a party favorable to the king, and the civil strife was then translated into civil warfare.

It was a confused, complex conflict in which the problems of England and Scotland became intertwined with religious and political issues. The radical group in Parliament, led by the Puritans, the moneymen in London, religious sectarians, and an important group of gentry came to be known as the Roundheads, since they did not wear wigs. In the course of the conflict their most important leader was the soldier-organizer of the Puritan army, Oliver Cromwell. Their opponents, the Cavaliers, were largely recruited from noble houses, Catholics, adventurers who supported the Stuarts, and men convinced of the divine right of kings. The Cavaliers were finally defeated on the battlefield; their king was captured, tried and executed; and their leaders were driven to Europe in exile. But the execution of the king, the establishment of the regime of the Commonwealth with a relatively narrow political base, and the rule of Cromwell and the major generals of the army alienated a large segment of English opinion. Cromwell and the Puritans ruled as long as Cromwell lived and controlled the army, but when he died there was no one capable of taking his place. His son stepped into his shoes for a few months, but he could not rule England. Major General Monk, with the support of the army leaders, managed to make a compromise with Prince Charles and his followers that provided for the restoration of the Stuart family to the throne and a stabilization of English politics that, at least for the moment, reestablished a measure of peace and tranquility in the land.

During the years of civil war, the dual monarchy of England and Scotland was largely removed from the high politics of Europe. At the same time, the revolts against Philip IV, the German war, the peasant rebellions and the advent of the Fronde in France, and the efforts to make peace at Westphalia largely prevented Europe from intervening in the affairs in the

British Isles. However, when Cromwell emerged as the Lord Protector of the Commonwealth, England was again able to act as a force in European affairs. Cromwell's first problem was with the Dutch. The Stuart connections of William II of Orange, and, after his death, of his English-born wife, the daughter of Charles I, made the Orange faction in the Netherlands a threat to the Commonwealth. Cromwell's first proposal was to unite the English and the Dutch Calvinist republics in a common state which would exclude the Stuarts; but the Dutch republican regents were almost as much opposed to such a proposal as the Orange faction would have been. Next, Cromwell forced a war with the Dutch over the Navigation Acts, which excluded Dutch ships from the carrying trade between English ports and from the fishing trade, and which refused to allow Dutch merchants to import the goods of countries other than their own into England. The war was one-sided, for there were many more Dutch merchant ships to be captured than English, and the Dutch therefore suffered great losses. The settlement shows, however, that political as well as economic factors were involved, for Cromwell made peace as soon as the rising Amsterdam politician DeWitt secured a law that would exclude princes of the house of Orange from stadtholdership in the Netherlands.

Cromwell's next intervention in continental affairs came with his alliance with Mazarin's France against Spain. The French needed a navy to conquer the Spanish Netherlands; Cromwell was willing to furnish one, and some land forces, in return for English possession of Dunkirk. It was hardly a decisive intervention, but it did give the English a foothold on the continent for the next four years (1658–1662). After the restoration of Charles II to his father's throne, new constellations and new combinations dominated England's relations with the rest of Europe.

REBELLION IN FRANCE; THE COMING OF THE FRONDES

Even before Richelieu decided that the kingdom of France must enter the war to prevent the emergence of a Hapsburg preponderance in Europe, the fiscal demands on the kingdom combined with weather unfavorable to agriculture to create a series of very serious peasant uprisings. In 1636–1637 peasant rebellions almost amounted to a full-fledged civil war; large-scale peasant revolts broke out again in 1643–1645, when fiscal demands drove the peasants to despair and again in 1648, when extremely bad harvests added an extra dimension to the fiscal crisis. In addition to these widespread rebellions, hardly a year passed without a local peasant uprising in some part of the kingdom. France was in serious economic condition. The kingdom needed increasingly large subsidies to support its military effort just at the time when chronic bad harvest made any increase in the fiscal burden unbearable. Against this economic background, the political crisis that overtook the kingdom assumed serious proportions.

There were other problems in the kingdom. Louis XIII and Richelieu, bent upon assuring the king's power, had broken the Huguenot republic, curbed the ambitions and powers of the great nobles, and invaded the traditional authority of the municipal governments—the *Parlements*—and the other so-called sovereign courts by the use of intendants of police, taxation, and "justice" who directly represented the king's council. These two redoubtable men ruled with an iron hand that did not hesitate to use the executioner's sword as an instrument of policy. As long as they lived they terrorized, imprisoned, or exiled the opposition and put down revolts with violent reprisals. But Richelieu died in December 1642 and Louis XIII followed him to the tomb a few months later. The heir to the throne, Louis XIV, was a small boy; his mother, Anne of Austria, persuaded *Parlement* to set aside her late husband's will and allow her to be regent unrestricted by the document's provisions. In return, she assured the *Parlement* that she would consult it in the future. Everyone expected Anne to reverse the policies of her old enemy, Richelieu, but the men and women who returned from exile or from prison soon learned that she depended upon one of Richelieu's creatures, Cardinal Mazarin, to govern the kingdom.

Mazarin, less brutal than Richelieu, relied upon guile and diplomacy rather than force, but he did not change the basic policies laid down by his predecessor. Nor did he solve the fiscal problems of the regime any more successfully than had Richelieu. The government had to introduce new taxes; when *Parlement* objected, the boy-king was brought to *Parlement* to impose the measure by a *lit de justice. Parlement* agreed but scolded. There were other conflicts with *Parlement.* The intendants of police, justice, and taxation, acting for the royal council, quashed *Parlementary* writs, interfered with legal actions, and took authority into their hands that *parlementarians* believed to belong to them. By 1648 the *Parlement* and the other Sovereign Courts were ready to attempt to impose a reform constitution upon the king's government. While the *robins* (lawyers and judges) were entering a confrontation with the regime, many of the great nobles also sought to reestablish their place in the government. Mazarin excluded them just as Richelieu had done. Subsequently, there was a plot to murder Mazarin. When it was uncovered, the principal conspirators, including an illegitimate grandson of Henry IV, were sent to prison rather than to the executioner. Clemency did not make Mazarin—termed the "Italian adventurer" in the propaganda of his opponents—any more acceptable. Thus, by 1648 pressures for a rebellion were developing from several sides. News of the English revolution, of a rebellion in Naples, and of the Catalan and Portuguese revolutions encouraged the dissident factions, and in 1647–1648 bad harvests that drove the price of bread to new highs added further fuel by threatening both peasants and town artisans and laborers with starvation. Many people were ready to man barricades and spark the civil rebellions we call the Fronde.

Barricades in the streets of Paris and deputations from the *parlement* waiting upon the queen regent were most embarrassing to the government. Mazarin was deep in negotiations for the ending of the German war by the treaty of Westphalia, and he could not actually throw down the glove to the rebels until the ratifications of that treaty were completed. The government temporized until the winter months of 1649, when the royal family and the ministers left Paris at night and besieged the city to force a surrender.

The following three years saw a confusion of political maneuvering. Princes of blood were jailed. Mazarin was forced into exile twice. The king's cousin, Condé, joined the Spanish. The king's armies were shut out of Paris while Spanish soldiers were sheltered there. Plots and counterplots excited the government, some rooted in Rome, others in Madrid. In the course of the crisis, the French were unable to continue adequate support for the rebel forces in Barcelona, but they were able to maintain their pressure on the Spanish Netherlands in spite of the fact that the prince of Condé commanded the forces of Philip IV.

By 1652 Mazarin returned as the first minister of Louis XIV, who had attained his majority during the crisis. The minister's success surely was the result of the fact that he alone of the politicians had a clear and largely unselfish political objective. The men in *parlement* were seeking to enhance their roles in the kingdom and to prevent the government from imposing new taxes upon them. The princes and great lords talked much about French liberties, that is, the preservation of their own special privileges to the detriment of the rest of the kingdom. Only Mazarin understood that the great problem of the day was to establish the power of the French king both throughout Europe and within the kingdom so that some order could be made of the disjunctive forces and security against Hapsburg domination could be assured in Europe. Mazarin's loyalties were to the house of Bourbon and to the authority of the royal government. By the time that the Fronde had collapsed in 1652 both of these goals were about to be assured.

The boy-king, Louis XIV, left the government of the kingdom in Mazarin's hands until his minister died in 1661. The great problems of the last years of Mazarin's rule were the settlement of the war with Spain and the establishment of peace in Europe. The Treaty of Westphalia in 1648 started the process; the Treaty of the Pyrenees (1659) and of Oliva (1660) completed it.

PEACE FOR EUROPE

The Peace of Westphalia. With the entry of France into the war in Germany and the Netherlands (1635) the pace of the conflict quickened. After the first French reverses, Richelieu was able to turn the tide against the imperials and the Spanish. French subsidies for Sweden increased, and the French king assumed responsibility for the army commanded by Bernard von Saxe-Weimer, one of Gustavus Adolphus' most talented generals. These were hard years for Germany. There was no front; most of the German princes, both Catholic and Protestant, allied to the emperor by the Peace of Prague, were confronted with the Franco-Swedish invaders whose armies ravaged the land. According to the lurid stories of nineteenth-century German historians, the German people were often reduced to cannibalism during these years. Whole villages disappeared, towns lost population, commerce ceased. These stories may have been exaggerated, but there can be no doubt that Germany suffered horribly from this conflict that had begun as a civil war and had become a struggle kept alive by French and Swedes for many different motives—most of which did not even exist in 1618. The men who had started the war were nearly all dead, and their projects had become meaningless. Everyone involved in the conflict insisted that peace was the prime objective, but each had ideas about the peace that were not acceptable to the others.

All parties to the conflict felt the economic pinch, for no state in the first half of the century had revenues equal to the demands of this war. When both Portugal and Catalonia revolted in 1640 and the treasure fleet from the New World failed to arrive in Spain, the Hapsburg powers were sorely strained, but their foes were not able to take full advantage of the situation because they, too, were in serious financial difficulty. The petty German princes were in even worse condition because the ravages of war had deprived them of the small incomes usually available from their lands. Thus, by 1640 all wanted peace; it was simply a matter of finding a series of formulas that would be acceptable.

In Germany, the first break came when Frederick William succeeded his father to the throne in Brandenburg-Prussia. This young man was a realist. He reorganized the tiny Brandenburg army, and, recognizing that Emperor Ferdinand III was seeking to establish the imperial power in Germany rather than to find peace, Frederick William opened negotiations with the Swedes for an armistice. The negotiations started in 1641, and by the end of that year all parties to the war had agreed to start peace negotiations in the Westphalian towns of Münster and Osnabrück. However, the agreement did not include an armistice, or even a cease fire, so the war went on without respite.

The actual negotiations did not get under way until the end of 1644. Richelieu's death, then that of Louis XIII, then the expected declaration of the majority of Christine, queen of Sweden, were the major reasons for delay; the minor ones were legion. As the delegates converged upon the Westphalian towns, it became evident that the peace negotiations would place a strain upon the city's resources. Food prices skyrocketed; conflicts between servants and underlings created disturbances; the babble of tongues led to confusion. When the French ambassador arrived, his first act was to plant a garden. Wags, noting that his wife was pregnant and considering the problems of the negotiations, were taking bets that his child would be married before a treaty could be written.

The Peace of Westphalia, as it is called, was largely a peace for Germany, and its terms, while important for all Europe, were essentially a settlement of the outstanding questions in the Holy Roman Empire of the German nation. Perhaps the treaty could not have been written if the Franco-Spanish conflict in the Netherlands, Catalonia, and Italy had also been included in the negotiations. The chief problem there was that of the Spanish Netherlands. In 1643, almost on the very day of Louis XIII's death, a French army under the duc d'Enghein, later known as "great" Condé, defeated, indeed practically destroyed, the Spanish army at Rocroi. This victory, added to the revolts in Portugal and Catalonia, caused the Dutch to revise their attitude toward Spain. They had been fighting the Spanish for almost eighty years; suddenly their enemy was revealed as a hollow giant; would not this weak Spain be a better neighbor than the rising Bourbon power in France? A few years later this concern was strengthened by the news that Mazarin and the queen regent in France hoped to marry the young king of France to the infanta of Spain, who would bring the Spanish Netherlands as her dowry. The Dutch relaxed their pressure on the Spanish and even made it possible for the latter to obtain needed military supplies so that they could defend themselves against the French. Thus, the two conflicts were separated, but Mazarin made sure that peace in Germany would remove the German Hapsburgs from the war in the Netherlands. His method was to negotiate with the more important German princes to set up a League of the Rhine, by which the king of France agreed to guarantee the princes' positions in return for the assurance that the Holy Roman Empire and the emperor would not become involved in the war between France and Spain. This separation of the German war from the Franco-Spanish war and the victories of the French and Swedish armies in the south of Germany made possible the writing of a treaty of peace satisfactory to France and to Sweden as well as to several of the more important princes of the empire. Emperor Ferdinand III was obliged to accept the treaty.

The French and Swedish negotiators both secured ambiguous footholds in Germany for their kings. The Treaty of Westphalia transferred the emperor's rights as Margrave of Alsace to France, but no one really knew what had been given to the king of France. The city of Strasbourg, the bishopric of Strasbourg, and some of the cities and many of the imperial counts and knights in both upper and lower Alsace assumed that they held power directly from the emperor, not from the Margrave of Alsace. The French also secured both Philippsburg and Breisack, strong points on the right bank of the Rhine from which an invasion of Germany could be launched. The treaty also recognized French possession of Metz, Toul, and Verdun, but the status of Lorraine was left unclear. Sweden secured a foothold on the southern Baltic coast in West Pomerania and the island of Rügen, the bishoprics of Bremen and Verden on the lower Elbe and Weser. One of the biggest problems with the Swedish treaty concerned the demobilization and return of the Swedish army which was quartered all over Germany. The empire finally paid five million reichtalers to be rid of these soldiers.

There were many changes within Germany. Frederick William, elector of Brandenburg, fared best of all. He acquired East Pomerania, the bishoprics of Minden, Haberstadt, and Kammin, and a complex of territories on the lower Rhine. Thus, his lands extended across north Germany from the Vistula to the Rhine. A number of the other important princes also added territory to their holdings. Bavaria retained the electoral dignity formerly belonging to the Palatinate, but an eighth electoral vote was given to Karl Ludwig, the son of Frederick v who had been the "Winter

King" of Bohemia, when he recovered the throne in Heidelberg.

The Westphalian treaty recognized that both the United Netherlands and the Swiss confederation were outside the boundaries of the Holy Roman Empire. It also gave to the German princes the legal right to make treaties of alliance with foreign powers, thereby admitting their sovereign status. The Holy Roman Empire of the German nation had been dealt a grievous blow during the Reformation when the princes obtained the right to fix the religion in their own lands, but this provision that permitted them to negotiate with foreign powers made the empire a hollow shell with little meaning or power.

The Treaty of Westphalia also recognized the right of anyone in the empire to practice the religious forms as they existed in 1624, but no prince could force a change even though he himself might alter his religious practices. The peace further recommended tolerance of all religious practices and provided a measure of protection for everyone who might dissent from the religion of the state. Henceforth, although the religious split created by the Reformation would continue to divide Germans, the intolerance of the preceding hundred years was considerably modified. After a conflict of the dimensions of the Thirty Years' War, it was hard to justify religious intolerance.

The Treaty of the Pyrenees. The Frondes interrupted the war between France and Spain, but the Spanish were unable to take much advantage of the civil disorders in France because their attention was diverted by their own efforts to reconquer Portugal and Catalonia and to suppress a rebellion that had broke out in Naples in 1647. Even the addition of the strength and skill that came when the prince of Condé, the very man who had overwhelmed the Spaniards at Rocroi, joined Philip IV's armies, did not give the Spanish a great advantage. On the other hand, even after 1652 when the Fronde was defeated, the French found progress against the Spanish in the Netherlands difficult because they could not control the English Channel. Mazarin attempted to make an agreement with the Dutch to use their navy, but he could offer no solution for the disposal of the Spanish Netherlands that was satisfactory to the men in Amsterdam. The latter feared either the partition of the provinces between themselves and the French or "cantonization" on the model of Switzerland; such measures would bring the French up to their frontier, and the Dutch believed that the French were good to have as friends but bad as neighbors. They preferred the weak Spanish regime. Mazarin finally made an alliance with Cromwell's England, and by the end of 1658, after Anglo-French victories on the Channel coast, the French armies stood poised to sweep the Spanish from Flanders, perhaps from the whole of the Spanish Netherlands. The only trouble was that that action might bring Dutch assistance to Spain, and such an extension of the war was the last thing Mazarin wanted to see.

There seemed no way to force the Spanish to make a peace that would satisfy the French—until Mazarin hit upon the ruse of pretending to make a marriage agreement between young Louis XIV and a princess of Savoy. Both in Madrid and in Paris it had long been assumed that Louis XIV would marry his cousin Maria Theresa, the eldest daughter of Philip IV. When the French court went to Lyons to meet the Savoyards, Philip IV sent his ambassador with a request for peace and a marriage agreement. The Treaty of the Pyrenees that followed was as much an agreement between the Bourbon and Hapsburg families as it was a treaty between the kingdoms of Spain and France.

While much of the discussion between the negotiators dealt with the problem of French acceptance of the prince of Condé, who had been both a rebel and a traitor in the eyes of the French, the fateful clauses of the treaty were embodied in the marriage agreement. As noted, Maria Theresa was Philip IV's eldest daughter; he did have sons, but they were sickly. If they should die, Maria Theresa was his heir. But Hapsburg pride in family could not willingly allow the transfer of the Spanish crowns to the Bourbons. Thus, Maria Theresa was forced to renounce her right to her father's throne on condition that she bring with her an enormous dowry. Much has been made of the dowry clause because it was never paid, but at the time both families believed that the right to a throne was the gift of God and that a princess might be able to renounce her own rights, but she could not dispose of those of her unborn children. Some forty years after the signing of this treaty, a Bourbon prince, Philip V, grandson of Louis XIV and Maria Theresa, mounted the throne in Spain. The conditions that led to his being asked to become king of Spain, however, included many considerations other than the presumed will of God.

By the Treaty of the Pyrenees, Philip IV ceded Russillon, a province on the north slope of the Pyrenees, Artois in Flanders, and a chain of towns and counties on the Franco-Spanish Netherlands frontier. But the most important political fact about the treaty was the tacit recognition that the kingdom of France had become the first power in Europe, that the crowns of the Spanish king no longer dominated the political scene. In a very important way, this family treaty was the end of the era that began when Charles V came into his inheritances and Luther announced both the freedom of the Christian man and the divine right of princes. It had been an era of international wars, but, even more importantly, an era when civil conflicts were fought over religious institutions and the rights of traditional liberties. As we have seen, princes everywhere were attempting to bring order into the chaotic political structure of Europe; they tried to do so by establishing their own power as supreme in their respective states.

SUGGESTED READING

The latter sixteenth and the first half of the seventeenth centuries are often treated as having the Counter-Reformation or the Baroque art style as their central motifs. R. S. Dunn, *The Age of Religious Wars, 1559–1689* (1970), Henri Daniel-Rops, *The Catholic Reformation* (1964), A. G. Dickens, *Reformation and Society in Sixteenth Century Europe* (1969), A. G. Dickens, *The Counter Reformation* (1969), R. M. Burnes, *The Counter Reformation* (1964), and C. J. Friedrich, *The Age of the Baroque, 1610–1652* (1963) provide useful introductions to these interpretations. T. R. Davies, *The Golden Century of Spain* (1965) written a generation ago, is still an excellent introduction to the kingdom of Charles v and Philip ii, but it should be used in connection with J. H. Elliott, *Imperial Spain, 1469–1621,* (1963). The "problem book" by John Rule, *The Character of Philip* ii, *The Problem of Moral Judgment in History* (1963), is much worth reading. For two of Philip's most serious problems see Pieter Geyl, *The Revolt of the Netherlands, 1555–1907* (1958) and Garrett Mattingly, *The Armada* (1962). R. S. T. Blindhoff, *Tudor England* (1950), J. E. Neale, *Queen Elizabeth* i (1967), and A. L. Rowse, *The England of Elizabeth* (1953) are excellent guides to Elizabeth's England. J. W. Thompson, *The Wars of Religion in France, 1559–1596* (1962) is an old book but still useful because it is in English. J. E. Neale, *The Age of Catherine de Medicis* (1957) provides a newer interpretation. For the rise of Bourbon France see J. Boulenger, *The Seventeenth Century in France* (1963), C. J. Burckardt, *Richelieu, His Rise to Power* and C. V. Wedgwood, *Richelieu and the French Monarchy* (1966). The Netherlands have an excellent historian for the great century in Pieter Geyl, *The Netherlands in the Seventeenth Century,* Vol. I (1961). Violet Barbour, *Capitalism in Amsterdam in the Seventeenth Century* (1963), is a nice account of the economic power of the United Netherlands. R. T. Davies, *Spain in Decline* (1957) and J. H. Elliott, *The Revolt of the Catalans, A Study in the Decline of Spain, 1559–1640* (1963) tell the tragic story of Spanish decay. Christopher Hill, *The Century of Revolutions, 1603–1714* (1966), Philip Taylor, *Origins of the English Civil War; Conspiracy, Crusade, or Class Conflict?* (1960), and Lawrence Stone, *Social Change and Revolution in England, 1540–1640* (1966) all offer extracts from other historians to illustrate the several controversies. C. V. Wedgwood, *The King's War, 1641–1647* (1959) has become a classic. Her *Thirty Years' War* (1958) is still the best account of the conflict in English. T. K. Raab, *The Thirty Years' War—Problems in Motive, Effect and Extent* (1964) is very useful in presenting several interpretations of the war. A. L. Moote, *The Seventeenth Century, Europe in Conflict* (1970) is the first attempt by an American scholar to write about Europe as a whole in this difficult period; it is a highly successful book.

TYCHO BRAHE* (1546–1601)

Tycho Brahe was born into the high nobility of Denmark in the year 1546. The Brahes had been great warriors since the fourteenth century: knights, country junkers, commanders of castles, boon companions of rough-and-ready kings. The

*Professor J. R. Christianson, whose work on Tycho Brahe is of the highest quality, kindly prepared a manuscript for me. The present biography was taken from that manuscript, and he has kindly granted me permission to use it here. Professor Christianson is Chairman of the Department of History at Luther College, Decorah, Iowa.

Billes, Tycho's mother's family, had been bishops and chancellors, university men, patrons of printing and scholarship, smooth diplomats and skilled Latinists. Tycho Brahe was raised to the lordly traditions of his house and his class.

Tycho's four brothers followed the military path which was their patrimony. All of them held prominent Danish fiefs and governorships; one ruled three provinces at once, and another sat in the regency council during the minority of the king. But Tycho, the second son, followed the learned path of the Billes.

Tycho knew enough Latin to enter the University of Copenhagen at the age of 12, and at fifteen he set off on an eight-year tour of the universities of Leipzig, Rostock, Wittenberg, and Basel. This is not to say that he was a peaceful bookworm. At Rostock, he quarreled with another young Danish lord, swords flashed in the wintry dark, and at the end of the duel Tycho had had his nose hacked off (he wore a false nose of gold and silver the rest of his life).

Around 1570, he returned home ripe with German learning, but instead of presenting himself at court to enter the royal service, he withdrew to his maternal uncle's isolated fief of Herrevad Abbey to lose himself in alchemical investigations and—inspired by the appearance of the New Star of 1572—astronomical observations and calculations.

King Frederick of Denmark was puzzled by this scholarly reticence on the part of a Brahe. He called him to court and spoke frankly, saying that he realized Tycho did not want to receive royal favor in the form of mighty castles because he did not want the affairs of administration to distract him from his studies. So, he offered Tycho the small and isolated isle of Hven as a place to live in scholarly tranquility, "and when I have finished my castle at Elsinore, I shall sail over to the island now and then to see your work in astronomy and I shall gladly support your researches. For I am king and you my subject. . . . I see it as my duty to support and promote your work in a fitting manner."

In such fashion, Tycho Brahe entered the service of the Danish crown without abandoning his scholarly pursuits. Fiefs and incomes were showered upon him until he became the best-endowed scientist of the sixteenth century and one of the richest men in northern Europe. In the midst of the little island of Hven arose the "celestial palace" of Uraniborg, an edifice of red brick and grey stone topped by a cluster of green copper spires that rolled back to reveal immense observational instruments. A flock of university graduates and young savants came to Hven to continue their studies and found themselves treated like the lackies and servants of a noble household, housed in an unheated garret, ordered hither and yon by the golden-nosed lord, kept up all night to peer at the stars and all day to labor in the fires of fourteen chemical ovens, write his letters, run his errands, and perform his calculations. But they stayed, because here they could learn things that the rest of the world did not know. A similar staff of paid artists and craftsmen answered to the master's beck and call: painters, engravers, printers, and type founders from Germany, architects from the Low Countries, bookbinders, papermakers, tanners, joiners and smiths, millwrights, and more.

In the midst of all this learned bustle stood the noble lord, Tycho Brahe, a scholar himself and patron of scholars but also a mighty man of the world. He was the constant host of distinguished guests: his own noble kinsmen, learned professors, foreign dignitaries and ambassadors, kings and queens, dukes and duchesses. Nobody of note passed through the Sound in those days without taking a trip to Hven. The learned King James VI of Scotland (later James I of England) delayed his courtship of a Danish princess to call upon Tycho Brahe. In the palace of Uraniborg there were marvels to dazzle the eyes: gigantic instruments of the lord's own manufacture, a huge celestial globe inscribed with data of un-precedented accuracy, running water and secret bell alarms, portraits and inscrip-tions, artistry and science, a Renaissance pleasure garden, a consort of sweet musicians, gallant wit and verse, bountiful feasts, and free flowing wine.

For twenty years under Tycho Brahe, the isle of Hven in Denmark was one of the foremost places in Europe. It was a center of technology and of Renaissance civilization in the north. It was a center of science and learning for the whole continent. And it was the first institute of advanced studies to emerge from the Scientific Revolution, a prototype which has remained viable to our own day.

In his old age, Tycho Brahe was forced by a combination of circumstances to abandon Uraniborg and depart the realm of Denmark. He entered the service of the Holy Roman emperor and thus came into contact with young Johannes Kepler, who inherited his manuscripts and carried on his work when Tycho died in 1601.

Tycho Brahe has long been famous for the bulk and amazing accuracy of his data. He died shortly before the invention of the telescope; but he solved the problem of quality in naked-eye astronomy by increasing the scale of his instru-ments, adding basic technical improvements, and by establishing the procedures of data analysis and refinement which are still basic to scientific observation. Nor did the great lord object to getting his hands dirty or working side by side with plain craftsmen when it came to astronomical instruments, and most of the improve-ments in this area were his own, just as much as those in the realm of observational method. He solved the problem of quantity in compiling a whole new body of astronomical data by the simple expedient of organizing a whole team of ob-servers, training them himself, and then riding close herd to see that they worked as a team. Recent research has shown that Tycho Brahe's accomplishments are no less striking in theoretical astronomy—he made the first original contribution to lunar theory since antiquity—and in the general cultural history of the late sixteenth century.

No other Danish scientist, not even Claus Römer, H. C. Orsted, or Niels Bohr, can approach the stature of this golden-nosed Renaissance lord whose data was both so massive and so scrupulously precise and whose mind was as broad as his age. ∎

[1]When her brother Henry III was killed in 1589, Philip tried to place her daughter on the French throne.

The Alba Madonna by Raphael (1483–1520). A master of space composition and design, Raphael here depicts the Mother and Child as ideal types in a classic pose. His influence remained very strong in Italy and France for almost two centuries. *National Gallery of Art, Washington, D.C., Andrew Mellon Collection*

The Wedding at Cana by Veronese (1528–1588). Veronese painted gigantic scenes, usually swarming with Venetian patricians, even though the title may be Biblical. The use of color and dramatic exposition of subject matter foreshadow the Baroque artists of Spain and the Netherlands. *Cliché des Musées Nationaux-Louvre*

Charles V Seated by Titian (1490–1576). Though still classical and idealized, the portrait gives insight into the character of its subject. *Alte Pinakothek, Munich*

FROM CLASSIC TO DRAMATIC: RENAISSANCE AND BAROQUE ART

The Renaissance tradition looked back to classical antiquity for its calm and balanced beauty, its naturalism, and its idealized types. But the artists in this tradition also experimented with tactile values, perspective, motion, space composition, and the use of color. By the opening of the sixteenth century, the great Italian Renaissance masters already dominated Italian art; in turn Italian art, combined with that of the Netherlands, became the chief inspiration for all Europe in the hundred years following the death of Michelangelo, Leonardo, and Raphael.

The new generations of painters, however, were not content to reproduce the forms of the earlier masters. The damp Venetian climate forced painters to experiment with oils rather than tempera on plaster, and this medium suggested more vivid color and the molding of form by color, light and shade. Painters thus turned to the problems presented by color, light and shade, and the single light source, as well as design. They also took a greater interest in the problems of presenting a

St. Peter's Basilica, (above) Rome (16th and 17th Centuries). A model for cathedrals and capitol buildings all over the western world, this breathtakingly grand structure was the product of several architects' vision. Michelangelo designed the High Renaissance dome, and Bernini created the Baroque circular colonnade. *By courtesy of the trustees of the British Museum, London*

El Escorial, (below) Spain (16th Century). Both a monastery and a royal palace, this massive building was probably the first ever constructed with standardized designs for windows and doors. Its central feature is the chapel; the king's personal chambers are to one side with a secret window giving on the altar. *Photo Mas, Barcelona*

dramatic story. There is often an abundance of activity, a sense of motion, in their works.

The painters who followed the great masters of the Renaissance have been called Baroque. At first this term was one of opprobrium; the critics simply assumed that these artists represented a decadent sort of Renaissance art. However, we now see the Baroque painters in a very different light. They did not follow the classic forms of their predecessors because they had different problems to solve. They were painting for courts that demanded monumental productions, for churches which required dramatic pictures, for wealthy patrons of art who desired art that would either proclaim the importance of the patron or provide him with an amusing picture for his wall. It is hard to generalize about this Baroque art, and the student will understand more by seeing the diversity as well as the unity

The Ambassadors by Holbein the Younger (1497–1543). Representing the German painters, Holbein's exactitude reveals minute details of his subjects' features and also something of their personalities. As the European state system took form, with many conflicts, ambassadors became increasingly important. *Reproduced by courtesy of the trustees, The National Gallery, London*

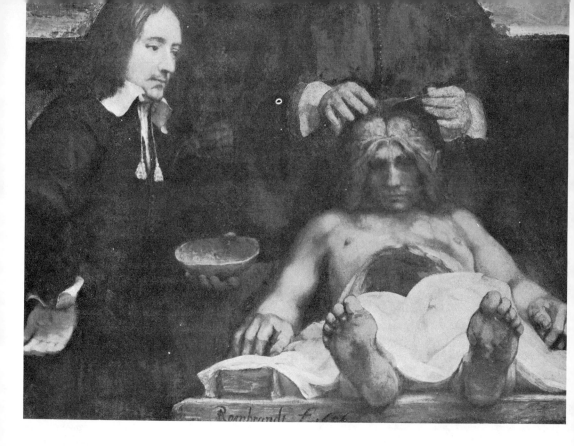

Anatomy Lesson (above) by Rembrandt (1606–1669). Rembrandt was a master of light and shade and of character study. He was much more sober, even Calvinistic, than Rubens. This picture shows a detachedly professional brain dissection, but it also suggests the tragedy of death in the representation of the corpse. *Ryksmuseum, Amsterdam*

Coronation of Marie de' Medici (below) by Rubens (1577–1640). Rubens, a Catholic painting for the Church and the Catholic kings of Spain and France, splashed color on his canvases with exuberance. As a dramatist, he could concentrate a whole story into a single picture, and he had a remarkable ability to portray motion. *Cliché des Musées Nationaux-Louvre*

Lorenzo de' Medici by Michelangelo (1475–1564). Sculptor, painter, architect, and poet, Michelangelo here gives a classic calm to his Florentine patron, Lorenzo. Contrast this with Bernini's realism and action. *Alinari-Art Reference Bureau*

Aeneas and Anchises by Bernini (1598–1680). Aeneas is taking his father and son from the ruins of Troy. The stone is realistically worked to contrast the emaciated father, the vigorous Aeneas, and the childlike son. *Alinari-Art Reference Bureau*

among the great artists of Italy (Veronese, Titian, Caravaggio), of Spain (El Greco, Murillo, Velázquez), of the Netherlands (Rubens, Hals, Rembrandt), and of France (Poussin, Lorrain).

There was a parallel development in sculpture and architecture. Sculpture moved from classic idealized beauty toward a more personal and realistic portrayal of action and emotion, often embodying a dramatic story. The contrast between Michelangelo and Bernini shows this well. Baroque architects, while still employing classical decorative details, achieved their dramatic effects by creating grandiose buildings which dominated the entire area of parks, ponds, and subsidiary buildings around them. ■

Chapter 3

A Constitution for Europe, 1660–1715

DIVERSITY OF POLITICAL EXPERIENCE

"Modern" princes in the first half of the seventeenth century saw the need to establish a form of absolute power over their lands. The traditional centers of power were so diffuse, so pluralistic, so varied in application as to make it *almost* impossible to govern and *quite* impossible to mobilize the resources of the state for any considerable political enterprise. One six-teenth-century ruler after another had gone bankrupt either because he could not tax his subjects or because the economy simply could not support his wars. Nor were fiscal problems the only ones that cried aloud for the centralization of power. Justice and police powers were arbitrary and irrational as long as the noblemen on their estates, the town courts in the cities, and Church tribunals and provincial courts contested with the king for the right to provide and control them. Police authority was even less effective. Occasional sallies might wipe out bands of marauders and thieves, but murder, kidnapping, robbery, and other crimes were common through-out every land and went largely unpunished. Furthermore, new areas for the operation of government emerged with the developing commercial civilization, and princes were naturally anxious to occupy them. The situation demanded the rise of a central authority, of power not shared with all the pluralistic centers that made police activity and justice impossible.

The traditional officers and authorities, however, were unwilling to surrender their positions without a struggle, and the efforts of princes to erect absolute, or undivided, power led to rebellions in the name of "liberties"—Flemish and Dutch liberties, French liberties, English liber-ties, Hungarian liberties, Catalonian liberties, to mention only a few. Not all added a flag of "religious liberties" to their demands for royal recognition of their "traditional" rights, although in some cases, the rebellion was actually a revolution attempting to establish a new situation. However, Dutch merchants and sea captains as well as English squires who revolted against their kings usually insisted that they were only fighting for their tradi-tional rights.

The issues involved in these struggles varied from place to place. Europe in the early seventeenth century was not a community. Geography and history gave great diversity to the political and economic structures under which men lived. Moreover, there were three major languages, each separated into many subdivisions; some parts of Europe had easy access to the sea, some parts were remote from the centers of commerce; the climate and the soil also contributed to differences. But most of all, the variations in the historical pasts of the European peoples made their lives very different. Thus, while we can see a common thread in the efforts of princes to establish their power over the diversities in their realms, the fact that Europe was not a community with common institutions and a common past accounts for the diverse solutions that had come into being by the mid-seventeenth century.

France, the Netherlands, and the British Isles. Of the three states that shared control over the Channel and the Atlantic approaches to the North and Baltic seas, the kingdom of France was the most populous and, potentially, the richest. The reigns of Henry IV (1587–1610) and Louis XIII (1610–1643), and the first years of that of Louis XIV had consolidated the authority of the king. The Huguenot minority and the great lords had been deprived of their power to rebel, and the apparatus of royal government, supported by military power unequalled in the kingdom, was unquestionably supreme. When Cardinal Mazarin died in 1661, young Louis XIV assumed control over a kingdom in which the royal revolution that resulted in the transfer of significant power from the traditional pluralistic centers to the king's government had been largely accomplished. France was still a "federal" monarchy, i.e., the provinces all had their own charters, liberties, and privileges, but within that framework the king's authority was absolute, that is, undivided.

The young king decided to be his own first minister; he called to his council three of Mazarin's trusted lieutenants, each an expert in his own area of competence. Under Louis XIV, LeTellier became minister of war, Lionne minister for foreign affairs, and Foquet controller general for finances; under the king's direction these men were to govern the kingdom. Fouquet was disgraced within a year—as much because Colbert wanted his post as because Fouquet had hoped to dominate the king and assume Mazarin's position as first minister, although the reason given was that Fouquet had stolen the king's money. In addition to the functions of foreign affairs, army, and finance, Lionne, LeTellier, and Colbert (who did get Fouquet's position) administered the provinces, the navy, the colonies, the Catholic church as well as the Reformed church, the king's court, the police, and many of the problems of justice. When the chancellor died, LeTellier moved into this high judicial post, and his son Louvois, who had been trained for the position, became minister of war and took on many other functions as well. When Lionne died, Pomponne was called from a diplomatic post to take charge of foreign affairs. Throughout his reign, Louis XIV tried to call to high positions men who had the expertise necessary to occupy those posts. In practice, this usually meant that the king chose the sons or relatives of his ministers who had acquired expertise by serving apprentice-

88

ships in the king's government. Louis XIV understood that his role was to find and appoint good men to office, support their efforts, and continually review their policies. The king did not need to be an expert; he needed to know which experts to follow. Louis XIV and his ministers set the constitution for the kingdom of France until the Revolution of 1789 overturned the pattern.

The king maintained an army strong enough to stop any domestic rebellions and to guard the frontiers from invasion. The formation of this army took several decades; it was no simple task to recruit and train clerks, administrators, engineers, and soldiers who would obey. Soldiers had to be trained to accept orders from the king's war ministry and to recognize the king's right to establish a table of ranks. This new army was not greatly different from the old condottieri armies of the Thirty Years' War, but in place of a free captain like Wallenstein or Bernard von Saxe-Weimar, the king's ministry governed the troops and regulated the military hierarchy under the direction of the minister of war. The war ministry's engineers and administrators established depots for supplies, organized siege trains—the carts or river boats for portage of war matériel and food for men and horses—and regulated training, weapons, and, by the 1680's, even uniforms. The French war ministry, ruled by LeTellier and later by Louvois, started a military revolution in Europe. This provided the king of France with an overwhelming force, and his neighbors had either to accept French hegemony or somehow build military forces that could cope with this French power.

Colbert, as finance minister, minister of colonies and commerce, minister for internal economic organization, and holder of many other titles connected with the economy of the kingdom, attempted to rationalize and control the economic order in France so that the king could pay for this army, support his diplomacy and his projects in Europe, maintain a brilliant court, and at the same time build such architectural monuments as the new Louvre or Versailles and subsidize poets, painters, scientists, and men of letters who would make the Age of Louis XIV as brilliant as had been the Age of Augustus. But Colbert's most important efforts were directed to the development of uniform tax and tariff schedules in the kingdom, the encouragement of industry, and the extension of French commerce both in Europe and beyond in Asia and the New World. The king's wars made it immpossible to accomplish these objectives, and yet Colbert did provide his king with the money needed to build the new Louvre and Versailles and to fight the so-called Dutch war. In the later years of the reign, when two great wars had exhausted the treasury, there was no one with Colbert's ability to manage the royal finances. Indeed, perhaps Colbert himself could not have pulled the kingdom out of the hole that these wars had made for it.

The third arm of Louis' government was his foreign ministry and diplomatic corps. Diplomacy had been Mazarin's principle interest; Louis XIV, Mazarin's student in the art of government, also gave it much attention. His successive foreign ministers, Lionne, Pomponne, Colbert de Crossy, and Colbert de Torcy, were able men, skilled in the art of negotiation; they were assisted by a corp of professional diplomats, trained in the school of Mazarin and Louis XIV, who acted as the eyes and ears of the king in Europe. Thus, Louis had the best machine for conducting the king's business in Europe that had been developed anywhere up to this time. This bureaucratic, military, police state that emerged under Louis XIV made its will felt in the kingdom through officials known as intendants for police, justice, and taxation. The word "police" really meant "civil administration." These officers not only executed the will of the king and his council in the provinces, but they also supervised local officers to be sure that the latter actually carried out their functions. Gradually, these royal officials forced the election or appointment of their favorites in the municipal governments and extended their controls to the countryside where the nobles previously had ruled without challenge. The intendant could depend upon military force to accomplish his missions in the provinces; in Paris a proper police department emerged to assure the tranquility of the city. According to this description, it would seem that a political machine had come into being. However, we must not forget that the kingdom of France was enormously large in terms of the time required to go from place to place and that the number of royal officials, even though it had increased considerably under Louis XIV, was still small by modern standards. The average subject probably lived out most of his life without ever seeing a royal official. Furthermore, as Colbert's correspondence clearly indicates, even those officers who did exist could not always be depended upon to carry out the king's will. Poor Colbert spent many hours restating his commands and reenacting his proclamations and his laws. He was always faced with the problems of time and space as well as with the venal, dishonest, corrupt, inefficient creatures who managed the king's government. Even so, this was the most effective political machine that had appeared in Europe up to that time, and it became a prototype adopted by other rulers who hoped to give their realms government as effective as that in France.

The mid-century civil war in England resulted in the execution of Charles I and the establishment of the Commonwealth government with Cromwell as Lord Protector. This government, however, could not command a majority of the politically potent people of England; it depended upon the army and the major generals. When Cromwell died in 1659, there was no one to succeed him; the obvious solution was the restoration of the Stuart dynasty as the legitimate monarchy of England but with guarantees that would prevent any recurrence of the arbitrary government that had brought about the revolution. In 1660, Charles II ascended to his father's throne after he had agreed to the Restoration constitution. Several important things were settled by this restoration, but there were still unsolved problems. The king could no longer rule without the consent of Parliament, and yet the king's prerogatives left him in full control of the administrative machine of the state. As long as the king and Parliament were in agreement over objectives, the government could be effective, but if they disagreed, the power of England would fall on dead center and nothing could be done unless the king could find sources of money outside his kingdom. This explains the fact that Charles II and, later, his brother James II had to accept subsidies from the king of France when their policies differed from the wishes of Parliament.

However, Charles II and the so-called Restoration Parliament got along famously at first. Both were anxious to erase the work of the Puritans, to reestablish the Church of England, and to take revenge upon their enemies. But there were real disagreements over both religion and politics that were not solved until the revolution of 1688 made it possible for the king and Parliament to cooperate in the mobilization of the power of the kingdom. Nevertheless, the years of the restoration government were important in the development of the English political system. Out of the civil wars emerged the two parties that were eventually to develop into an effective political machine for the direction of state policy.

These political parties were neither well defined nor disciplined; in a general way the divisions of the civil wars between the Roundheads and the Cavaliers tended to be perpetuated in the Whig and Tory political orientations. The Whigs, more or less heirs to the revolutionary tradition, tended to emphasize the rights of Parliament to control the realm. They drew support from the nonconformist religious groups in the kingdom, city men, and lords who had emerged from the revolution. While no less anti-Roman Catholic than their opponents, they were more inclined toward toleration of Protestant groups outside the Church of England. The Tories tended to be very pro-Church of England and most respectful of the rights of the crown. They drew their support from the country gentlemen who had suffered from Puritan intolerance during the Revolutionary and Commonwealth eras and from the lords who had been loyal to the crown. They could count upon the bishops in the House of Lords and the country members in the House of Commons.

The grave difference between the two groups came to the fore when the Whigs attempted to exclude Charles' brother James from the succession on the ground that he was a Roman Catholic; the Whigs were quite willing to set the succession to the throne by an act of Parliament, but the Tories, staunch believers in the divine right of kings, refused to go along. There was a Test Act which prevented anyone who would not take communion in the Anglican church from holding office. This excluded James from the admiralty, but his birth assured him the right to mount the throne if Charles should die without heirs. Thus, it became possible for England to have a Catholic dynasty.

Local government in England remained in the hands of the local gentry and nobility. The sheriffs, justices of the peace and lords-lieutenant were appointed by the crown from men of the shire. This gave the king's government a great deal of leverage in securing the election of a friendly parliament. Many of the towns that had two seats in Parliament were the private property of great lords, the other towns and the shires had so narrow a suffrage that bribery or threats could often influence the outcome of elections. Nonetheless, England was a kingdom in which the great lords and gentry ruled in the countryside and the moneymen governed the commercial cities. They could all be bribed to do the king's "will," providing they did not object to his policies and the king did not interfere with their government of their own communities.

The English fiscal system did not strain the resources of the kingdom largely because Parliament was reluctant to vote new taxes. When a king mounted the throne, Parliament voted him a subsidy that was expected to be enough to maintain his household and his government and support his projects. As we have seen, kings after Elizabeth I found it nearly impossible to live on these revenues, and the last two Stuart kings were no exception. Thus, both Charles II and James II were obliged to seek funds from Louis XIV when they could not secure them from Parliament. As we shall see, the solution to the problem of king and Parliament came after 1688 when a revolution created a new situation in which it became possible for the English government to mobilize the wealth of the kingdom for purposes that both king and Parliament wished to accomplish.

By 1660–1680, France had developed a bureaucratic, military, police state under the control of the king and his ministers, and England had found a new compromise between the power of the king and the authority of Parliament. But in the Netherlands the *Stände-stadt* that had been developed by the men who rebelled against Philip II continued almost as an anachronism. Each of the seven provinces had its own legislature (Estates) which controlled the affairs of the province. However, these provincial legislatures were frequently subordinated to the governments of the important towns within the province. To govern the union of the seven provinces, there was a General Estates in which delegates from the several provinces sat to deliberate on common problems. Since the province of Holland was overwhelmingly the largest in the Union, its delegates had a decisive vote in the General Estates. In turn, the city of Amsterdam could control the Estates of Holland, and with it the General Estates of the United Netherlands. The most serious bar to decisive action was the fact that there was no executive authority in the sense found elsewhere. There was no king or prince in the Netherlands, and yet there was the office of stadtholder, which, when occupied by the head of the house of Orange, could encompass an executive function. Each of the provinces had a stadtholder, who was a military officer and governor, and in several of them this office was hereditary in the house of Orange. Each of the seaward provinces had its own admiralty which might be coordinated by the stadtholder but was not necessarily so. This ambiguous political situation was further complicated by the socioeconomic structure of the United Netherlands.

The governments of the great commercial cities, the Bank of Amsterdam, and the Dutch East and West India Companies were largely under the control of a patrician class of wealthy, bourgeois families who ruled through interlocking directorates. This regent class occupied the positions of economic power and was usually able to control the municipal governments, the provincial estates, and the General Estates. The men of this class were primarily interested in their economic projects, but they also were much concerned to retain control of the state. During the rebellion against the king of Spain, they had provided the money and the ships to win independence, but they, like other sixteenth-century men, could not imagine a military enterprise not subordinated to a great nobleman. Thus, they were quite willing to accept the military leadership of the prince of Orange, but they were unwilling to allow the Orange family to establish itself as hereditary rulers of the land. However, an Orange political faction emerged in the Netherlands, supported by the noble families who readily served in the army under the prince and by the artisans and workers in the cities who allied with the house of Orange against the wealthy bourgeoisie. By the mid-seventeenth century, the Orange faction could also count upon the radical Calvinist ministers who objected to both the regent's religious liberalism and the fact that in the rural areas of landward provinces and in those parts of Brabant that were acquired by the Peace of Westphalia and administered as common property of the United Netherlands, the Roman Catholic religion was commonly practiced by a majority of the people. The radical Calvinists wished to end this "scandal"; the regents prevented them from doing so, but with such bad grace that they gained little support from the Catholics while they lost the favor of the radical Calvinists. The regents also ran into conflict with Calvinist preachers because of the former's willingness to espouse Cartesian philosophy and the new physics and astronomy; the radical Calvinists were conservatives in the academic world as well as in the religious one. With its hold on workers, the clergy's support to the Orange faction against the regents was important.

In the mid-seventeenth century, Prince William II of Orange seemed about to establish his dynasty as the real rulers of the land, but his untimely death left a posthumously born son and no other male members of the family capable of assuming control. This family crisis came exactly at the time of the first Anglo-Dutch commercial war and played a part in its conclusion. As we have seen, Cromwell feared the Orange faction because of the relation between the house of Orange and the Stuarts, and he was willing to make peace only after an act of exclusion deprived the Orange family of its traditional place in the government of the United Netherlands. This act of exclusion was not easy to secure since in some of the northern provinces the house of Orange held hereditary rights to the provincial stadtholderate, and in most of the provinces the Orange faction was strong enough to block any such action by the General Estates. DeWitt, however, secured the act from the Estates of Holland, and since Holland, the largest and richest of the provinces, could veto any action of the General Estates, the pretentions of the Orange faction were, at least for the time, blocked by this measure that had the approval of both Cromwell and the regent class in the Netherlands.

Since William III was only a child at the time, and there was no other male member of the family capable of becoming stadtholder, the act could not arouse great objections. And the fact that it brought peace gave the regents, under the leadership of DeWitt, the opportunity to attempt to organize the government of the United Netherlands without a stadtholder. Their success proved to be shortlived. They were able to weather the second

Anglo-Dutch war (1665–1667), but when Louis xiv's armies invaded the Netherlands in 1672, the DeWitt brothers were murdered, the seats in the Holland Estates and the General Estates were reshuffled, and Prince William iii became stadtholder. He held that office until his death in 1702 when the regents again had the opportunity to attempt to establish a stadtholderless government since William iii did not leave a male heir who could step into his place.

Students of recent European history are often much surprised to discover that the United Netherlands provinces, occupying a tiny scrap of land on the estuaries of the Rhine, Maas, and Scheldt rivers, could play the role of a great power in the seventeenth century. These people successfully made war on equal terms against Spain, England, and France; their diplomats played important roles at the peace conferences of the era; and the words of their leaders were decisive in the politics of Europe. The reason for this of course, lay in the commercial position that these united provinces occupied in the total European economy. As we have seen in the preceding chapter, the United Netherlands formed an *entrepôt* for all the goods of Europe as well as for the commodities that came from beyond the seas. It was a center for all sorts of merchandise, for banking, for insurance, for refinishing, and for both the shipbuilding and carrying trade. All this brought wealth into the land, and with wealth, seventeenth-century men could buy cannons, soldiers, warships, and allies. When William iii became king of England he could not understand why the English Parliament forced him to send his Dutch guards back to Holland; in his land, foreign soldiers were the rule rather than the exception. The Dutch hired Germans, Frenchmen, Scotsmen, Swiss, and men of other nations to fight their battles; Dutch noblemen might be the officers, but only a few Dutchmen were in the ranks since recruiting could create shortages of labor.

The United Provinces maintained fortifications and stationed soldiers on the upper reaches of the river systems that flowed through their lands—in some cases with, and in others without, the consent of the cities and princes upon whose territories they intruded. These bases, particularly along the Rhine and the Maas, were regarded as necessary for the protection of commerce as well as for the defense of the United Provinces themselves. When the French threatened to take the Spanish Netherlands, Dutch occupation of "barrier fortifications" in those provinces became a political demand, and the peace settlements of Ryswick and Utrecht each recognized the right of the United Provinces to station soldiers in these fortifications in the provinces of the Spanish, later Austrian, Netherlands. These outposts of Dutch military influence were much the same as the American military bases that were established after 1945 in Spain, Italy, Tripoli, and many other places on the globe. The difference, however, was that the Dutch used their military presence to further the economic interests of their merchants and, wherever possible, forced the local inhabitants to pay for the "protection" that they afforded.

In times of war, the Dutch could also bring together naval power that could operate on a level of equality with its rivals; this was true until almost the end of the seventeenth century when the Dutch navies weakened relative to those of France and England. In wartime, too, the economic power of the united provinces allowed them to pay subsidies to foreign princes; even the Holy Roman emperor sought these subsidies, and most of the German princes could not have had an army without them. This was an era when princely revenues were slender and difficult to expand under any conditions; the Dutch, with a vigorous economy from which to draw money, had power available to few other states in Europe.

The Spanish and German Empires in Decay. In the years following the Treaty of the Pyrenees, it became increasingly evident that the great period of the Spanish crowns had come to an end. Barcelona did return to its allegiance to the Hapsburg king, but Portugal successfully maintained its independence in spite of all that Philip iv could do. Spain's grip on her Italian holdings in Naples and Sicily, the Tuscan ports, and Milan became so relaxed that these territories, like the Spanish Netherlands, were largely self-governing and contributed little or nothing to the common interests of the crown. The Indies, too, ceased to be as important as formerly; the silver mines were almost played out, the "gold-rush" economy dwindled to a stagnant economic situation that witnessed the decay of the port cities and a serious loss of revenue to the agricultural communities that had furnished meat, grain, horses, and fodder for the miners. The countryside in Spanish America was destined to be inhabited by largely self-sufficient haciendas governed by a landlord who ruled over his peons. The wealth that had produced beautiful Baroque churches, cathedrals, and palaces was gone. Most discouraging for the future of the Spanish crowns was the further fact that Castile could no longer carry the financial load for its king. Heavy taxes; debased currency; bad government; loss of men and women to monastic institutions, in military adventures, or to the New World; and foreign competition that ruined native industries all contributed to the decline of Castile. The population dropped rapidly in the seventeenth century; the country began to look like a land occupied by a hostile army. At the death of Philip ii when the century turned, the Spanish crown was still the foremost power in Europe; when Philip iv died in 1665, leaving a sickly child as heir, Spain was not even a "hollow giant"; all Europe understood that Spain could no longer play a leading role in the politics of Europe.

As we have noted in connection with Spanish Italy and the Spanish Netherlands, the inner organization of the crowns of Spain tended to revert to the status of the period before Philip ii had attempted to make a proper empire of his many crowns. As the central power weakened, local authorities assumed more and more responsibility for whatever government did exist, but this trend did not mean better government. The local powers were usually under a municipal patriciate or a grandee, and either one was more concerned for its own interests than for those of the men it ruled.

For more than a decade after the death of Philip iv, a regency government in Madrid governed in the name of the sickly, dim-witted boy, Charles ii. Decisions were made in his name in Brussels, Milan, Naples, and the capitals of the Spanish kingdoms, but the fate of his realm was decided in Paris, The Hague, London, and Vienna. When he came of age the situation did not change. He could neither make decisions nor sire an heir. All Europe watched and wondered when he would die and plotted for the disposition of his realms. When he finally did die in 1700, the disposition of those crowns led to one of the great wars of modern times.

After the Treaties of Westphalia, the Holy Roman Empire of the German nation was even more dilapidated than the empire of the Spanish Hapsburgs. The Diet of Augsburg (1555) placed the control of the Church in the hands of the princes; the Peace of Westphalia gave the princes the right to deal directly with foreign powers and to negotiate treaties of alliance outside the Empire. The emperor's powers were thus severely reduced. He had no effective army except the forces he could command as king of Bohemia and Hungary and prince over the Hapsburg *Erbländer* on the Danube and in the Alps. His court could still decide questions of succession and he could grant titles and honors that were becoming more and more hollow, but his real power came from the lands that he ruled as prince rather than from his position on the imperial throne. The Diet was no less unfortunate. It met perpetually at Regensburg, attended by representatives of the princes since it was no longer important or useful for a prince to attend in person. Most of its time was taken up with endless wrangles over precedence and gossip about the courts of Germany. Only when the French encroachments in the Rhineland and the Turkish invasion on the Danube in the early 1680's posed threats to all central Europe did the Diet and the emperor succeed in raising an imperial army to defend the frontiers.

The century following the Treaties of Westphalia, however, was a great period for the German princes. In a dozen or so of the larger principalities, in some of the richer cities, and in a number of the ecclesiastical states a court life flourished as the princes learned to manage their estates and govern their treasuries. These were the years when princes developed bureaucratic machines inspired by the Cameral doctrines that taught princes how to govern their subjects in the spirit of German Christian civilization. At its best, the bureaucracy that Cameralism inspired did provide better government than had been known before, but unhappily most of the petty capitals did not achieve this "best" and the result was often enough a sordid, corrupt tyranny. However, in Brandenburg-Prussia, in Hanover, in Bavaria, in Saxony, and elsewhere princes were able to repeat on a petty scale the achievements of the enlightened rulers of France who were trying to rationalize the decentralized, confused political and economic forms they found all around them. The princely authority, often exercised in the name of "German liberties," was usually founded on the destruction of the "liberties" of noblemen and towns within their principalities. The record of Frederick William, electoral prince of Brandenburg, is most striking. He built an army and a bureaucracy to manage it by overriding or suppressing the *Landtage* in the principalities that he ruled and by ruthlessly crushing rebellions of the noblemen in Prussia and other of his territories. The counterpart of this violence was the erection of the bureaucratic and military machines for which he recruited the sons of the

96

landowners as soldiers or officials. By drawing personnel for his army and government from the Rhineland, from Brandenburg and the other principalities in north central Germany, and from Prussia, he began to develop a group of officials and soldiers inspired with *esprit de corps* and loyalty to his family, the Hohenzollerns. Frederick William did not make a single state out of his several provinces, but he did give them a form of unity and he built an army that was the best in Germany.

The story of the rise of princely power in Bavaria, Saxony, Hanover, and the Rhine Palatinate is not so striking as that of Brandenburg-Prussia, and yet in each of these electoral principalities we see a process of development similar in outline but different in detail. Saxony, the Palatinate, and Bavaria were more closely attached to France than were Brandenburg and Hanover, but all of them accepted subsidies from Louis xiv and, in a way, modeled their bureaucratic forms after those of France. The problem, however, was a difficult one. None of these German princes occupied territory that could be considered rich, and the commerce that passed through their lands was relatively slight and usually in the hands of Dutch merchants rather than their own subjects. They all had to depend very heavily upon the income from the agricultural production of their own princely lands, supplemented by dues, fees, fines, and other income of feudal origin and some excise taxes on spirits, candles, cards, taverns, and the like. None of these princes had an income that could assure independence even though legally they had all mounted to the status of quasi-independent rulers. What was true for the secular states was even more true for those governed by bishops or abbots. None of the ecclesiastical states could escape the need for begging subsidies, nor could they force the Dutch to withdraw their troops from the electoral cities and towns on the river systems of western Germany. After 1660 the most important of these states, Cologne, became, in fact if not in law, almost a province of the kingdom of France because the elector owed the French king so much more money than he could repay.

Baltic and Eastern Europe. By the mid-seventeenth century, the kingdom of Sweden and the Baltic empire under its control ruled the north of Europe. After Gustavus Adolphus, there was a regency government for his daughter Christina, but when she came of age, she resigned her throne, converted to Catholicism, and spent the rest of her life in France and Italy. Her cousin, Charles x Gustavus, came to the throne in 1654; his short reign was largely concerned with the war against Poland which ended with the Treaty of Oliva (1660). In 1660 another regency government for the child-king Charles xi put control of the Swedish empire in the hands of the great lords of the land. This regency was discredited after its disasterous participation in the so-called Dutch war when Brandenburg troops defeated the Swedish army and expelled it from Pomerania. After 1680 the young Charles xi managed to oust the great lords of the regency from his council and then reoccupy the crown lands that they had appropriated for themselves. Charles xi, by this "reduction" and the creation of a bureaucracy and an army, placed new powers in the hands of the king so that Swedish historians refer to this period as the "time of strength." Charles' son was Charles XII, the soldier-king who spent most of his life fighting the War of the North that ended Swedish hegemony in the north and brought Peter the Great's Russia into the balance of European power. With the rise of Russia, Sweden sank to a third-rate position in Europe.

The kingdom of Poland-Lithuania began to decline in power during these same years. This dual monarchy was made up of a dozen or so large provinces or palatinates, each with a local Diet and a palatine elected from the important local nobility. For all intents and purposes, these units were nearly independent in everything except foreign affairs; they even had the right to combine with each other to make war on the king. The central authority was vested in the king and a Diet, but the existence of the so-called *Liberum veto* made the sessions of the Diet futile and the powers of the king nearly nonexistent. While other states were developing bureaucratic organizations that strengthened the powers of the central authority, vis-à-vis the great nobles, Poland took the other direction, and prepared itself for absorption by its neighbors. Without a strong army organized by a ministry of war and supported by adequate tax revenues, Poland was unable to defend herself.

The Turkish wars of the sixteenth century had created three Hungarys: Hapsburg, Turkish, and Transylvanian. In all three, the great nobles were the important political powers; they largely controlled the Diets of Hapsburg and Transylvanian Hungary; they governed the countryside in all three. The big problem, of course, was the reunificiation of the three into a single kingdom of Hungary. There were several great families that aspired to the throne and were even willing to become vassals of the sultan to acquire it. For these magnates, the Hapsburg kings were enemies who would impose German rule on the Hungarian nobility. Throughout the seventeenth century, Hungarian malcontents carried on more or less undercover warfare against the Hapsburg rule. They were Calvinist by religion; they were opposed to the development of bureaucratic power; they disliked the German variety of Christian civilization. In the third and fourth quarters of the century, they made common cause with the Ottoman invasion of the Danube basin and suffered the fate of rebels when Leopold's armies routed the Turks and conquered the whole of Hungary. It was not until the mid-eighteenth century, however, that the Hapsburgs were able to trust their Hungarian subjects, and then only by giving way to the latter's demands for local autonomy.

In the mid-seventeenth century, the Ottoman Empire seemed to recover from the decline that had set in shortly after the death of Suleiman the Magnificent. A series of reforming viziers assumed the power that had formerly been the sultan's alone and gave new impetus to the state by probing at the frontiers. These viziers from the Kiuprili family realized that the power of the Turkish state was related to its ability to continue conquests; they also understood that the conquests they could make were relatively limited. The heroic age of Islamic expansion was over. The first probing up the Danube in the early 1660's met with a resounding defeat

98

when an imperial army, supported by a strong contingent from France, met the Turks at Saint Gottard. By 1664 they were willing to make a twenty-year truce with Emperor Leopold and turn their efforts east and southward where their neighbor's military power was somewhat less than their own. However, in 1683 a Turkish armament again invaded the Danube basin and reached Vienna only to be thrust back and driven from all of Hungary. Like Poland, the Ottoman Empire began its period of decline in these years when the Christian armies under the banners of Emperor Leopold drove the Turks from the middle Danube.

In the eastern borderlands of Europe, the Russian empire was bogged down by great spaces without roads leading westward and in archaic political and military organizations unsuited for contests with the West. In the eyes of Europeans, it remained an isolated, distant, partially understood state. European military and commercial adventurers had penetrated Russia, but their influence was not great except in a limited circle around Moscow. The reforming influences that had freed the Muscovite state from the Tartar powers had been dissipated in the "Times of Trouble" in the early seventeenth century when there was a contest for the crown. The Romanov family had come to the throne under the influence of the Church, and its early members often carried out a quasi-religious role in their governing of the state, leaving the power in the hands of the great nobles. The Russian armies were no match for Western soldiers nor was Russia's political order geared to develop Western-style military power. Indeed, both the Polish and the Swedish governments maintained a sort of quarantine on their frontiers with Russia to prevent the Russians from acquiring Western arms. By the last quarter of the century, however, the Russian government did have about 4000 men armed, trained in the Western military manner, and under the command of Western soldiers. These men, as we shall see later, were very important in the revolution made by Tsar Peter I in the opening decades of the eighteenth century. But before Peter's time, Russia could hardly be said to be a part of Europe. Its religious orientation was toward the Orthodox community; its political and economic orientations were either primitive or turned in upon themselves and quite unrelated to most of the developments in the West.

Consequences. If we look at the spectrum of mid-seventeenth century political societies—ranging from vigorous "modern" powers such as the kingdom of France, the dual monarchy of England-Scotland, and the realm of the United Netherlands through the varied experience of the Hapsburg Spanish empire and the Holy Roman Empire of the German nation to the anarchic situation in Poland and Hungary and the archaic structure in Russia—it becomes quite clear that any idea of Europe as a political entity with common characteristics and forms must be discarded. The diversity of Europe's medieval past could not be brushed aside in an age that still depended upon the power of men, animals, and wind for transportation. Indeed these differences, rooted in the remote past, were so pervasive that they were not to be wiped out even when men had steam, electricity, and the twentieth-century's adaptations of power to transportation, communication, and production. The diversities, however, may be at the center of the story of the fantastic development of the civilization we call European for they were responsible for many of the conflicts that forced European men to consider the institutions and ideas of their neighbors and adopt or modify them for their own use. These frictions were military, political, and intellectual; they resulted both from political ambitions and from the development of new ideas, and they were evident in both the movement of armies and the migrations of scholars, artists, engineers, and diplomats from one part of Europe to another. The last country considered thus far in this chapter was Russia. At the very end of the seventeenth century, European soldiers, merchants, architects, scholars, shipbuilders, cannon founders, and other technicians were invited to Russia in large numbers. These people did not remake Russian civilization, but they did give it a Western orientation through the impact of their ideas and methods. Nonetheless, even in the late twentieth century, the divergences are strongly marked when one crosses political and linguistic frontiers in Europe; but the friction created by war, ideas, methods, and competitions has broken down some of these differences and has acted as a creative force in the formation of a larger society of Europe.

HIGH POLITICS

The Question of Frontiers. The treaties of both Westphalia and the Pyrenees were more or less intentionally vague about the actual transfer of territory; it was not customary to define a lineal frontier, and these treaties spoke of the transfer of the "rights and territories" belonging to the Hapsburg house as Margrave of Alsace, of the province of Artois, or of this or that county or city and "its dependencies." In the past, this had been a satisfactory method of defining frontiers; indeed, a lineal description would have probably been impossible anyway because of the enclaves and projections of territories on both sides of any frontier in Europe, particularly along the frontiers of the Holy Roman Empire. At Westphalia and in the Pyrenees agreement, Mazarin had been quite willing to accept this solution for establishing frontiers—in part because there was no other way to write the treaties and in part because the vagueness opened opportunities for the future. But Louis XIV and his advisors needed a more exact definition. Louis' council was made up of men of the pen who supplanted the noblemen and soldiers who had advised kings in the past. They were deeply concerned with tariffs, taxes, frontier fortifications, administration, and police. Even more than Richelieu and Mazarin, who had been anxious to secure the "gates" to the kingdom, these men wanted to know where the king's rule stopped and his neighbor's began, and they wanted that line to be defensible. Louis shared their concern for he had come of age in the era of the Fronde and the war with Spain when his frontiers had been violated, when the Spanish Army had been in Paris; he, too, wanted frontiers that could be defended or that could be used as a springboard for any future offensive action that might become necessary.

In the first years of his personal reign, Louis succeeded in buying Dunkirk from Charles II of England (1662), and he thought that he had secured French control over Lorraine by a treaty with its duke, but these were only two of the minor questionable frontier positions. The important problem was the frontier between the kingdom of France and the Spanish Netherlands. Here was France's most dangerous frontier, for there were no natural barriers between France and the Spanish holdings. Mazarin had hoped to add the entire Spanish Netherlands to the kingdom of France as dowry of Maria Theresa, but that had been impossible because of Dutch opposition. Louis and his advisors did not give up the dream of acquiring these territories, however, and when Philip IV died in 1665 they found an excuse that might allow them to bring at least part of their dream to fruition. In some of the Spanish Netherlandic provinces, there was a law that provided for a female of the first bed to inherit a part of her father's goods even though there might be a male heir. This "law of devolution" seemed to be an excellent pretext for depriving the Spanish King Charles II, then a baby, of part of the Netherlands. The time seemed most appropriate. England and the United Netherlands were locked in a trade war in which the French king was an ally of the Dutch; thus, Louis might hope that there would be no serious objection to his plans. Naturally, the Spanish regency refused to surrender any part of Charles' inheritance on so specious a pretext, and so a French army marched, almost unopposed, into the Spanish Netherlands to secure the French queen's "just pretentions." Louis announced in advance that his objectives were limited to the lands belonging to Maria Theresa, but his formidable army and the ease with which it made conquests did not reassure his neighbors.

The Dutch did not want Louis XIV's France for a neighbor; they did not want the port of Antwerp to be opened to the traffic of the world under French control. The English city-men shared some of the same fears. As a result, the Anglo-Dutch war was quickly ended, and English and Dutch statesmen agreed to try to check the ambitions of the French king. Assurance of a Spanish subsidy persuaded the Swedish regency government to join England and the United Netherlands in the Triple Alliance, which proffered its "good offices" to the belligerents and assured Louis XIV of support for his claim to limited annexations. They also agreed among themselves to use military force if Louis XIV should demand more. However, since the French demands were essentially met, and since Mazarin had often warned against arousing a coalition against the kingdom, Louis XIV agreed to peace. It was concluded by the Treaty of Aix-la-Chapelle of 1668. But the frontiers of France were made even more insecure and indefinite by that settlement, and, when the French learned the full terms of the treaty of the Triple Alliance, Louis and his advisors realized that those frontiers could not be made secure as long as the United Netherlands were in a position to prevent it.

There seemed no alternative to the destruction of Dutch power. This would remove a block to the "rectification" of the northern frontier; it would also remove a commercial rival that Colbert regarded as his ultimate enemy. Between 1668 and 1672, therefore, the full power of French diplomacy was set in motion to isolate the Dutch and secure allies for the kingdom of France. Both Sweden and England were detached from the Triple Alliance and tied to an alliance with France. The Holy Roman emperor and several of the German princes agreed to remain neutral; several others of them joined the French alliance.

By 1672 all seemed ready, and the most powerful army ever to march on European soil up to that time moved down the Rhine and invaded the United Netherlands from the rear while the Anglo-French navies harassed their foe from the sea. It seemed inevitable that the United Netherlands would be crushed never to rise again. But the French had made a miscalculation: They had failed to capture the sluices that allowed the Dutch to let in the sea and make Amsterdam and much of Holland into an island. Even so, the Dutch offered terms extremely favorable to the victors, but they could not accept the Carthaginian peace that the French demanded of them. There was a revolution in Amsterdam. The DeWitt brothers were murdered; Prince William III of Orange became Stadtholder and raised a cry to Europe for aid.

The invading army of 1672 gave all Europe a fright; in 1673 the impression of urgency was further reinforced when the French besieged and took Maestrick in an unbelievably short time. That fortification had been built by the Dutch in the city belonging to the archbishop of Cologne to control the traffic on the Maas river. It was believed to be the most powerful fortification in all Europe. The designer of the siege was a young engineer, Vauban, who had attracted the king's attention and confidence; Vauban captured the fortification with an army "under the orders" of the king himself. (Only with Louis in command could an engineer direct the siege; prestigious soldiers who were marshals of France would not have accepted his suggestions otherwise.) But this siege proved to men beyond the Rhine, in Spain, and even in England that the kingdom of France was dangerous. The elector of Brandenburg forgot that the Dutch had driven his little African company from the African coast; the emperor decided that if the Dutch were destroyed, he would be the next target of the French king; the Spanish were sure that their Netherlandic provinces would be absorbed into France unless the Dutch were saved. By the first months of 1674, it was no longer a question of whether the French would withdraw from the Lower Rhine; men were making bets on the day that the withdrawal would begin.

The year 1674 proved to be a critical one. England made peace with the United Netherlands—in part because of a rising fear of France, in part in hopes of taking commercial advantage of the two rival trading nations. The Holy Roman emperor, Spain, and the German princes declared war on France. Only Sweden remained a French ally and the Brandenburg army crushed the Swedish forces at Fehrbellin in June of 1675. The French managed to occupy Franche-Comté, establish a foothold in Sicily, and hold off the enemy that invaded Alsace, but it was obvious that they must soon go

102

on the defensive. In 1675 Turenne was killed, the French army retreated from Germany in rout, another French army was defeated in the middle Rhine, and French forces on the Spanish Netherlandic frontiers were on the defensive. If the Triple Alliance of 1667–1668 was the first coalition against France, the alliance that came into being in 1673–1675—including the United Netherlands, Spain, and the German powers—was the second; and it was much more dangerous than the first, for William III of Orange managed to marry the niece of Charles II of England, and thus English intervention against France also became a possibility. With Turenne dead and Condé ready to retire because of his failures, the king of France stood in dire need of military and political advice.

The course of the war combined with Vauban's genius as a soldier and an engineer provided the solution to the problem of frontiers for France. As early as 1673, Vauban made a tour of the Flanders frontier and came back with the recommendation that it should be made more rational. He found French and Spanish fortifications, some strong and some weak, scattered pell-mell along the border; what was needed, he insisted, was a well-marked "dueling field." The French invasion of the Rhineland in 1672 also taught an important lesson: The Dutch forts intruded along the Rhine collapsed one after another; at one point four of them surrendered in one day. Such fortifications were not worth the powder, shot, and cannon they required even for a token resistance. A strong fortification, on the other hand, could withstand an assault. In 1676, William III of Orange besieged for months the fortification that Vauban had constructed at Maestrick and finally had to lift the siege. A further important lesson of the war stemmed from the fact that it had proven impossible to break Dutch power, therefore making it improbable that France would be able to annex the Spanish Netherlands. All this pointed to the obvious solution: The French military effort should be directed in such a way as to clear up the enclaves and other irregularities along the Flanders frontier so that a defensible line could be established by the peace. And, indeed, this was the strategy of the French army between 1676 and 1678.

There was more to the war than the battle over frontiers. It was seemingly an endless, expensive venture that was draining both France and the enemies of France of wealth and manpower. There were "peace parties" in every government, but there seemed to be no possible peace. The emperor and Prince William of Orange were convinced that, if the war could be continued, England would join them and Louis XIV's France could be properly humbled; there were other men, both in Germany and in the United Netherlands, who wanted to end the conflict as soon as possible. In France the peace party was strong, but the king and his most important advisors were committed to some sort of victory even though it undoubtedly would be less than they had hoped to achieve. As was characteristic of those years, negotiations for peace continued while the soldiers made war. But the negotiations could be successful only if the coalition against France could be broken by the defection of one of its members. Prince William and Emperor Leopold wanted to hold firm, but the French found the weak link in their opponent's armor: The bourgeois regents of Amsterdam were tired of the war that had cost them so much and was ruining their commerce to the advantage of the English. In 1678 Louis XIV and a majority party in the General Estates reached an agreement to end hostilities.

The peace was made at Nymwegen after the French and the regents in the General Estates had reached a compromise. This peace reaffirmed the Treaty of Westphalia by which the French had secured a hold upon Alsace. The frontier between France and the Spanish Netherlands was "rectified." The French returned the enclaves that they had acquired by the last treaty and retained the "line" that the French army had forged between 1676 and 1678. The king of Spain also ceded the province of Franche-Comté to the king of France. The French had occupied this province during the war of the Devolution and again in 1674; it was essential for the defense of the eastern frontiers of France and next to useless to the king of Spain. As an aftermath of the peace, the French forced Frederick William, elector of Brandenburg, to return to Sweden the German territories he had conquered during this war. Sweden was Louis xiv's only faithful ally, and the French king was quite unwilling that it should suffer a loss. After this treaty, Louis' subjects called him "Louis the Great," but he understood that the terms of the peace were a considerable modification of the aims that he had had in 1672.

The Flanders frontier was not the only one that had been threatened during the war. Indeed, the most serious threat had come when Strasbourg had acted as a "gate" for the imperial armies' invasions of Alsace (1674 and 1675). When the war was over the lesson of the lineal frontier obviously also had to be applied to the east as well as to the north of the kingdom. The ink was not dry on the treaties when Louis xiv sent Vauban and Louvois on an inspection tour of the frontiers from Franche-Comté to the Channel. At the same time, the French courts at Besançon, Breisach, and Metz opened proceedings to examine the territorial rights of the king of France as ceded by the treaties of Westphalia and Nymwegen. The objective was simple enough; the French king wished to annex any additional territories needed to establish a lineal frontier from Franche-Comté to Flanders.

These were the famous "reunions," so named because the section of the *Parlement* of Metz that handled the problem was named the "Court of Reunion." By studying ancient charters, commissions, grants, and other such documents, the courts "found" that the territory needed to connect Franche-Comté with Alsace really belonged to the king of France rather than to the duke of Baden. Further, they "discovered" that the towns, seignories, and ecclesiastical holdings in Alsace owed homage to the king of France and not to the emperor, and in the tangle of territories between the Rhine and Luxembourg, they "found" that many of the lands were dependencies of the bishoprics of Metz, Toul, and Verdun. The electors of Cologne, Trier, and Mainz, the kings of Sweden and Spain, the emperor, and dozens of petty German princes were summarily deprived of territories that they had believed were theirs. The king of France may have thought that he was merely rounding out his frontiers by securing territories that rightfully belonged to him, but his action stirred up a hornet's nest of antagonism in Germany. The climax, as far as Germany was concerned, came when a French army forced the capitulation of Strasbourg. After what had happened in 1674 and 1675, this probably should have been expected, but the Germans were not ready to accept it. When the French began to move to annex Luxembourg, the tension in Germany and in Europe ran high. Leagues and alliances began to emerge, and the Diet at Ratisbon even consented to the creation of an imperial army.

The Crisis of 1683 and the Hungarian War. Emperor Leopold, however, was threatened by more than the armies of France. In 1683 a powerful Turkish force supported by Hungarian malcontents and irregular troops from all over the Ottoman Empire marched up the Danube and laid siege to Vienna. The Ottoman Empire was suffering from internal decay, but this was not evident when the mighty armament directed by the grand vizier, Kara Mustapha, suddenly appeared in central Europe. There were many factors behind this effort: The reforming viziers knew that the empire must expand or it would die; the Hungarian malcontents had persuaded Kara Mustapha that he would obtain an easy victory; the French king had promised not to interfere to protect Emperor Leopold; and Kara Mustapha seems even to have dreamed of a new Moslem state in central Europe under his personal rule. These and perhaps other things brought the Turkish army into Europe; now what would Europe do in the face of this threat?

The king of France did withdraw his army from around Luxembourg so that "those who should defend the empire could do so"; however, he not only refused to listen to the pope's appeals for French aid, but he also tried to prevent the king of Poland from joining the Germans in defense of Vienna. Louis XIV was playing for high stakes in 1683. If the Turkish army should overrun the Hapsburg Danubian states, Germany would be open to invasion and there would be no army except the French to defend it. Mazarin had unsuccessfully attempted to secure for Louis XIV the election to the imperial crown, but if the French king should become the sword and shield of Christendom, his election as emperor could not be denied. For the moment, Louis XIV allowed this prospect of universal empire to overshadow his policy. The Germans, unshaken by the French refusal to aid in their defense, raised an army, and Jan Sobieski, king of Poland, also brought forces to fight the Moslem invaders. Sobieski and Karl of Lorraine fell on the Turkish army at Vienna and completely defeated it. Vienna was saved. As soon as the combined Polish and imperial armies raised the siege and drove the Turkish armies down the Danube in full retreat, Louis gave up the dream of the imperial crown and returned to the policy of securing defensible frontiers for his kingdom. A French army again appeared before Luxembourg when the Turks were defeated, and other French forces invaded the Spanish Netherlands. Louis XIV announced that his price for peace was the recognition of the annexations by the Courts of Reunion as well as French sovereignty over Strasbourg and Luxembourg. In other words, if the emperor and his German allies wished to fight the Turks, they must first of all satisfy the king of France.

The Spanish king bravely declared war on France, but he had no armies with which to fight. The decision was up to Emperor Leopold. There were many factors involved. Leopold's closest advisors believed that the time was ripe for the reconquest of all Hungary and the building of a powerful Danubian state complex; the most powerful prince in Germany, the elector of Brandenburg, was willing to use his army to fight the Turks, but not the French; William of Orange was unable to secure consent for an alliance against France from the regents in the General Estates—some of whom were bribed by the French, others of whom were merely timid or fearful for their commerce. Obviously, Emperor Leopold was in no position to fight on two fronts, and so when Dutch intermediaries suggested a twenty-year truce rather than a definite treaty, he was willing to reach an agreement with his cousin, the king of France. The twenty-year truce was signed at Ratisbon in 1684; it recognized tentatively the French occupation of all the territories that Louis XIV had annexed, but it reserved the making of a formal treaty for a future date.

This truce suited Pope Innocent XI who wanted a crusade against Islam; he immediately worked for the creation of a Holy Alliance signed by the emperor of the Holy Roman Empire, the king of Poland, the doge and senate of Venice, and the regent in Russia. Innocent also tried unsuccessfully to persuade the ruler of Persia to create a diversion on the eastern frontiers of the Ottoman Empire. He did not mind connection with Russian schismatics, north German Protestant heretics, or even Persian Moslems so long as they were willing to fight the Ottoman Turks.

This war of the Holy League proved to be fateful for all Europe; for slowly but surely the balance of power shifted against France as the German armies overran Hungary and Transylvania and the Venetians occupied the Morea. At Versailles, Frenchmen watched the progress of the imperial armies unbelievingly. Each spring they were sure that the Turks would be able to withstand the attack, but by 1686–1687 they had to face the fact that all Hungary was under Emperor Leopold's control, and in 1688 his armies were ready to besiege Belgrade. The French ambassador in Constantinople sent wild reports of the disorders in the city and of his fears that Emperor Leopold himself would appear there to dictate peace unless the French intervened in the war.

The Crisis Year of 1688. After 1686 the shifting balance of power in Europe was building up to a crisis in the Rhineland, and in 1688 it allowed Prince William of Orange to cross the Channel and drive his father-in-law from the throne of England. There were two points of conflict in the Rhineland: the electorate of the Palatinate and that of Cologne. Beyond these was the unresolved problem of a definite treaty recognizing French annexations on the Rhine and Netherlands frontiers. As the German armies made progress down the Danube, German statesmen were less and less willing to accept the French pretentions. They discussed and negotiated agreements for defense against France; the League of Augsburg was only one of the several alliances and agreements that came into being to resist the French demands. The French, on the other hand, fearful of the growing strength of the German emperor, were anxious to impose a solution for all political problems.

The situation in Cologne was complex. French subsidies and a huge loan that he could hardly hope to repay, had long forced the electoral archbishop of Cologne to accept the leadership of France. The elector, however, was old and ill, and Louis wished to place one of his own creatures, Cardinal William Egon von Fürstenberg, in position to become the next elector by making him coadjutor archbishop. The archbishopric of Cologne, however, had long been occupied by a member of the Bavarian house of Wittelsbach, and, even though the only male member of that family who could aspire to the office was too young for the position, the family wanted him elected to it, and since his brother was Prince Max Emanuel, commander of the imperial armies in Hungary, the pope also would favor his cause. Furthermore, Emperor Leopold announced that he could not tolerate a French agent as an elector in the empire. Fürstenberg managed to get himself elected as coadjutor, but before his appointment could be approved at Rome, the archbishop died, and Innocent XI, no friend of France, refused to appoint a "coadjutor to a dead man." When the election to the throne at Cologne was held, neither Fürstenberg nor the young Bavarian prince had enough votes to win, and the case was referred to Rome just at the time when Max Emanuel, brother of the Bavarian candidate, captured Belgrade. There was no doubt about Pope Innocent XI's action; the Bavarian prince became the elector of Cologne.

This case arose almost simultaneously with the problem raised by the death of the elector of the Palatinate. There was no question about the succession to that electorate, but there was a possible question about several other territories belonging to the late elector, who happened also to be the brother of Elizabeth Charlotte, Louis XIV's sister-in-law. Could she claim part of the Palatinate inheritance?

The problems of both Cologne and the Palatinate were combined with the French desire to transform the twenty-year truce of Ratisbon into a definitive peace. But the German emperor, flushed with victories in Hungary, was unwilling to yield on any of these counts. His hand had been strengthened considerably since 1684 when he had made that truce. Victory in Hungary had given him prestige and a battle-trained army. Louis XIV's revocation of the Edict of Nantes in 1685 had turned the powerful elector of Brandenburg against France so much that he had joined with the others in forming alliances to check French pretentions. Leopold felt sure that he could count upon the German princes, William of Orange in the Netherlands, and the kings of Sweden and Spain. With Belgrade about to fall, the emperor could look to the future with confidence. Indeed, he seemed about to realize the dream that his ministers had had in 1683 when they urged war in the Danube basin to create a powerful Danubian state complex that would be the military equal of France.

The victory in Hungary was more than a victory over the Turks.

Hungarian malcontents had joined the Ottoman army in hope of establishing a Hungarian kingdom as a vassal state of the sultan. Like the Turks, they were defeated, and when the sultan's armies melted away, Leopold sent both Jesuit priests and royal officials to consolidate his conquests. The estates of the rebels were forfeit, but more important than that, Leopold could not redraw the Hungarian constitution. Instead of the elective monarchy that it had been, the crown of Hungary became hereditary in the Hapsburg family; the ancient right of the magnates to rebel against their king if they disagreed with his policies was revoked; finally, Leopold's eldest son, Joseph, was crowned king and signed a coronation oath dictated by Leopold. Henceforth, the Hungarian chancellory was in Vienna, and bureaucrats subservient to the king administered the kingdom; the Diet continued to exist, but it was much more docile before the orders of the king. This was a revolution in a very real sense, but a revolution in the mold of Hapsburg tradition: Existing institutions were modified to strengthen the crown, not destroyed.

After the battle of White Mountain in 1621, Ferdinand II brought Bohemia under closer supervision from Vienna; he also had been the author of the changes in the German Hapsburg *Erbländer* that had strengthened the rulers' power. With the reorganization of Hungary during 1686–1688, the Hapsburgs at Vienna governed a complex of states—German, Bohemian, and Hungarian—each with its own constitution and government and yet all under the direction of the emperor's council. At the same time that Leopold saw his son crowned king of Hungary, he also secured for young Joseph election as king of the Romans, that is successor to the imperial crown. The German Hapsburg state was obviously emerging as a great power in Europe, even though it was not actually fully consolidated by the events of 1683–1688. The Hapsburg monarchy still lacked the inner cohesiveness necessary for a state; nevertheless, it could provide its ruler with strength that assured him a place as one of the important military powers of Europe. It continued to be a counterweight in the maintenance of the European balance of power until its destruction in World War I (1914–1918).

The emergence of the Hapsburg Danubian monarchy and the imminent defeat of the Turks forced Louis XIV and his advisors to make some decisions about their course of action. In late September 1688, after news came from Belgrade that Max Emanuel had taken the city, the French decided to invade the Rhineland in order to force the Germans to agree to change the Truce of Ratisbon into a definitive treaty of peace. The council of war recognized that French finances were in such bad condition that they could sustain only a short war, what we might call a *blitzkrieg,* but Louis and his advisors were sure that the French army was the best in Europe and that the German princes, once they were confronted with French power, would quickly "accommodate" themselves to French demands. In the first week of October 1688, therefore, the Dauphin, assisted by Vauban and a stellar cast of French generals, invaded the Rhineland and set siege to Philippsburg, and Louis' diplomats announced to all who would listen that their king's aims were modest; he merely wanted the Truce of Ratisbon made into a definitive treaty of peace. He gave the German princes until January 1, 1689, to agree to his proposals.

THE "GLORIOUS REVOLUTION" IN ENGLAND

As we noted earlier in this chapter, the restoration of Charles II to his father's throne in England did not produce a political settlement that would allow the English government to organize its potential military power unless the king and Parliament were in complete agreement; moreover, it provided no mechanism to compel either king or Parliament to reach agreement. The English king could not act independently of all parliamentary controls, but neither could Parliament impose its will upon the king. This situation reached a crisis in 1688 when England was confronted with the possibility of a Catholic dynasty—the re-establishment of the Roman Catholic church and a government controlled by Roman Catholics.

When Charles II died in 1685, James II mounted the throne; he was an avowed Roman Catholic, but his two daughters Mary and Anne who were his heirs were both Protestants, so the danger of a Catholic dynasty seemed remote. James, however, caused his Anglican subjects considerable worry when he discovered that it was legal for him to grant exceptions to the Test Act to allow Roman Catholics and dissenters to hold office without taking communion in the Anglican church. He also forced some of his officeholders to become Catholic, employed Irish Catholics in his army, and introduced Roman Catholic priests into Oxford University. Even the pope at Rome and Louis XIV at Versailles warned him that he was moving too fast. The crisis came when his young wife, Princess Mary of Modena, gave birth to a son. Roman Catholics regarded the birth as a miracle; the Protestants were sure that the child was an impostor introduced into the queen's bed in a warming pan. However, there was no doubt that this little boy, James Edward, was next in line to his father's throne, and that if James II continued his policies, it might soon be possible to staff all the offices of the kingdom with Roman Catholics, rig an election to Parliament, and make legal all the "illegal" proceedings by which James had reintroduced Roman Catholicism into England. The political leaders of the kingdom, both Whig and Tory, had to face this situation.

There was no easy solution. The Tory politicians and the vast majority of the clergymen of the Church of England, were completely committed to the doctrine of divine right of kings. In good conscience they could oppose the king, but they could not question his right to the throne. A decade or so before, when the Whigs had attempted to exclude James from the throne on the grounds that he was a Roman Catholic, the Tories had sustained his divine right to succeed. The Whigs, on the other hand, had no such respect for hereditary succession; they knew that James' father had lost his head and saw no reason why James could not lose his throne. Even before the birth of the male heir, Whig politicians had approached Prince William of Orange, the husband of James' eldest daughter, Mary, with the suggestion that he should intervene in the affairs of his father-in-law's kingdom. After the birth of the heir, these suggestions became more and more pressing. The Whigs could assure Prince William that the leading Tory politicians would "look aside" rather than support James II, while the Whigs would enthusiastically assist in forcing James "to obey the law" in England.

William III of Orange had interests in the problem of the English throne that transcended those of the Whigs or the Tories. He was deeply involved in the political maneuvers directed against France. As long as James was on the English throne, England would be either neutral or pro-French unless some measures could be taken to compel him to join in a grand alliance against Louis XIV. But William's situation was complex. In 1688 France unquestionably had the most powerful military force in Europe. The bulk of the German armies were far down the Danube at Belgrade. This left the Netherlands in a defensive position vis-à-vis France, and William and the politicians in the General Estates well understood that the polyglot army of French Huguenots, Germans, Scotchmen, and Netherlanders could not be transferred to England as long as the French army was uncommitted. They believed that Louis XIV could be depended upon to attempt to prevent any action against his cousin James II, especially if that action seemed likely to increase the power of Prince William III of Orange. Thus, William had to be evasive to the suggestions that he bring an army to England to coerce his father-in-law. He had the army ready, but as long as there was French military pressure on the Netherlands' frontiers, that army had to stay on the continent.

In the summer of 1688 French intelligence noted William's assembly of an army that could be used to invade England, and the French government attempted to warn James of his peril. But the English king, anxious not to appear before his subjects as a client of Louis XIV, refused to believe that he was in any danger. Obviously, the French could not "save" James against his will, so at Versailles men had to consider the consequences of a possible invasion of England by a Protestant army. The French could not know that James' soldiers, some of whom he had loaded with high honors, would not support him. They did know, however, that in the earlier English civil war the king and Parliament had fought a long duel, and several important men in the council believed that if William did invade England, a long civil war would effectively keep both England and the United Netherlands out of any continental conflict. It was this conviction that persuaded the French that it was safe to invade Germany to redress the balance of power that the Hungarian war was so seriously altering in Emperor Leopold's favor. It was a fateful decision with consequences for England, Germany, and all Europe.

When the French army laid siege to Philippsburg, it could no longer be used against the United Netherlands; therefore, it became possible for Prince William of Orange to sail with his army to England. The intervention was much easier than anyone had believed possible. James II proved to be indecisive, many men around him quickly deserted his service, and, in confusion, he fled his kingdom for refuge in France. This was an unexpectedly complete victory for the Whig position; it was not even possible to consider a "regency" government to bring James II into line with the realities of English politics. Early in 1689 a Parliament met to revise the constitution of England. It called William of Orange and his wife, Mary, to the throne that had become "vacant," established firmer laws for the convocation of Parliament and for the relations between king and the two Houses of Parliament, and, in a series of laws that followed, gave the English constitution its new course. Instead of granting William and Mary the usual subsidy, the Parliament provided a royal income suitable for the dignity of the court, but not enough for any program of action. Thus, the king's treasury officers were henceforth annually obliged to present their money bills along with the projects of the government to the Parliament for a money grant. This meant that any royal policy had to have the support of a majority of the House of Commons to succeed; it also meant that henceforth royal policies were also Parliament's policies, and Parliament would provide the money to effect them. Another important measure was the Mutiny Act. Parliament had always been suspicious of the royal army, for soldiers could be used for tyrannical purposes; this act, passed for only one year at a time, provided for the creation of courts-martial; without them, the king's officers could not enforce discipline on their troops except through appeals to the civil courts. Thus, the king's army, dependent upon the annual repassage of this act, became in effect also Parliament's army.

Perhaps the most important fact about the Revolution of 1688 was the establishment of the principle that the throne was not necessarily the gift of God. The English Parliament, in its need to maintain what the political leaders of the kingdom believed to be the fundamental law of the land, had changed the succession. No amount of sophistry could cover the fact that James II and his son were still alive when Parliament installed William of Orange and Mary as king and queen. It was true that William was the grandson of one English king and Mary the daughter of another, but neither could claim the throne by any right save that given by Parliament. This fact bothered the tender consciences of many Tory leaders, who accepted the new sovereign *de facto* but not *de jure;* it also allowed William and Mary to pack the House of Lords with their followers, for most of the Anglican bishops refused to take the oath to the new rulers and therefore were forced to withdraw from their sees. Interestingly enough, this situation also bothered William, who disliked both the English Parliament and the United Netherlands' General Estates because they were checks upon his authority. William's wife and her sister, Anne, were also bothered because they suspected that they had usurped the rights of their little half-brother now exiled in France. These doubts were not shared by the Whigs. Their most important intellectual, John Locke, had generalized the doctrine in an important statement on political theory in which he justified the revolution that forced the king to obey the law.

For the political structure of Europe, however, the most important result of the English revolution was the fact that William was able to bring England into the war against France as soon as Louis XIV espoused the cause of the exiled James II.

THE WORLD WAR OF 1688–1697[1]

The French campaign of October 1688 bogged down in a sea of mud as the rains impeded the siege of Philippsburg and slowed up the march of the armies into the Palatinate. The French decided to take up winter quarters in Germany, but they were forced to give up the idea by the arrival of imperial cavalry from Hungary. The German princes showed no sign of "accommodating themselves" to Louis XIV's demands. By December 1688, the French were in an awkward position; they had failed to impose their will upon Germany, and now they found themselves committed to a war that they were not really prepared to fight. At this point, Louis XIV and his advisors decided upon a plan to ravage a broad belt of German territory opposite the French frontiers so that the Germans could not use the towns, villages, and châteaux as bases for operation against France. Several men in the French council were sure that the ravaging of German territory would bring the German princes to heel; they did not understand what anger this "war crime" would evoke. To Louis' astonishment and irritation, a number of his general officers failed to execute the commands to burn and raze, but their neglect did not make the Germans less horrified at the results of the destruction that did take place. This ravaging of the Rhineland assured Louis XIV's armies the unified hostility of the Germans; indeed, it has been pointed to as the beginning of German nationalism.

The earlier coalitions had been slow to develop, but the third coalition against France was more quickly organized. The emperor and the German princes, the United Netherlands and England, Spain, and Savoy were brought together in a Grand Alliance (1689–1690) against France. The allies all pledged not to make separate peace and to force France back to the frontiers of the treaties of Westphalia and Nymwegen. The English and Dutch treaty with Emperor Leopold also assured him of Anglo-Dutch support for his second son's succession to the thrones of the Spanish Hapsburgs should Charles II die without heirs. As in the later years of the Dutch war, the kingdom of France was again alone against a coalition of the rest of Europe. True, the Ottoman Empire did not make peace when the general war broke out in the Rhine, but even though the sultan's armies might retake Belgrade, they did little more than occupy the attention of a part of the German armies. The fact that Emperor Leopold was at war with the Ottoman Empire, however, was embarrassing to the Anglo-Dutch statesmen, for they wanted no part in a war with the Turks that might

[1]Sometimes called the Nine Years' War, King William's War, the War of the League of Augsburg, the War of the English Succession, the Anglo-Dutch War against French Trade, or the War of the Rhine Palatinate.

endanger their commerce. Thus, the two wars ran on more or less congruently, but Louis XIV did not ally himself with the Turks nor did the Anglo-Dutch governments make war against them. The Russians and Poles also were technically at war with the Turks, but they failed to play any important role in the conflict.

The war against France was fought on the French frontiers with the Spanish Netherlands, Germany, Italy, and Spain as well as in India, on the West African coast, and in North America. It was the first European war that spilled over to all parts of the world. In the first years, the French armies in Flanders and in Italy won indecisive victories that allowed them to occupy small enclaves of territory but did not destroy their foes' will to resist. In 1692–1693 the weather took a part in the struggle; bad harvests led to famine and decreased tax revenues. Both sides were severely affected, but the Anglo-Dutch navy had wrested control of the seas from the French and so was able to bring more grain from the Baltic and elsewhere than the French. Thus, Anglo-Dutch suffering was somewhat less. By 1694 the military advantage was with the allies; Louis had to announce sadly that he could not supply the money needed for a French offensive and therefore his armies must simply defend the frontiers. However, Vauban's fortifications and the stout French lines made an assault on France difficult and costly. The war simply stalled without much hope for advantage on either side. But peace negotiations could not get started because William III and Leopold, in control of the Grand Alliance, were sure that the king of France could be humbled.

This war of attrition was more of a disaster for France than for the allies, for the expenses of this conflict, added to those of Louis' earlier wars and his building of Versailles, grossly overtaxed his treasury. On the other hand, while the Germans and the Dutch were greatly embarrassed by the growing costs of war, the English found the "secret weapon" that financed the war. English treasury officials persuaded Parliament that the war was an important English venture, and Parliament voted the money to finance it. This money came in part from a very stiff tax on the income from land, in part from loans based upon excise taxes, and in part from the new financial institution that became the Bank of England. Englishmen may not have liked paying so much for war, but they did so nonetheless, and it was this flow of revenue that kept the alliance together for the long conflict. Her ability to mobilize the wealth of the kingdom for war made England a great military power in the world. This may have been the most significant result of the so-called Glorious Revolution of 1688.

French diplomacy, remembering its success in separating William from the majority of the regents in the General Estates in 1678, probed for a similar victory over the king-stadtholder, but William's position was too strong to break. However, there was a weak link in the alliance against France. The duke of Savoy understood that his position between the emperor and the king of France was a hazardous one, and that his role as "porter of the Alps" put him in position to balance the political situation either for or against these two important political figures. In 1695, when

French weakness made the German armies relatively stronger, Emperor Leopold decided upon a siege of Casale. At this point, the duke of Savoy secretly contacted Marshal Tessé to see whether it might not be possible to have the French army in Casale surrender to the Savoyards with the understanding that the fortification would be razed and returned to the duke of Mantua; he was most interested in preventing this strong place from falling into Emperor Leopold's hands, for the emperor could use it to control Italy even more effectively than Louis XIV could. Thus began the negotiations that finally ended in the Treaty of Turin (1696) that was the first breach in the coalition against France.

The Treaty of Turin also signaled a serious reverse for France. It provided for the surrender of the fortifications of both Casale and Pignerol, and with them the results of almost three quarters of a century of French policy in Italy. In return, the duke of Savoy withdrew from the war and agreed, in effect, to guarantee France's frontier with Italy against attack. This released the French army in Italy, but the duke's attitude did not allow the Germans to reduce theirs significantly. A Savoyard princess, Adélaïde, journeyed to France to become the wife of Louis' grandson, the duke of Burgundy. Her presence and her love somewhat made up to the old king for the losses he had suffered by the treaty.

Once the solid front was broken, the pieces for a general treaty of peace began to fall in place. William III ordered one of his confidants to negotiate with Marshal Boufflers for an agreement about outstanding problems between William and Louis XIV. Both rulers had personal as well as political fears that had to be removed by negotiations. When the treaties were ready, the Peace of Ryswick, like that of Turin, gave evidence of the fact that the French king was no longer the only great power in Europe. The French "rectified the frontier" of the Spanish Netherlands in favor of the Spanish; they returned Lorraine to its duke and several of the German territories, including the fortifications of Philippsburg, Brisack, and Landau in the Rhineland, to their original owners. The overseas provinces were returned to the status quo ante, but the French hold on her overseas positions had been weakened. The Dutch were allowed to occupy the barrier fortifications in the Spanish Netherlands.

The treaties of Turin and Ryswick said nothing about the war that was still raging in the lower Danube basin, but it, too, was on the verge of coming to an end with a treaty that would further indicate the changes in the European balance of power. The imperial armies in Hungary were commanded by Prince Eugene of Savoy, the son of one of Mazarin's nieces and a French nobleman of the house of Savoy, who had joined the emperor against Louis' will to help save Vienna in 1683. When Prince August of Saxony was elected king of Poland, Eugene became commander of the army in Hungary, a change in command that replaced a mediocre soldier with one of the great captains of all times. Eugene lost no time in fighting the sultan; at Zenta (August 1697) he destroyed a large part of the Turkish army, captured its treasury, and took over much military booty. The Ottoman Empire had to sue for peace.

The treaty between the members of the Holy League and the Ottoman Empire was dictated at Carlowitz by the imperials and the Venetians. All Hungary and Transylvania went to the Hapsburgs; the Morea went to Venice; and both Poland and Russia were accorded territorial advantages on their frontiers. But the Hapsburg Danubian monarchy was the great gainer; it emerged as a major military power in the arena of European politics. When the war began in the 1680's, only France was a great military power; by 1700 both England and the Danubian monarchy were also great powers in the world. The fact that Leopold's candidate for the Polish throne, rather than the French prince proposed by Louis xiv, won that election was proof that the power structure in central and eastern Europe had tipped against France.

THE THRONES OF THE SPANISH HAPSBURGS

Had Charles ii of Spain died before the Peace of Ryswick, the Archduke Karl, second son of Emperor Leopold, would undoubtedly have mounted the throne in Madrid as Carlos iii. But Charles ii did not die, and the Treaty of Ryswick did nothing to avert a crisis that was bound to occur if he died when Europe was at peace. This was a thorny problem to settle. The male line of the Spanish house of Hapsburg was obviously coming to an end, for Charles ii was sickly, ill-favored mentally, and without hope of having children. The thrones therefore had to pass to an heir tracing his inheritance through the female line. Charles ii's eldest half-sister was Maria Theresa, wife of Louis xiv and mother of the Grand Dauphin; she had waived her right to the Spanish throne in favor of her sister in return for a huge dowry, which had not been paid. Philip iv in his will specifically disinherited her in favor of her sister Margaret Theresa, wife of Leopold i. The Bourbon case rested both upon the fact that the dowry had not been paid and upon the assumption that a princess could not waive a throne for an unborn heir. However, if the French claim to the throne were not valid, then the only daughter of Margaret Theresa and Leopold i should be in line for the throne, but that daughter, Maria Antoinette, upon her marriage to Max Emanuel of Bavaria had renounced her rights to the thrones of Spain in favor of her half brothers Joseph and Karl. These two princes were the grandsons of Marie Anna, daughter of Philip iii and wife of Emperor Ferdinand iii. Marie Anna was the elder daughter; Anne of Austria, mother of Louis xiv, was the cadet. But if the rights to the throne went back to the children of Philip iii, the princes of the house of Orleans were also heirs, for their father, Philip, was the second son of Anne of Austria and Louis xiii. Thus, when the Treaty of Ryswick brought peace to western Europe, there were three principal contenders for the right to inherit the thrones of Charles ii of Spain: the Grand Dauphin or second son, Philip, duke of Anjou; Archduke Karl von Hapsburg, whose elder brother Joseph was destined for the thrones of the

German Hapsburgs; and Joseph Ferdinand, Prince of Bavaria and son of Maria Antoinette. Unless some agreement could be reached, it was improbable that any one of them could ascend the throne without provoking a new war.

As early as 1671 when Emperor Leopold signed a treaty with Louis xiv to pledge his neutrality in the forthcoming Dutch war, there was an agreement between the two monarchs for a partition of the Spanish inheritance between the German Hapsburgs and the French Bourbons; but in 1699 Emperor Leopold, flushed with victories over both the king of France and the sultan of Turkey, and assured by the treaty of 1689 of Anglo-Dutch support for his son's candidacy to the Spanish thrones, was no longer in a mood for compromise. Louis xiv, on the other hand, chastened by the defeats that he had been forced to recognize by the treaties of Turin and Ryswick, was anxious to find some way by which his house could be assured of part of its "just pretentions." Both the kingdom of France and Europe needed peace; Louis xiv and his advisors were more than ready to compromise their demands to secure it. If the emperor would not talk about partition, at least William iii might be willing to do so for England and the United Netherlands. Louis approached the English ambassador at Versailles with a plan; when he could make no progress there, he ordered the French ambassador in London to deal directly with William iii.

The real difficulty was that William did not see any part of the Spanish inheritance as suitable for France, but he did recognize Louis' assertion that, without a treaty to regularize the succession, Europe could be drawn into another disastrous war. After long negotiations, William iii and Louis xiv finally came to an agreement embodied in the First Partition Treaty (October 1698) between France, England, and the United Netherlands. It made the young Bavarian prince, Joseph Ferdinand, the principal heir to Charles ii with the "consolation prizes" in Italy for the German Hapsburgs and the French Bourbons. When the Spanish learned of the treaty, they were shocked that foreigners should presume to regulate the affairs of their king and persuaded Charles ii to make a testament by which he gave all his crowns to Prince Joseph Ferdinand; the Spanish wanted no partition of the inheritance. Unhappily, a few months later Joseph Ferdinand sickened and died (February 6, 1699).

Some suspected poison; Charles ii was delighted that he had outlived his "heir"; Louis xiv and William iii were shocked to have their months of negotiation wasted. There was nothing to do but return to the task. In due time, a Second Partition Treaty came into being (March 1700). This one was more difficult to write, for there were only the two heirs representing the two big continental powers, but finally it was agreed that Archduke Karl should inherit Spain, the Indies, and the Spanish Netherlands, while the Spanish crowns in Italy should go to the French crown with the understanding that there would be exchanges between the dukes of Lorraine and Savoy and the king of France. Emperor Leopold refused to sign the treaty; he believed that Charles ii would make a testament leaving the entire inheritance to his son Karl. Charles ii was a Hapsburg and his wife was a

German princess, Leopold's sister-in-law. As a matter of fact, Louis xiv made the same assessment, for he was convinced that the weak-willed king would try to disinherit the Bourbon heir. This seems to be the reason he was so anxious to make a treaty of partition that would assure his house a share in its "just pretentions."

In Spain, however, the problem seemed quite different. The grandees and officers of the crown, who for almost two centuries had regarded their king's estates as their own preserves for wealth and fame, and who had great pride in the "empire upon which the sun never set," were appalled at the idea of partition. Those with a practical turn of mind asked the question: "Of the two possible heirs, which one could defend the empire better?" This question had only one answer: France had frontiers with Spain, the Netherlands, and Italy; France also had a navy; the Danubian monarchy had none of these things. The only problem was to convince the superstitious, dim-witted king that he should make a testament in favor of the duke of Anjou. This was a formidable task, for Charles was a Hapsburg, and Louis xiv and the kingdom of France had done him great evils in the three preceding decades. The pope, the important high clergymen, a press of the members of the court and government, even the opening of the grave of Charles' French wife—all featured in the process that resulted in the decision. Finally Charles ii consented, signed the will, and, a few weeks later on All Saints' Day 1700, died.

The issue of the Spanish succession was squarely up to Louis xiv and the court of France, for a Spanish envoy appeared at Versailles armed with instructions to offer the throne to the duke of Anjou; if he should refuse, to the duke of Berry, his brother. If he, too, should refuse, the envoy was to proceed to Vienna and offer the throne to Archduke Karl. Testament or the Partition Treaty, which should the king of France choose? Louis learned that both in England and in the United Netherlands there was a considerable body of opinion that favored the testament over the Partition Treaty, for the testament would give nothing to France, and the duke of Anjou, as King Philippe v, would undoubtedly become a Spaniard and follow Spanish interests. This seemed better to many Englishmen and Dutchmen than installing the French in Italy. Louis also learned that it was unlikely that William iii would go to war to force Emperor Leopold to recognize the Partition Treaty and allow France to occupy part of Italy. Thus, if Louis should accept the testament, it was probable that England and the United Netherlands would recognize Philippe as king of Spain but that France would have to fight the Danubian monarchy. If France stood by the Partition Treaty, the crown would go to Archduke Karl, and France would have to fight the Danubian monarchy *and* Spain for the share of Italy, and no help could be expected from either England or the United Netherlands. It was a difficult dilemma; Louis XIV decided to accept the testament and the chance of a war with the Danubian monarchy, which was obviously to come no matter what he did.

Had the French been willing to let Philippe v assume the thrones in Madrid without securing advantages for themselves, it is possible that the war between the Danubian monarchy and the crowns of France and Spain could have been somehow settled, but Louis xiv did not show wisdom, and within a year of Charles ii's death, a new coalition emerged to place limitations on the ambitions of the kingdom of France.

In quick succession, Louis xiv committed a series of provocative acts. A decree registered in the *Parlement* of Paris assured Philippe, duke of Anjou and king of Spain, and his heirs of his "rightful" place in the succession to the throne of France. French soldiers, in agreement with Max Emanuel, governor of the Spanish Netherlands, expelled the Dutch soldiers from the barrier fortifications and assured Europe that the French would withdraw as soon as Philippe v could find soldiers to replace them. The Spanish government, at the request of Louis xiv, granted French merchants special privileges, not open to Dutch or English merchants, in the Spanish colonies. These acts shocked into action those Englishmen and Dutchmen who preferred the testament to the Partition Treaty. They first demanded that France should withdraw; then they authorized William iii to make an alliance with the emperor and the Germans. By the first of September 1701, the alliance had been completed; on the 16th of September James ii died in France and Louis xiv, contrary to the Treaty of Ryswick, recognized his son, James Edward, as king of England. If there were still those who doubted the wisdom of fighting a new war, this act dispelled the doubts. The War of the Spanish Succession, sometimes known as the War of the Two Crowns, that was to last for more than a decade, was ready to begin.

THE WAR OF THE SPANISH SUCCESSION

The French king, his ministers, and his soldiers accepted the coming of the war with confidence. They were in possession of all the real estate in question: Philippe v's uncles, the electors of Bavaria and Cologne, were allies in Germany, which gave the Franco-Spanish armies control of the Rhine and the upper Danube; the alliances with the duke of Savoy, Philippe's father-in-law, and with the king of Portugal seemed to assure control of all Europe west of the German Hapsburg empire and south of the United Netherlands. Furthermore, the French believed that their army, made up of veterans of the preceding war, would be quite superior to the Anglo-Dutch armies, since both the English Parliament and the Dutch General Estates had compelled William to disband most of his military after the Peace of Ryswick. The French in Italy bragged that the imperial army would have to learn to fly if it were to cross the Alps, and Louis sent Boufflers into the lower Rhine under "the orders of the duke of Burgundy," the king's young grandson, to convince the German princes that they would be wise to accommodate themselves to the two crowns. Louis had not learned the lesson that soldiers are not the best prognosticators about the course of a conflict.

The French had not counted upon all the factors involved. In the first place, Vauban's lines of fortifications were created to defend the kingdom of France, not the lower Rhineland, the Spanish Netherlands, Bavaria, and northern Italy. In all these territories the fortifications were either nonexistent, weak, or directed *against* France. Perhaps even more important than the lack of good fortifications was the unhappy fact that the two crowns did not have soldiers with the skill and boldness necessary to counter the two men who were to command their foes' armies. In the preceding war, the French commanders were as good as, or even much better than, those directing the enemy; in the war that broke out over the Spanish crown, the allied commanders, Prince Eugene of Savoy and John Churchill, duke of Marlborough, were soldiers of the very first order, while those available to command the Franco-Spanish efforts were capable officers but not the equals of Marlborough and Eugene. Finally, even though the French potential wealth as well as its population was much greater than that of England, the political and financial institutions that had emerged from the English Revolution of 1688 gave the island kingdom an immense advantage in a war of attrition that required money and men and more money. This did not become so apparent in the first six years or so of the war when good harvests eased the financial pressure, but in the later years the English political and fiscal institutions along with her control over the seas became decisive. This latter fact was very significant, indeed, perhaps even as important as the genius of the allied commanders. French neglect of seapower after 1691 gave the allies a great advantage in the war both for the conduct of military operations and for the procurement of supplies.

Almost from the outset, the war went badly for the Franco-Spanish crowns. In 1701 Eugene inflicted a severe defeat on the Franco-Spanish armies in Chiari and seized the initiative in Italy. The following year Marlborough drove Boufflers out of the Rhineland and occupied the electorate of Cologne. In 1703 both Savoy and Portugal deserted the two crowns and joined the Grand Alliance. The next year came the first great disaster: Marlborough and Eugene teamed up to attack Bavaria, and at Höchstadt-Blenheim they crushed a Franco-Bavarian army, captured a marshal of France, and occupied all Germany up to the Rhine. At the same time, the English fleet established itself at Gibraltar and assumed control over the western Mediterranean. The French king put out peace feelers. His enemies, however, were not willing to listen to peace proposals; they were intent upon a victory that would humble Louis xiv and his kingdom.

The year 1705 saw the first allied invasion of Spain. With control over the seas, the allies landed an army in Catalonia, where disaffected elements of the population immediately rallied to Carlos iii (Karl). Spain had not carried any appreciable share of the war up to this time. Louis xiv had sent French advisors to reorganize his grandson's kingdom, but they had been unable to reform the system. When they tried to do something with the tax structure, the Spanish cried that the "French are bleeding us white"; when they withdrew their efforts, the Spanish cried that "the French are abandoning us." Philippe was both too young and too weak-willed to govern, and Louis xiv was too far away to do so effectively.

It took an invasion of their country before the Spanish began to realize that the war really concerned them and their future. The invading armies were commanded by an English lord and a French Huguenot; the men in the ranks were English, Scotch, Dutch, German, and French Huguenots. The archduke-king, Carlos III (Karl), was a Roman Catholic, but the invading army was largely Protestant. To these men, Spanish Catholicism was superstition, even idolatry; to the Spanish these foreign soldiers appeared as barbarians who violated their shrines and scoffed at their customs. It took the allies until the end of 1706 to arouse the Spanish from their lethargic attitudes, but the occupation of Madrid and the violation of their churches finally did bring the Spanish into the war. In 1707 Philippe's fortunes turned for the better; the Franco-Spanish armies defeated their enemies and forced them back to the seacoast where the English fleet could assure their survival. For the first time in the war, Philippe could begin to assume an independent position toward his grandfather, for even though his enemies occupied all of Spanish Italy, they had not been able to place Carlos III (Karl) on the throne in Spain. This fact was eventually to be an important one in the discussions for peace.

While this drama was being acted out in Spain, the situation of the two crowns in the Netherlands and Italy deteriorated badly. In 1705 Marlborough might have driven the French from the Netherlands had he not been "chained" by the Dutch civilian commissars attached to his army. The battle of Höchstadt-Blenheim in the preceding year had been a great victory, but there were many men in both England and Holland who felt that the "butchers' bill" (casualties) had been too high and shuddered at the thought that the decision on the field might have been just the reverse. Marlborough and Eugene had won Bavaria and all southern Germany "in an afternoon," but they could have lost it just as well. In 1706 the situation changed rapidly. In the spring Louis gave his childhood friend, Marshal Villeroi, and France's ally, Max of Bavaria, a powerful French army to operate in the Netherlands. They met Marlborough's Anglo-Dutch army at Ramillies; it was a disaster for the French. Villeroi asked to be relieved, and Louis XIV called his most prestigious soldier, Vendôme, from Italy to command in the Netherlands. Whether Vendôme could have saved Italy or not is an open question, but when he left for France, one French army was "observing" Eugene, and another was set to besiege Turin to punish the duke of Savoy for his treason. Eugene managed to bring more troops over the Alps, to immobilize the French army of observation, and, with a mobile detachment, to slip around the French and join the duke of Savoy in an attack on the besieging army at Turin. The French were utterly defeated, and all Italy soon fell to the Austrian forces.

In 1707 the French had a short "breathing space." Dutch rapacity in the occupied Spanish Netherlands convinced the inhabitants that the French were the lesser of the two evils, and Vendôme was able to recapture a number of strongpoints. In Germany, Villars also won limited victory, and when Eugene and the Savoyard armies attempted to take Toulon, they were forced to lift the siege. Since these events were contemporary with Philippe's successes in Spain, the French felt that they could hope for an honorable peace. But the next year blasted these hopes. In 1708 Louis entrusted the army of Flanders to his grandson, the duke of Burgundy, and Marshal Vendôme. Burgundy was supposed to accept Vendôme's superior judgment, but the two men, quite different in temperament, soon were at odds. Unhappily, they encountered the combined armies of Marlborough and Eugene at Oudenarde. The two French commanders disagreed; Burgundy ordered retreat. The result was another disaster for the French. Eugene besieged and finally took Lille while Marlborough commanded an army of observation. The French, confounded by the bitter quarrel between Vendôme and Burgundy and their respective supporters, looked helplessly on. When the winter set in, only old Marshal Boufflers, who had so ably defended Lille, came through with his reputation unscathed.

Then came the real disaster: the winter of 1708–1709 when the grain froze in the fields; birds, beasts, and men died of the cold; and the harvests of 1709 completely failed. At Versailles it seemed that there was no alternative but to accept the terms of the enemy, even if that should mean that Philippe would be deprived of his throne. But when the French asked for terms, there was no end to the escalation of demands; each member of the coalition produced maximum war aims to be achieved. Louis was willing to give up everything that France had won during his reign, including Alsace and the gains of the Treaty of Westphalia, but he hoped to secure some compensation for his grandson Philippe, perhaps a kingdom in Italy. His enemies knew about France's distress, and they were determined to exploit it to the limit.

Their problem was Spain. The English Whigs had a treaty with Carlos III (Karl) that gave English merchants enormous advantages in the Spanish markets as well as provided England with naval bases at Gibraltar and in the Mediterranean. For the English, it was "No peace without Spain!" and they persuaded their allies to accept the dethronement of Philippe V as a condition for peace. But Philippe V was not dethroned; indeed, he was more firmly established on the throne in 1709 than he had been in 1702. He was not asking for terms, and to force him to accept dethronement would require a very large military expenditure. The people of England and the United Netherlands, however, would take it much amiss if they were forced to continue to fight this burdensome war after Louis XIV had achieved a peace settlement—even a disastrous one—for his kingdom. Thus, the Anglo-Dutch side conceived the demand that Louis XIV dethrone his grandson as a condition for peace. This Louis would not do; he offered to pay a subsidy to the allies while they fought in Spain, but he could not accept the terms they offered him. As Villars put it, "We have nothing left to do but pray to the Mother of God and strike as hard as we can."

While the allies were waiting for Louis to accept their terms, Marshal Villars rebuilt the lines and somehow held the army together. The troops had more wheat than did the villages, but neither had enough to prevent starvation. Finally Villars insisted that only a battle could save the situation. It came at Malplaquet. The first news was that the French had been defeated, that their commanders had been seriously wounded, and that they were in retreat. But further assessment indicated that the French had withdrawn in good order, leaving the allies in command of the field upon which the flower of their armies was strewn dead. "Sire," wrote Villars, "if God gives us the grace to lose another similar battle, your Majesty can count upon your enemies being destroyed." The battle of Malplaquet did not immediately make Louis' enemies less demanding, but it did make them more cautious. They were careful not to give Villars the opportunity to bring them to battle again.

The next year (1710) was the fateful one. The allied armies continued to press the French fortifications, taking them one by one but not allowing Villars to fight a battle. In Spain, an allied army again marched from Barcelona to Madrid, and Philippe seemed again in danger of being driven from his kingdom. But the allies had overreached themselves, and again they failed to get the support of the Spanish people. In December of 1710 the allies were in full retreat when Vendôme, commanding Philippe's army, shattered Carlos III's chances of becoming king by defeating both the English and the imperial forces.

The other important event of 1710 was a change in the ministry in England; the Whigs were ousted and the Tories brought to power. The Tory ministers, wishing to end the war as quickly as possible, entered into negotiations with Louis XIV. Early in 1711 Emperor Joseph I died without direct heirs; his brother Karl (Carlos III) succeeded him on the thrones of the Danubian monarchy and the empire as Charles VI; there seemed to be no good reason in England or the Netherlands to continue a war simply to give him another throne in Spain. The process of making peace between England and France went on apace; England's allies were shortly forced to follow the same path.

A new order in western Europe came out of the peace settlements of 1713–1714. In a very real sense, these treaties were the final agreements partitioning the thrones of the Spanish Hapsburgs. Philippe V was left in control of Spain and the overseas empire. Karl secured the Spanish Netherlands, Milan, the Tuscan ports, and Naples. The duke of Savoy was given Sicily. The English acquired Gibraltar and Majorca and special trading privileges in the Spanish colonies (the Asiento) from Spain as well as Hudson's bay, Arcadia, Newfoundland, and St. Kitts from France. While Emperor Karl became lord of the Austrian Netherlands, the treaties left the garrisoning of the important fortifications in those provinces to the United Netherlands. These "barrier" fortifications not only protected them against the French, but also allowed the Dutch to exploit their southern neighbors and cripple their economy. The peace of 1713–1714 contains many complex conditions regulating things from the separation of the thrones of France and Spain to recognition of the Hohenzollern elector of Brandenburg as king in Prussia. But the most important aspect of the settlement was the general recognition of the fact that there had emerged in western Europe a balance of power regulated by the relations of France, the United Kingdom of England and Scotland, and the Danubian monarchy with each other and with the lesser states of the area.

This balance of power, tested and developed by coalition warfare and systems of alliances, formed the core of a new "constitution" for the community of European states that was to last as a fundamental assumption of European statesmen and diplomatists from 1715 until after the Treaty of Versailles at the end of World War I, 1914–1918. It was seriously questioned as the constitution of Europe only once in that two-hundred-year period; that was when the French Revolution and the subsequent rise of the Napoleonic empire again posed the problem of a universal empire dominating the continent. This experiment in empire, however, was defeated by exactly the same political-military mechanism—alliances and coalition warfare—that had checked the rise of Louis xiv's kingdom of France in the period before the Peace of Utrecht.

THE EMERGENCE OF RUSSIA AS A POWER IN EUROPE

Russia's first tentative entry into European affairs came with the Holy League against the Ottoman Empire, but Russia's part in the war that followed was negligible. Before the opening of the eighteenth century, the geography, history, and culture of Russia largely oriented its people southward and eastward. In part this was a result of the direction of the important rivers of Russia; in part it stemmed from the hostility of the Swedes and Poles who were Russia's western neighbors. At the end of the seventeenth century, however, a prince, Peter I, came to the throne after a coup d'état that displaced his half sister as regent. Peter's experience and interests turned him westward. Peter I learned about the West from friends in the "German quarter" of Moscow, a ghetto for foreigners whose habits, ideas, and ways of life, religious men feared might corrupt the Orthodox religious patterns of living. Peter did not feel the need to wash his hands after contact with a Westerner, and he did recognize the superiority of their technical culture. Soon after he had displaced his sister on the throne, he tired of playing at war and agreed to attack the Turks at Azov (the war of the Holy League was not yet over so there was reason to revive Russia's part in that conflict). The first assault was a disaster. Azov was miserably defended, but it was more than a match for the Russian army. The next year (1696), armed with Swedish cannon, foreign officers, and Dutch-built river gunboats, the Russians were more successful. Azov fell, and Peter went back to Moscow to hold a victory celebration. He also sent the first contingent of the sons of his noblemen to western Europe to study.

The decisive event, however, seems to have been Peter's own trip to the West in 1697–1698. He visited Germany, the United Netherlands, England, the Danubian monarchy, and Poland. This trip opened his eyes to the differences between the culture of his own lands and that of Europe, and he resolved to attempt to introduce European ways into Russia. On the trip he made great efforts to encourage Europeans to go to Russia to teach their skills. There had long since been a small European colony in Moscow, and Peter hoped to enlarge it and generalize its influence throughout the Russian lands.

At Vienna (1699) he proposed an enlarged joint effort against the Turks but discovered that Emperor Leopold and his advisors were interested in peace in the lower Danube so that they could be ready to contest their share of the Spanish inheritance.

When he arrived in Poland, Peter found the opportunity he sought. August the Strong was a proper companion for Peter's drinking bouts, his carousing, and his adventurous foreign policy. August, Peter, and the king of Denmark joined in an alliance to make war on Sweden and partition the Swedish Baltic empire. The time seemed ripe for this adventure in international piracy for the king of Sweden was a mere youth. They did not know that this youth was, in fact, Charles XII, who was soon to be known as one of the great military captains of the era.

This war with Sweden was the driving force for the reforms known as the Petrine Revolution in Russia. Charles XII quickly forced Denmark out of the war; then he journeyed across the Baltic to punish the Russians for their invasion of his Baltic provinces. On November 30, 1700, a Swedish army only a fraction of the size of its Russian opponent burst into the Russian fortified camp at Narva and completely routed the Russian forces. Peter, who had had the wisdom to slip away before the battle, learned the hard lesson that his people could not fight with the men of the West until they had learned Western military techniques and were supplied with Western equipment. Fortunately for Peter, Charles XII gave him nine years to acquire the needed skills.

Charles XII next turned his attention to Poland to punish Augustus. The Poles insisted that they were not at war with Sweden. Their king August, electoral prince of Saxony, they explained, made wars of conquest as a Saxon, not as a Pole. In 1704 Charles forced the Polish magnates to dethrone Augustus and elect Stanislas Lesczynsky as their king, but it took another four years of fighting in Poland and an invasion of the empire that brought Charles XII into Saxony before August could be forced to make a treaty of peace with Sweden and accept the loss of the Polish throne. During these years, the War of the Spanish Succession raged in western Europe. The two wars—that in the north and that of the Spanish Succession—were never united—in part because of the great distances and the problem of transportation, but perhaps more importantly because Charles XII was a Francophobe and allied to England and the United Netherlands, while August was an ally of the emperor and Peter, an admirer of the United Netherlands and England and also somewhat of a Francophobe. In any case, Louis XIV was never able to persuade either Charles XII or Peter I to create a second front against the German empire.

After the treaty of Alt-Randstadt with August of Saxony-Poland, Charles decided to invade Russia. In the years between the battle of Narva and 1708, Peter's Russia had made considerable progress in westernizing her army. European officers taught the Russians Western drill, European cannon founders at Tula forged Western-type cannon, and European gunsmiths manufactured muskets to supplement those bought in the West. Even more important, perhaps, was the fact that Peter reformed, in fact revolutionized, the Russian government to allow him to collect more taxes and to administer his own army. He forced his *boyars* to learn to be Europeans so that they could fill his diplomatic posts, the officerial ranks in his army and navy, and the cadres of his bureaucracy. It was no easy thing to regroup a vast land and reform people often quite unwilling to be reformed. Historians who have studied the archival evidence explain to us that the process was always in disorder, nearly in chaos, and yet out of it came a considerable alteration in the political and military structure of the Russian lands. By the time that Charles was ready to invade Russia, Peter's armies had captured a part of the Swedish Baltic provinces, had established a new city at St. Petersburg, and had developed an embryonic Baltic navy. Moreover, the Russian army was better armed than the Swedes and much larger. The Russian soldier in the ranks had not yet learned to fight as effectively as the Swedish soldier, but the difference between the two armies had shifted greatly in favor of the Russians. The Petrine Revolution was largely a reorganization of Russia to make an army.

Charles XII not only did not recognize that the Russia of 1708 was more dangerous than Russia had been at Narva, but he also failed to understand that in Russia the winter "fought" for the Russians, and that in Russia the peasants' xenophobia made the task of invasion enormous. Napoleon, Hindenburg, and Hitler, each in his turn, had to learn the same lesson. Charles XII thought that he would have the support of the Cossacks; he believed that his army could defeat any Russian force. But when the contest finally came in 1709 at Poltava, the Swedish army was defeated. Most of it was made captive and put to labor in Russia, and Charles himself became a fugitive exile in the Ottoman Empire. This left Peter another breathing space to continue the reorganization of his bureaucracy and his army.

As a guest of the Ottoman Empire, Charles proved himself to be almost as good a politician as he was a soldier. In 1710 he managed to provoke a war between the Turks and the Russians. This was perhaps a fateful event: Russia's important rivers drain into the Black Sea, and Russia's easiest outlet to the oceans in this era before rail transportation was through the Bosporus and the Dardanelles. Thus, Russia's rise to power unquestionably was as much a threat to the Ottoman Empire as it was to the Swedish empire in the north where Peter also sought an outlet to the ocean. The Russians had secured a foothold in the Black Sea basin in 1702 by a treaty that recognized their possession of Azov. When Charles managed to involve him in conflict with the Ottomans in 1710, Peter proposed himself as the champion of the Christians in the Ottoman Empire, thus combining the military and economic drive into the Black Sea basin with the religious and racial interests of the Orthodox Slavic peoples. In other words, this war of 1710 might have turned Peter away from the north toward the south, which was to become the important Russian objective in a later era. However, instead of victory, Peter found himself and his army in a military trap on the Pruth River, and he happily settled for a peace that removed Russia from the Black Sea basin for a generation or more. Charles XII accused the Ottoman vizier who made the peace of treason to his sultan, but the Turks of 1711 believed that they had secured their northern frontier by the Peace of Pruth and saved themselves from a dangerous situation. They could not be expected to know that later in the century the Russia of Catherine II would start a southward march that would continue until the Ottoman Empire was destroyed.

In 1714 Charles XII managed to return to Sweden, but he was quite unable to reverse the process of disintegration in the Swedish Baltic empire. Peter's Russia was well established in the Baltic provinces, and the Russian navy was soon to be the important seapower in those waters. August of Saxony had re-entered the war and had driven his Swedish-supported rival from the Polish throne, and Denmark, Prussia, and Hanover had all joined against Sweden. Charles was still a formidable foe, but the odds were all against him. In 1718 he was killed by a bullet from a fortification in Norway, and his sister succeeded him on the throne. With the "Lion of the North" no longer in command, the Swedish government moved to make peace. Treaties of Stockholm and Nystadt ended the war. The real victor was Peter's Russia, which now had an army of 100,000 men, a Baltic navy, and a "window" to the West at St. Petersburg. Sweden was no longer the important power of the north; Peter's Russia was not yet a great military power on the scale of France, England, and the Danubian monarchy, but this new Russia had become a part of the European power structure and in time would achieve great-power status.

THE BALANCE OF POWER

The wars against Louis XIV taught European statesmen the important lessons necessary for fighting coalition warfare. In each case the coalitions were finally broken by the defection of one or more of the allies, but in 1688–1697 and again 1701–1713 the coalitions held together long enough to force the king of France to recognize that the European community, not just one of the powers, would determine the government of the continent. The familiar alliance of England, the United Netherlands, and the Danubian monarchy against the kingdom of France and lesser powers in both Germany and the Mediterranean basin had been the seventeenth-century pattern of the balance of power; there was no reason to assume that this pattern would necessarily continue, but the lessons of the War of the Spanish Succession were not lost on succeeding generations who strove to govern the European anarchic community by systems of alliances and, when necessary, by military force. There was no other way to govern a community of sovereign states.

SUGGESTED READING

Three volumes of the *Rise of Modern Europe* series deal with this period: Frederich Nussbaum, *The Triumph of Science and Reason, 1660–1685* (1962), John B. Wolf, *The Emergence of the Great Powers, 1685–1715* (1962) and Penfield Roberts, *The Quest for Security 1715–1740* (1962). My most recent study, John B. Wolf, *Toward a European Balance of Power, 1620–1715* (1970) and Ragnhild Hatton, *Europe in the Age of Louis xiv* (1969) should be useful. Lloyd Moote, *The Seventeenth Century: Europe in Ferment* (1970) is well worth reading. This book may be contrasted with David Maland, *Europe in the Seventeenth Century* (1966). For the English Revolution of 1688, G. M. Straka, *The Revolution of 1688—Whig Triumph or Palace Revolution?* (1963) presents several conflicting interpretations. G. N. Clark, *The Later Stuarts, 1660—1715* (1955) is probably the best general account. There is no good general paperback account of later seventeenth-century France available in English. My biography of Louis xiv is a study of the king rather than an account of the reign: John B. Wolf, *Louis xiv*, (1968). S. G. Baxter, *William iii and the Defense of European Liberties* (1966) provides an interesting picture of Louis' greatest enemy. Ferdinand Schevill, *The Great Elector* (1965) and Vasili Klyuchevsky, *Peter the Great* give us pictures of other important rulers of this era. Since there are so few paperback books for this period, we suggest that the student should consult the volumes in the *Cambridge Modern History* and the *New Cambridge Modern History* that deal with this period. Both of these series present topical discussions of politics, religion, economics, etc., that are very interesting.

WILHELM EGON VON FÜRSTENBERG (1629–1704)

Wilhelm Egon von Fürstenberg was born into an illustrious German family prominent in imperial affairs since the thirteenth century. Since war was the order of the day in Germany when he was young, he and his brothers Ernst and Franz decided first upon military careers. Ernst Egon was killed fighting France in the service of Spain, but his brothers, seeing the coming end of the Great German War, decided that they could do better in the Church than in the army. Thus, Wilhelm and Franz Egon von Fürstenberg left the army and sought political careers as clergymen.

The two boys had been educated at Cologne in company with a young Bavarian Wittelsbach prince, Maximilian Henry, who was destined to become electoral archbishop of Cologne. Wilhelm also went to Rome to the Jesuit Collegium Germanicum Hungaricum, and then traveled widely in Europe to complete his education. When Maximilian Henry mounted the throne in Cologne, he called Franz to join him as his first minister and Wilhelm to act as a roving diplomat. Cologne, however, was too small a stage for the Egonites; they needed to serve a great prince. Mazarin met them first in 1651 and apparently decided to attempt to enlist them into the service of the king of France, much as Richelieu had earlier enlisted him. This was not an era of national loyalties; the Fürstenbergs, like other noblemen of the era, felt free to seek a career and fortune wherever it might be found. They were able and avaricious, ready to sell their services to the highest bidder. Both the emperor in Vienna and the king of France were anxious to have them as political agents, but Mazarin could outbid the emperor with money and offices and prospects for the future. Nineteenth-century German historians called the Egonites "traitors," but such a judgment overlooks the fact that they had no "country" in their day. There was no Germany, only the Germanies, and the Fürstenbergs could make careers only by taking service with a prince willing and able to reward them.

In the next decade or so, both brothers wore several hats. They were the minister and the diplomat of the archbishop of Cologne; they also were the trusted confidential agents of the king of France. Their position is mirrored in a piece by Austrian Lisola, the great polemicist against Louis XIV who described the actions of Prince Wilhelm at the Congress of Cologne (1673) thus:

> "A false, cunning minister who played so many roles . . . who changed into more figures than Proteus himself. . . . Sometimes he was seen armed, the colonel of a French regiment who recruited and reviewed troops, preparing them for combat and displaying the artillery so as to make the French presence felt everywhere. Soon after he would appear wearing the miter and the habit of a canon, insolently intruding into the peaceful deliberations of the cathedral chapter. Next he would arrive wearing the mask of a prince of Germany, acting as an emissary of France and attempting to entice German princes into the lair of the enemy. Suddenly he would be in the guise of a polemicist, disseminating tracts and libels against the emperor, only to return and introduce himself with an olive branch while at the same time weaving new alliances and lining up new enemies for the emperor and the empire: always changed, always changing, yet always the same in the midst of so many roles and malicious designs. . . . "

With such a picture, it is not surprising that Emperor Leopold imprisoned Wilhelm when he happened to fall into imperial hands (1674). Five years later, one article of the Treaty of Nymwegen provided for his release. Leopold gave him an audience before he left Vienna and presented him with a cross set with diamonds in an effort to enlist his services, but the wily politician preferred to work for France. When he arrived in Paris, Louis XIV assured him of his affection as well as provided him with a handsome pension and promised to seek for him a cardinal's hat. One French historian has called Wilhelm Egon von Fürstenberg Louis XIV's "assistant secretary for German affairs." The title is correct so far as it goes, for Louis' ministers regularly consulted Wilhelm on all problems concerning the German empire, and he bombarded them with memoirs on Germany, German statesmen, and German politics.

However, Wilhelm von Fürstenberg provided one of the problems that led to the war of 1688–1697. When Franz Egon died in 1682, Wilhelm took his place as Archbishop Maximilian Henry's first minister at Cologne. He also became dean of the chapter at Cologne and bishop of Strasbourg, and in 1686 Louis XIV secured for him a cardinal's hat. In all these roles, as well as in that of a French diplomat and agent, Wilhelm so well served the king of France that another French diplomat wrote, "The more I advance in the knowledge of the internal and external affairs of this country [The German Empire] the more I understand the necessity of [Fürstenberg's] ministry, without which we could do nothing. If God were to carry him off we would not retain our present position more than twenty-four hours." Both the king of France and the new cardinal wanted to culminate this brilliant career with Fürstenberg's elevation to the electoral throne at Cologne. But would

Emperor Leopold allow a man who had spent his life in the service of France, to the detriment of the house of Austria, to become an electoral prince in the empire? Would this not merely mean that the kingdom of France had established a salient in the Rhineland as the first step toward control over that empire?

The route to the electoral throne seemed to open when Maximilian Henry's illness made it evident that he needed a coadjutor to help him administer the affairs of the electorate. Wilhelm Egon was in a key position for the post. He understood the politics of the electorate, he was able to use French money to bribe the cathedral chapter, and he had the support of the French king both at Bonn and in Rome. Furthermore, there were French troops close at hand to prevent any military objection to his candidacy. The fight in the cathedral chapter was a bitter one because two other German princely families as well as Emperor Leopold opposed his elevation for fear that, upon Maximilian Henry's death, Wilhelm would become the electoral archbishop. This post had long been held by a cadet of the Bavarian house of Wittelsbach, and the family had a candidate to succeed Maximilian Henry; the only trouble was that Joseph Clement von Wittelsbach was still a teenage boy and not yet a priest. The house of Pfaltz-Neuberg also had a cadet son, already a bishop, who hoped for the election. When the votes were finally taken, Wilhelm Egon was postulated for the post, and the case went to Rome. The situation was far from simple. Emperor Leopold was opposed to the Fürstenberg candidacy, and Emperor Leopold had great influence with Pope Innocent XI because Leopold was fighting and winning the war against the Ottoman Turks in Hungary. Furthermore Joseph Clement's elder brother Max Emanuel, electoral prince of Bavaria, was the commander of the imperial armies in that contest. Innocent stalled. Then came the news that Maximilian Henry had died, and the pope calmly announced that he could not appoint a coadjutor to a dead man.

The contest in Bonn at the cathedral chapter's meetings was now between the three hopefuls, but Wilhelm Egon and Joseph Clement divided the vote so that neither of them could be postulated as electoral bishop. The case was thrown into the lap of Pope Innocent XI. Almost at this same moment Joseph Clement's brother, Max Emanuel, forced the surrender of Belgrade and established Christian control over Serbia. Innocent XI, even had he not hated Louis XIV for his refusal to assist in the war against the Turks, for his unwillingness to allow the pope to police the city of Rome, and for his stubborn Gallican position, would have been hard pressed not to give the throne to Joseph Clement. And that, of course, is just what he did.

A few weeks later, the French armies invaded the Rhineland. Wilhelm Egon von Fürstenberg gave them all the assistance possible, but by the opening months of 1689 it was clear that they could not stay in Germany. His hopes for the electoral hat along with his power in Bonn went up in smoke as the French armies devastated the Rhineland in preparation for a general withdrawal behind the lines that guarded the kingdom. Fürstenberg had to follow Louis' armies into France. The king received him warmly and made him abbot of Saint-Germain-des-Prés, one of the richest sinecures in the kingdom. There he lived out his life with his mistress, Countess von Marck. He spent much of his time restoring the abbot's palace and gardens, aiding historians to find entrée to the archives of princely families, and squandering his immense personal fortune. Before he died he must have taken some satisfaction in the fact that Joseph Clement and his brother Max Emanuel became allies of Louis XIV and their nephew, Philippe V in the War of the Spanish Succession. O'Connor remarks, "As a connoisseur of German politics and diplomacy, Wilhelm could hardly have been surprised." ■

EUGENE OF SAVOY (1663–1736)

Prince Eugene was the son of Eugene-Maurice de Savoy, Comte de Soissons, and Olympe Mancini, niece of Cardinal Mazarin. Eugene's family was a cadet line of the house of Savoy, domiciled in France as princes with connections with sovereign families outside of the kingdom. The young Eugene early developed a slight hunchback condition that convinced Louis xiv that he should become a priest and seek his fame in the Church. Eugene rejected the idea that he was the "little abbé," but he could not convince the king that he should be considered for a military career; even his family prestige and his relationship with Mazarin were not enough to obtain his goal. When he was twenty, his chance arrived. The Ottoman Turks were pounding at the gates of Vienna, and both the pope and the emperor called to all Europe to come to the aid of Christendom. Eugene with a company of young French noblemen, including a prince of the blood, ignored Louis xiv's orders, and made for Vienna to join the crusade. He earned the disfavor of his king but soon won the admiration of Karl of Lorraine who commanded the imperial armies in Hungary.

The next decade saw the young prince of Savoy move up rapidly in the imperial service. He was a fearless commander, indeed reckless when he led his troops, and he soon proved also to be a skillful tactician and master of military logistics. Thirteen years after he left Paris as a youth of twenty to join the imperial army, he emerged as lieutenant general in command of the imperial army in Italy. The peace of Turin prevented him from demonstrating his talents against the French, but three years later when August of Saxony, who commanded the imperials in Hungary, became king of Poland, Eugene took his place on the middle Danube. In August 1697, Eugene caught the Ottoman army in a difficult maneuver crossing a river at Zenta; under the eyes of the sultan and the grand vizier, the imperials practically annihilated half of the Turkish army, captured the treasure chests, and took over much booty. Europe knew that there was a new soldier in command of the emperor's forces.

Belatedly, Louis xiv offered the truant a command in the French army, but Eugene could not forget that Emperor Leopold had loaded him with honors, wealth, and power. He now called himself Eugenio von Savoie; the combined Italian, German, and French spelling of his name indicated his imperial loyalties.

130

When the War of the Succession began, Eugene again was in command of the imperials in Italy. He was not supposed to be able to cross the Alps because the French had sealed off the passes, but he did. In addition, he harassed the French until Louis sent Villeroi to fight him, and then at Chiari he inflicted a bloody defeat upon a French army larger than his own. A few months later, with an elite corps he invaded the French winter quarters at Cremona and kidnapped marshal Villeroi. In the next decade, Eugene and Marlborough taught Europe new lessons in the art of war. Blenheim, Oudenarde, Turin, Malplaquet, and dozens of lesser adventures introduced a more vicious, more mobile, more effective use of soldiers on the battlefield. By the end of the War of the Spanish Succession, the king of France and all his soldiers had reason to regret that Louis XIV thought the young prince of Savoy should be a priest.

In the meantime, Eugene grew more and more important in the emperor's councils. President of the imperial war council, the most prestigious soldier in the imperial armies, and the strongest voice in the emperor's entourage, Eugene was a pillar of strength for Emperor Leopold and his two sons, Emperors Joseph I and Karl VI. He ended the war with Louis XIV by making the Treaty of Rastadt with Marshal Villars, and then he turned his attention to the problem of the Ottoman control of the lower Danube. Eugene's last war against the Turks took the imperial power into Serbia, the greatest Hapsburg penetration into the lower Danube. By the Treaty of Passarowitz (1718) the Hapsburg empire crossed the Danube and included large Serbo-Croatian populations practicing the Orthodox religion.

Eugene was a soldier, but he was more than a soldier. His palace, the Belvedere in Vienna, is one of the most beautiful of the new Baroque-Rococo châteaux of Europe. He patronized artists, literary men, and scientists and enjoyed the talk of philosophers. He died in Vienna, respected as the soldier-statesman who had been most responsible for giving the emperor a modern army that had assured the Austrian Hapsburgs of their share of the Spanish succession as well as extended their empire into the lower Danube. Like Mazarin, the Italian, or Fürstenberg, the German, both of whom had taken service in France, Eugene, a Savoyard-Frenchman, had no conflict in taking service in the Hapsburg empire on the Danube. These men considered themselves free agents rather than subjects; they followed their star and sought fame and fortune where it led them. ∎

FROM DRAMATIC TO ELEGANT: BAROQUE AND ROCOCO ART

As long as princes of church and state were the principal patrons of the artist, art works were monumental in character: impressive palaces or churches, religious tableaux and statues, dramatic historical and mythological pictures, and substantial statues for royal gardens. By the end of the seventeenth century, when standing armies and organized police forces made the countryside more secure, the wealthy nobles and bourgeoisie built country chateaux and comfortable town houses that no longer were first of all places of security. The nobility, deprived of its traditional function, sought substitute in play.

The Rococo period—especially the first half of the eighteenth century—was the era when French taste pervaded the upper crust of all European society. French art in the Baroque period had been heavily influenced by Raphael, as in the works of Poussin and Lorrain, both of whom spent much of their life in Italy, painting for the wealthy nobles and merchants of France. Lebrun, as the head of

The Death of Germanicus by Poussin (1594–1665). Typically French Baroque, this is a historical theme presented with the dramatic action concentrated on the central figure. Poussin also painted religious and mythological themes. *The Minneapolis Institute of Arts*

The Raising of the Cross (above) by LeBrun (1619–1690). LeBrun was accused of stifling French art in his insistence on following Raphael and on glorifying his king. *Musée des Beaux-Arts, Troyes-Giraudon*

Landscape with Merchants (below) by Lorrain (1600–1682). Lorrain's land and seascapes usually emphasize the grandeur of nature and insignificance of man. *National Gallery of Art, Washington D.C., Samuel H. Kress Collection*

The Lover Crowned by Fragonard (1732–1806). Fragonard was one of the more successful artists who decorated the homes of the rich and powerful with paintings of bucolic elegance, innocent pleasures and fashionable youth. *Copyright The Frick Collection, New York*

Louis XV by Rigaud (1659–1743). The foremost French portrait painter of his era, Rigaud liked to surround his subjects with evidence of their position, and occasionally, of their fatuity. *Cliché des Musées Nationaux-Versailles*

The Kitchen Maid by Chardin (1699–1779). Chardin knew little of the fanciful aristocratic world and painted everyday objects and domestic scenes. *National Gallery of Art, Washington D.C., Samuel H. Kress Collection*

the French Academy, insisted that French art must follow Raphael's emphasis on design rather than Rubens' and the Venetians' emphasis on color. After Lebrun's death, a great battle broke out between the followers of each school. The results were ultimately to free artists from both and to facilitate the development of the new Rococo style.

In place of the typical Baroque painting of a crucifixion or a triumphant royal exploit, the Rococo painting might depict the change of seasons, the pleasure of a party in the country, or a fanciful scene of love and beauty. Thus, there was a change from heavier or nobler modes to lighter, often exquisite paintings that featured the frivolous play of the rich, the familiar daily activities of ordinary people, sensuous scenes to stimulate the imagination, or land and seascapes designed to please. This refined and worldly art seemed to suit the more gracious social life that followed the new architecture. Interior decoration typically featured mirrors, French doors, crystal chandeliers, and lighter, more delicate furniture. All manner of ornamental handicrafts and industries developed.

Schönbrunn, Grosse Galerie, Vienna. Less grand than Versailles, its
French counterpart, this Austrian Hapsburg palace must have been more
comfortable. Like the former, it is set in a beautiful park with reflecting
ponds, *allées,* and even a small zoo. There are both a "ruin" reminding
us of Italy and a chapel that could be occupied by a hermit. *Bavaria-
Verlag*

In the eighteenth century, sculpture was typically required less for tombs and churches than for gardens and parks. This accentuated the trend to realism, for the patrons wanted pieces that would amuse or tell a story. Like the Rococo painters, the sculptors of the eighteenth century centered their attention upon the charms of life on earth. They were reflecting the homocentric world that the elite sought to bring into being. Their works tended to be intimate and decorative.

As the wealthy noblemen, war profiteers, and men newly rich in the expanding commercial society of the eighteenth century increasingly demanded homes of comfort and elegance, rather than grandeur, these social groups became more important purchasers of art than kings. There was a burst in construction of new country chateaux and town houses. There was also a much-enlarged market for pain-

Der Zwinger, Middle Section, Dresden. This was one of the first chateaux in the new Rococo style, and it became a model for princely hotels in and near cities. *Bavaria-Verlag*

Sans-Souci, Central Oval Salon, Potsdam. Built by Frederick the Great to entertain personal friends, this was the princely counterpart of a weekend cottage by the lake. *Edwin Smith*

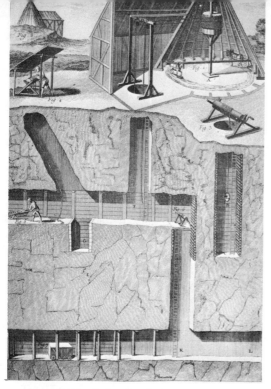

Mining in Diderot's *Encyclopedia*. This cut-out of a mine shows the timbering of tunnels and use of horse-powered windlass for raising ore. The first steam engines were used to pump water out of mines. *Encyclopedia*

Antoine Lavoisier and His Wife by David (1748–1825). This portrait was painted before David perfected his art; its subject was a tax farmer and financier as well as an important eighteenth-century chemist. *Art Reference Bureau*

tings; the eighteenth century witnessed a great increase in the number of art dealers and in commissions for family portraits. The introduction of pastel chalk portraits in the mid-eighteenth century created a "craze" in which grand portraits for rich noblemen and their families became a stable source of income for the important artists of the day.

The Rococo was romantic, fanciful, even unreal; toward the end of the eighteenth century, the sterner realities of the French Revolution and the Napoleonic era encouraged another shift in style. This is exemplified by David, who turned back again to the classic mode for a heroic style befitting his emperor. While the romantic interest in nature continued strong, art regained more emotional depth and moral concern. Depictions of the simple and lowly could be demands for reform. ■

Chapter 4

From a Static to a Dynamic World View

Historians have long been fascinated by the intellectual and artistic movement subsumed under the title "Renaissance," and they are unquestionably correct in assuming that the recovery of the texts of classical authors, the intellectual ferment of the Italian urban society of the fifteenth century, and the astonishing artistic development that culminated in the sixteenth-century master painters and sculptors had powerful effects upon the emerging culture of European men. However, if we seek to discover the intellectual sources of the "miracle" that gave European civilization the turn that fundamentally distinguished it from other civilizations, both past and present, we must look to the seventeenth- and eighteenth-century scientists, mathematicians, scholars, philosophers, and men of letters who overthrew the authority of Greek and Roman tradition and provided European men with a new cosmology, a new epistemology, and a totally new way of looking at the world. Seventeenth-century scholars wrenched the earth from its static position in the center of the universe and sent it spinning around the sun; they provided new explanations for the structure and functions of the human body, new insights into mechanics and motion, the weather, the tides, and even the psychology of man himself. Before the eighteenth century ended in a political revolution, the scholars, mathematicians, and natural philosophers had forced the intellectual elite of their society to recognize the relativity of manners and morals, of social and political forms, and had shaken the ground beneath the political and religious institutions that European men had inherited from their forefathers. The world in 1550 had been static and composed; two centuries later it had become a dynamic, moving thing, and men looked expectantly and optimistically into a future that they believed would reveal more of the secrets of the world and assure for mankind a happier existence.

Two books published in 1543 are often hailed as opening up the modern era: Copernicus' *On the Revolution of the Heavenly Bodies* and Vesalius' *On the Fabric of the Human Body*. Neither of these books, by itself, would have started a revolution. Copernicus simply accepted the assumptions of certain Greek astronomers who recognized that the apparent movement of the sun could be better explained by assuming that it, rather than the earth, was the center of the universe. He used star tables that had been prepared by Greek and Arabic astronomers and a few observations of his own to demonstrate that the same evidence that Ptolemy had used to support the geocentric pattern of the universe could also provide proofs for the heliocentric thesis. Furthermore, this heliocentric explanation was simpler than the geocentric one, which had become more and more complicated in the writings of astronomers of the fifteenth and sixteenth centuries. Copernicus' method was essentially the same as that of his predecessors: He was a mathematician who worked over the star tables prepared by others, not an observer who studied the phenomena of nature directly.

The anatomist Vesalius did examine the human body in preparing his text, but he was so aware of the imposing figure of his Greek predecessor, Galen, that he apologized whenever his findings differed with those of the master. There can be little doubt about the importance and the learning of the great Greek teacher, but Galen was not allowed to dissect the human body, so his findings were based upon studies of other animals, mostly the ape. But Vesalius did dissect the human cadaver; thus, it is not surprising that his findings differed from those of the Greek scientist. Vesalius' most important contributions were his excellent observations and, even more important, the beautiful illustrations that accompanied his text. Those illustrations often even went beyond the textual material in accuracy and observation.

Although these two books of 1543 undoubtedly were starting points for new approaches in both astronomy and anatomy, neither was unique in method or assumptions, and neither really challenged the accepted authorities with evidence that effectively discredited them. Furthermore, there were other astronomers and anatomists contemporary with Copernicus and Vesalius who shared their views. Nevertheless, these men were important in the development of man's understanding of the universe and of the human body.

It was later in the sixteenth century that an astronomer actually undertook to examine the course of the stars and the planets by direct observation. The Danish nobleman-scholar Tycho Brahe (1546–1601) (see pp. 77–79) opened a new chapter in the history of astronomy when he decided that the star tables inherited from the past were hopelessly in error, and, with the support of his king, established what might be called the first scientific institute. Brahe developed new instruments that would allow more accurate observation and, with his students and colleagues, spent a lifetime amassing information. His tables were very accurate considering that he was only able to use the naked eye. (A Samarkand astronomer, Ulugh Beigh, came near to Brahe's accuracy in the early fifteenth century, but the Dane did not know of Beigh's work.) Brahe believed that the earth was the center of the universe while the other planets revolved about the sun and that the sun, with these planets, revolved about the earth. The observations possible in his observatory could be used to support this theory as well as either the usual geocentric or the heliocentric ones. No one believed that it would be possible to prove conclusively any theory of the universe.

However, Brahe's tables were accurate evidence of the paths of the stars, and one of his student collaborators, Johann Kepler, used them to demonstrate mathematically the heliocentric structure of the universe. Kepler was the last of the old mathematician-astronomers who pored over tables; he did so with long hand arithmetic for he had neither trigonometric tables nor calculus. His first discovery came from an analysis of the path of Mars. All astronomers had assumed that God made the world as a "perfect" system and that all movement in the skies was thus necessarily circular and constant, but Kepler's calculations demonstrated that the planet Mars moved in an ellipse, with the sun as one focus, and that its movement was not constant. Indeed, this latter discovery was remarkable because Kepler could demonstrate that the area between the sun and the planet, swept by its movement in any set period of time, was the same even though the speed of the sweep might be different. A third discovery was most important: Kepler found that the square of the time required for a planet to move around the sun was as the cube of its mean distance from the sun. This relationship held true for Jupiter as well as for Mars and Earth. Kepler's laws were largely unappreciated by men of his day for they were hidden in three difficult books, written in Latin and obscure to anyone not skilled in mathematics: *The New Astronomy* (1609), *Epitome of Copernican Astronomy* (1617), and *Harmony of the Worlds* (1621). Nevertheless, Kepler's laws were fundamental to Newton's great thesis, and Kepler's third law was dramatically demonstrated in the eighteenth century when it became the basis for the prediction and discovery of the existence of the unknown planet beyond Jupiter, Uranus.

Kepler, like Copernicus and Vesalius before him, wrote and probably thought in Latin. Indeed, over three-fourths of the books printed in Europe before 1620 were written in Latin; the remaining 25 percent were divided among Italian, German, French, Flemish, and English—in that order. Since the majority of the books were in Latin, it must be assumed that they were written and read by the tiny minority who could easily use that language, the elite trained by the Church or in the Latin schools that were springing up in the urban centers of Europe. But even this elite undoubtedly had trouble with the mathematics of Copernicus and Kepler; so only a very small percentage of the total population could read and understand their writings. This probably accounts for the fact that the conservatives were not alerted to the threat posed by men like Copernicus and Kepler; too few could or would read their books. Indeed, as Luther remarked, Copernicus was a "fool who wished to overturn the whole science of astronomy," and no one would listen to a fool. However, in the seventeenth century when other men undertook to explain the new discoveries and postulates of the scientists in the vernacular languages, the danger to the established order became apparent and the conservatives rose to defend their traditional beliefs.

To read and understand Kepler required an understanding of mathematics far beyond most men. But Galileo did not depend upon mathematical proofs; he turned his newly invented telescope on the planets. There, for anyone who would look, was the evidence of the heliocentric universe. The planets not only had to circle the sun, but the perfection of the stars came under question when the telescope revealed that the moon unquestionably was "corrupt," that is, imperfect and irregular, not smooth. Moreover, a view of Jupiter revealed the moons that circled that planet. This upset the age-old belief that there were only six moving objects in the night skies. The way the planets as well as the moons of Jupiter "phased" left no room to doubt the fact that their source of light was the sun and that they circled that star. The conservatives simply refused to look, but Galileo insisted. Further, he presented his arguments in a most provocative form—and in Italian. Galileo used a literary device familiar to his day; he explained ideas through a dialogue between an Aristotelian (Simplico) and two other characters (Segredo and Salviati) who obviously considered Aristotle a fool. This was a direct assault on Saint Thomas as well as on Aristotle, for Saint Thomas always referred to Aristotle as "the Philosopher." The theological faculties of Europe were outraged.

In one dialogue, Galileo made a direct assault on Aristotle's physics. In the course of his studies, Galileo had discovered that the mysterious force that we call gravity was responsible for the fact that a projectile fired from a cannon moved on a parabolic line. This was quite contrary to the Aristotelian explanations which assumed that impetus was given to a cannon ball, much as heat might be given to it by fire, and that its movement continued until the impetus was exhausted, or that an object fell to the earth because it wished to rejoin it, or that water ran downhill because of its urge to go to the sea. Galileo's explanations for the new mechanics were not always correct by later standards, but he was on the right track. Perhaps more important for the time, he also was a debater who did not hesitate to show his opponents how obtuse they were in their refusal to see the light. Aristotle taught that nature "abhorred a vacuum." Galileo shyly remarked that after thirty-two feet the theory broke down.

Galileo was not the only one to raise a hue and cry at the heels of the Aristotelians. Some, like Bruno, soared into speculation about other solar systems and other gods that led to condemnation for heresy; Bruno was not a scientist nor did he talk like one. Others, like Gilbert, who demonstrated that the earth was a huge magnet, held ideas about the existence of other universes similar to our own, but such speculations were more restrained. A number of Galileo's students were in this company; Torricelli, for example, turned his telescope on the sun and found the spots that "Aristotle never mentioned." Political figures such as the lord chancellor of England, Francis Bacon, who was also a philosopher, and talented amateurs such as the duke of Tuscany, joined in the attack on the conservatives. It is small wonder that the disciples of "the Philosopher" became alarmed. They believed that the Aristotelian conception of the world and the Christian religion were inseparably bound together. The attack on Aristotle's physics and cosmology seemed to be an assault on Christian doctrine.

The *cause célèbre* of the period was Galileo's trial and forced recantation. Galileo had powerful friends in Rome, including members of the college of cardinals and intimates of the pope as well as important figures in other Italian courts, particularly in Florence. Nonetheless, his *Dialogues on the Systems of the World* so affronted the Aristotelians and so frightened the theologians that he was brought before the Inquisition and forced to recant. Some critics have suggested that he should have refused to do so, but it is hard to see what good could have been accomplished by his insisting upon severe punishment, perhaps even death. He knew that the earth turned and that it would not stop simply because a court held that it did not do so.

In the fourteenth century, natural philosophers had asked many of the same questions that proved to be so fruitful in the development of seventeenth-century scientific thought, but the earlier philosophers were unable to answer these questions—in no small part because they lacked both the mathematics and the instruments necessary for an assault on the secrets of the natural world. The sixteenth century witnessed an explosion of mathematical knowledge. Greek and Arabic geometry and algebra, Archimedean methods for analysis, and Euclidean logical deductions joined to make mathematics a popular study. By the seventeenth century, practically every philosopher or thinker was also a mathematician. In rapid succession, the secrets of algebra, the trigonometric tables, the logarithms, and Descartes' analytical geometry, which made geometry susceptible to arithmetical analysis, became tools for the scientists. The laws of probability and, later, the calculus that would allow the definition of a motion of varying speeds and changing directions crowned the efforts of mathematical research. The fact that both Leibniz and Newton independently discovered calculus is evidence of the importance that mathematical thought had in this era. Fontenelle could exclaim that any book, be it on theology, history, ethics, or physics, would be better if it were written by a geometer. This was the faith men developed in the *esprit géométrique* that permeated the period.

But mathematics alone would not have allowed these seventeenth-century men to "weigh, measure, and take the temperature" of the world. They needed instruments: scales, clocks, thermometers, barometers, telescopes, microscopes, pumps, glass tubes, and other devices for establishing numerical data that could be analyzed. Space, time, heat, air pressure, light, motion, extension, weight—these were phenomena susceptible to measurement, and therefore to mathematical analysis, only when instruments were available. The "institute" that Tycho Brahe founded on his island off Copenhagen included carpenters, metal workers, glass blowers, and other skilled craftsmen. In the course of the seventeenth century, such skilled workmen provided the scientists with pumps to exhaust air from a cylinder; they made globes of metal, cut in half but fitted so exactly that after the pump exhausted the air from them, horses could not pull them apart. This demonstrated the power of air pressure. They made glass tubes for thermometers and barometers; they made balance scales and clocks that could measure time and weight exactly. Without these craftsmen, whose elegant instruments for astronomical as well as physical explorations can be seen in museums today, the scientists would have been unable to unlock the secrets of the physical world.

Also important to the rise of scientific activity in the seventeenth century was the climate in which the natural philosophers were able to work. There were not so many of these men that it was impossible for them to know or at least correspond with each other, and in the course of the century the massive correspondence that passed among the more important figures was supplemented by the appearance of journals that provided regular outlets for scientific information. Moreover, princes and governments were willing to patronize the natural philosophers by founding and supporting scientific societies and even supplying scientists with the laboratories needed for their research. The first of the societies came into existence in Rome and Florence where, under the auspices of the pope and the dukes of Tuscany, learned men met regularly to discuss their own findings as well as those of other students. The duke of Tuscany provided laboratories where experiments made elsewhere could be repeated to test their validity. The most important of these societies, however, were founded in the seventeenth century: the English Royal Academy and the French Academy of Sciences. These two societies, supported by their respective kings, published journals and furthered research that could be described as both pure and applied. Seventeenth-century kings and their ministers did not make the distinction: They wished to use the efforts of learned men to improve all sorts of activities from the manufacture of cannon to the development of agricultural machinery. Through the efforts of these academies, observatories were established, laboratories subsidized, and the scientific activities of their members publicized and popularized. By the end of the seventeenth century, scientific societies were springing up all over Europe; some of them were superficial and amateurish, but others, like the Academy at Berlin or later the one at St. Petersburg, became almost as famous as their prototypes in London and Paris.

The story of the discoveries made by physical scientists in these years is an exciting one, but its full significance will be missed unless we realize that these men were exploring a great unknown about which there was much false information and observation. The barometer, for example, gave the first proof that nature did not "abhor a vacuum," but more importantly it introduced men to the problems of varying air pressure and weather— which had not even been conceived of before. Boyle's laws on gas (elastic air) concerned an unknown world in which men did not even know the elementary facts needed to develop chemistry. Others experimented with

144

the trajectories of cannon, of water shooting from a small hole in the side of a barrel, etc., to establish areas in the science of mechanics. Astronomers worked out reasons for the change in seasons as well as definitions of the orbits of the planets that had been established by telescopes. Men measured, weighed, and otherwise tested air and other substances. Hooke was on the verge of discovering oxygen when he found that a candle would be extinguished or that a mouse would die if either were placed in a glass inverted in water, but he failed to make the last induction from his evidence. Other searchers were able to prove that the water in the rivers and streams could be explained by the rain without positing underground streams from subterranean depths. The study of light produced the two theories (wave and particle) that still vie with each other for dominance. The microscope revealed the microworld to be as interesting and as worthy of careful research as was the macroworld of the planetary system.

One of the most important discoveries of the era was Harvey's announcement about the circulation of the blood in the human body. Anatomical artists and anatomists who followed Vesalius produced more and more accurate descriptions of the body; the problem that eluded them was the mechanism that made it function. Harvey's Italian teachers at Padua had exposed the valves in the arteries, but they had not been able to take the final step to show that the heart was the pump that propelled blood through both the lungs and the rest of the body. This discovery was probably responsible for the increased emphasis upon bleeding as a cure for fever and other diseases, but it was also fundamental to the understanding of the functioning of the body.

Unquestionably, the most astonishing discovery of the century, perhaps of all time, was Newton's proclamation of the universal law of gravitation. There had always been the problem of explaining what held the solar system together; a problem that had confronted both the Ptolemaic and the Copernican hypotheses. Following Aristotle, men posited a subtle substance, perfectly clear, perfectly fluid, perfectly solid, indeed perfect in every way, in which the earth and the planets of the solar system floated or were suspended. Descartes improved upon this by explaining that in this subtle substance there were vortices: The sun was the center of a huge one that included the planets, but the earth with its moon, Saturn with its rings, etc., were, in turn, also smaller vortices. One could liken the vortex to the spinning of water in a whirlpool. Fontenelle felt that this was a superior explanation to the Indian belief that an elephant somehow supported the earth, but it was not one that lent itself to empirical analysis. It remained for Newton to put into a grandiose system founded upon physical law the ideas developed from the days of Tycho Brahe, Galileo, and Kepler.

Newton's evidence demonstrated that the moon was obviously moving in its orbit under the influence of two forces: one which impelled it toward a line parallel with the earth, another which pulled it toward the earth on a perpendicular line and prevented it from flying on a tangent to its orbit. When he had the observational data to provide him with an exact measurement of the diameter of the earth and the distance between the earth and the moon, Newton, using Kepler's third law, was able to demonstrate that the moon was falling toward the earth at a rate comparable to the speed of falling bodies on the earth. He then turned his attention to the planets and discovered that they, too, were held in orbit by a force that acted with the same intensity as the pull of gravitation on the earth. With this he had a huge time-space machine responding to the law of universal gravitation. There were still some problems to explain, but these did not invalidate his grandiose conception. In Newton's first edition of the *Principia,* in which this time-space machine was described, he left in doubt the question of the subtle substance in the universe, but in an edition early in the eighteenth century, he cleared up the subtle substance mystery. He posited that the universe was empty and held together by the mysterious force of universal gravitation.

It is interesting to note that many Cartesian-oriented scientists refused to listen to Newton until well into the eighteenth century. The idea that the universe was held together by "gravitation" seemed to them to be most superstitious. Descartes had given his life fighting such things! However, the eighteenth century, as we shall see later in this chapter, saw the Newtonian thesis vindicated by scientific expeditions to Lapland and Peru so that by the middle of that century Newton's thesis was accepted by learned men throughout Europe.

While some men explored the problems of astronomy and physics, others struggled with those implicit in the structure of the earth and studied the fauna and flora that live upon its surface. These latter, however, were seriously handicapped by assumptions common to all seventeenth-century thinkers. In the seventeenth century, the world was considered only a few thousand years old. Both scientists and theologians believed that it had been created about four thousand years before the birth of Christ; this belief blinded men in their efforts to understand the earth and the biological world. It was most difficult to understand how fossil remains came into being, how clam shells were deposited upon the sides of high mountains or deep in pits that were far below the levels of the sea. John Ray once remarked that if he did not know that the earth was of recent origin, he would believe that these shells were very, very old. Stratification of rocks uncovered by mines, river beds, and faults also presented serious questions. Robert Hooke suggested that these strata might be a calendar, but he failed to follow up the idea.

The big problem confronting biological students was the fact that the explorations of the sixteenth and seventeenth centuries exposed the enormous variety of plant and animal life. True, no one found a unicorn, but they did find unbelievable numbers of butterflies, birds, animals, insects, trees, and flowers. The Roman books on plants and animals simply did not indicate the rich variety that seventeenth-century men were forced to consider and attempt to classify. Perhaps it is not surprising that they found this problem of naming and classifying so difficult that they had little time to reflect upon the origins or processes of the biological world. The biologists did make some important discoveries: Evidence of the sexual reproduction of plants and disproof of the idea of spontaneous generation cleared the way for further studies. But the most important biological work was in the field of taxonomy. Before any serious biological studies could be made, the plants and animals had to be classified and named. John Ray was the first to propose the binominal system of nomenclature, and his many books became the partial basis upon which eighteenth-century biological scientists erected their systems.

The geologists were not fortunate enough to find a John Ray. In their view, if the earth were really just a few thousand years old the "disorder" on the earth could only be explained by a cataclysm. Theological geologists stepped into the break; Noah's flood became the event that scattered clam shells about, that upset rock strata, indeed that explained everything. Perhaps this was about all that could be done as long as the earth was seen to be only fifty-seven hundred years old.

NEW EPISTEMOLOGY

Men have always asked the question: "How do you know?" Thus, it is not surprising that the generation which repudiated Aristotle's physics and Ptolomy's astronomy should ask whether or not Aristotle's epistemology should also be re-evaluated. Many men tackled the problem; we can only discuss three of the seventeenth century's most important suggestions. The lord chancellor of England, Francis Bacon (1561–1626), proposed that the deductive method of discovering truth should be abandoned. Logical inferences from "common-sense knowledge" or given truths had long provided the underpinnings of metaphysical systems based upon rational deductions. Bacon suggested that a better method would be to gather evidence about the world from all directions and sources and then attempt to discover truth by induction. In other words, he advocated allowing evidence to pile up and provide the solution to the question: "How do we know?" Bacon's method is most useful to biologists, geologists, historians, and others who see "process" as the key to understanding, but it did not suit a generation of mathematicians who were bent upon discovering a physical-world machine. Harvey remarked that Bacon reasoned like a lord chancellor; indeed, he was a mediocre mathematician.

The philosopher whose ideas most excited the imaginations of late seventeenth- and eighteenth-century men was the son of a French "robin" family. René Descartes (1596–1650), whose forefathers were judges and magistrates, moved into the soldier-nobility class. He found in mathematics and the new physics a philosophical methodology that nicely fitted the intellectual climate of the era. He himself was a profoundly religious man, anxious to relate the new science to the revealed religion of his ancestors. It had not been his intention to make Cartesian philosophy dangerous to the Christian doctrine a century after his death.

Descartes insisted that everything must be doubted, everything questioned, and that truth could only be established when there was evidence that could not be disproved. The fundamental truth of his system is best summarized in the exclamation: *"Cogito ergo sum!"* or "I think, hence I am!" In other words, he could not doubt his own reality, and upon the assumption that his mind, which was real, could penetrate the reality of the world, he erected a system of philosophy. Descartes believed that "experience" (experimentation) was necessary to establish basic truths, but he felt it would not be necessary to experiment to establish every truth. Logical conclusions could be drawn from the evidence.

Descartes' discussion of methodology proved to be his most important contribution. His physics, astronomy, and other scientific ideas had to be discarded, largely, perhaps, because men followed his method of uncovering truth. It is never easy to condense a complex idea into a few words, and Descartes' *Essay on Method* is no exception to this rule. However we can simplify it; in effect he proposed that the route to knowledge about the world and its laws should start with the formulation of an hypothesis. This hypothesis then must be tested, much as a geometer tests a proposition, by experiment and other known truths. If no evidence emerges that would prove it to be invalid, then this hypothesis could be considered to be a thesis, and subjected to even more rigorous experiments and tests. Finally, if the evidence becomes overwhelming, the proposition then can be considered to be a law. In cases where it is impossible to prove or disprove the proposition, it can be made into a postulate that can be considered to be tentatively a truth. The rigor of this system made it self-correcting, for at its center is the proposition that all conclusions, all laws, all truths must be subject to question and correction if evidence drawn from experiment proves them to be in error. This idea had within itself the possibility of eroding any metaphysical system, including Descartes', that had been erected on purely rational thought.

With his basic geometric assumption, Descartes himself found that the world and everything in it, except the soul of man, was mechanical. This mechanistic frame of thought fitted well into the physical researches of the era. From Galileo to Newton and beyond him into the eighteenth century, men set their thought patterns in the form of mechanics. These patterns yielded interesting results when translated to the fields of morals or theology. A great moralist like Spinoza saw morality as a series of geometric propositions and discovered a conception of God that was pantheistic. God was everywhere and in everything. Theologians (both Protestant and Catholic) believed in the ultimate unity of all truth and attempted to incorporate the Cartesian ideas into the doctrinal theology of the Christian religion. They, like Descartes, had to start with proof of the existence of God, rather than faith in His existence. The chemist Robert Boyle left money for lectures by theologians who would expand this point; their efforts at the end of the seventeenth century evoked the skeptical remark: "No one ever doubted the existence of God until the Boyle lecturers tried to prove it." Even more difficult was the mechanistic conception of the universe. In this view, the universe was created by a God, a figure perhaps vaguely resembling Jehovah of the Old Testament, but it responded to law. Thus, God became a sort of constitutional monarch who reigned over a universe governed by law. More unfortunate, it was difficult to find a place for Christ, the man-God, the gentle man of sorrows and forgiveness. Descartes himself was a thoroughgoing believer, a student of Saint Thomas, but his philosophy became a dangerous threat to Christian teaching before the eighteenth century was over.

Descartes' system depended upon a belief in "innate ideas" established in the mind of man by God; it also assumed that rational deductions could actually uncover truth. At the end of the seventeenth century an English philosopher, John Locke, questioned both of these assumptions and insisted upon an empirical approach to the problem of truth. The human mind, Locke argued, is blank at birth; it is like a piece of paper. The experiences of the human being are "written" upon it throughout life. Thus, the only "truths" that man can discover are those that he can experience. He cannot, so to speak, explore the depths of the ocean because his "sounding apparatus" will not reach so deep, but he can explore the coastlines and harbors. Locke insisted that men should limit their attempts to discover truth to those areas in which they can have experience (experiment). By this proposition, Locke provided the next generation with a new psychology and a new vision of man, as well as with a new epistemology. Locke himself was too much of a man of common sense to draw the most rigorous conclusions from his own assumptions, but in the eighteenth century, as we shall see later in this chapter, Berkeley and Hume were willing to push these ideas to logical extremes.

TRAVELERS IN TIME AND SPACE

While the Keplers, Newtons, Descartes, and Lockes of the world were providing Europeans with a new science and a new philosophy, other men explored places and civilizations that were distant in space and in time. While their impact was not as striking as that of Galileo or Newton, the stream of books on travel and history nonetheless had an erosive effect upon the given assumptions of European men.

The first waves of travelers to explore Asia and the Americas in the sixteenth century were usually soldiers, merchants, sea captains, and missionaries. Most of them were not sensitive men, willing to recognize and appreciate differences between themselves and the people they visited; furthermore, they were usually not able to describe their adventures with graceful pens. In the seventeenth century, more sensitive men went out to see the world, to collect exotic animals or plants, to learn languages, to study customs. They soon discovered that their predecessors had given the name "European" a bad reputation. In many places it meant cheat, robber, blasphemer, and other such unsavory things. This should have been no shock to anyone who had seen the behavior of European sailors and merchants in foreign lands, but to men in Europe, this mirror held up by "heathens" came as a surprise. The seventeenth-century traveler also often found that his hosts beyond the seas were highly civilized men, that they had morals and manners as lofty and gentle as those of Europeans, and that they practiced religious observances and maintained patterns of life different, perhaps, but no less laudable than those practiced by European men.

These discoveries were especially important because seventeenth-century men did not have the imaginative literature available to our society today. There were long-winded and essentially stupid romances, poetry, and some drama but little literature that dealt directly with problems of life. Thus, travel literature became a fad. In the seventeenth century, the number of travel accounts published in Europe doubled every two decades, so that by the end of the century the flow of this genre of writing had become a mighty river. Nor was it confined to travels that actually took place. By the end of the century, men could sit at home in Europe and write imaginary travel accounts; others brought together compendiums in which they lined up the accounts of many different writers about travel in this or that land; still others produced "geographies" that were in effect descriptions of the world drawn from the writings of the travelers. The total impact of this literature was impressive, and it led directly to the new idea that Europe was not unique as a civilized society, nor did Europe have any monopoly on morality and ethical behavior. This was the first time that any considerable number of European men had questioned these assumptions, but it was not long before European writers began to use the non-European societies to criticize the patterns of behavior of their own. In the eighteenth century, Swift's Gulliver visited Lilliput, Montesquieu's Persian traveler wrote letters home about the bizarre customs in European society, Voltaire's Huron arrived in France to be converted to Christianity, and a large company of other "exotic" people found their way into the presses of Europe, where they used the culture of non-Europeans as a rapier with which to prick the pretensions of Western Christian civilization.

While travelers brought back stories that were to develop into a pattern demanding the recognition of "relativism" in manners, morals, and society, scholars questioned the mythical background of history and asked for more exact information. In the sixteenth century, a school of French historians refused to accept the story that France had been colonized from Troy, thus laying the foundation for a more accurate account of the history of the French kingdom. In the seventeenth century, many scholars frankly recognized that the myth and the reality of Roman and Greek history also should be separated; and some even realized that the Hebrew Biblical stories might be of the same mythical origin. One of the most dramatic finds of the historians, however, was the work of scholarly Jesuit and Benedictine priests who attempted to write the lives of the saints. These clerics insisted upon scholarly evidence that soon removed hundreds, indeed thousands, of names from the rolls of the saints. In so doing, the priests also set up standards for the critical study of documents that were to be the bases for later historical investigation and that inspired the collection and editing of masses of documents for the study of antiquity. The great documentary collections that were started in the seventeenth century became the foundations for a new understanding of the European past that proved to be as disturbing as the discovery of the various civilizations of the non-European world.

One amusing incident indicates the problem that historical evidence could present. Seventeenth-century chronologers were scholars whose labors were used to prepare books for daily devotion. They fixed the day and year of important events like the birth of Moses, the temptation of Joseph, or the creation of the earth. It was this latter date that caused trouble, for the calculators could not agree. Was the date 4000 or 4004 B.C.? When they turned to the evidence that could be discovered from the historical documents available from non-Jewish antiquity, the scholars found that both the Egyptians and the Chinese had had a long history, replete with the names of the kings, that seemed to pre-date the creation of the earth. According to these stories, Adam was a "latecomer"! Hermann Moll, who wrote one of the best geographies of the period, "solved" the problem by refusing to accept any evidence that placed men on the earth before the creation of Adam; he also declined to credit any account of European men before Noah's son first "colonized" Germany. However, the problem would not be brushed under the rug. Bishop Bossuet, a learned and honest scholar, finally decided to move back the date for the creation of the earth to one that could be justified by the Greek Bible rather than one indicated by the Vulgate used by Roman Catholics.

The study of history also brought home to many European intellectuals the fact that the world of men was in flux, in the process of change. Western men had long recognized that the classical past of Greece and Rome was a golden age, presumably never again to be repeated. The civilization of the Roman past was, indeed, a massive backdrop for the stage of the present, but by the seventeenth century when Aristotle, Ptolemy, Galen, and other great figures of that past were discovered to have made errors that modern men could correct, it could be expected that other aspects of the Greek and Roman civilizations would be compared to those of later Europe. The result was a battle between the "ancients" and the "moderns" that first broke out in Italy during the opening years of the seventeenth century and continued to rage until the end of that century. One side maintained the superiority of ancient civilization and ancient authors; the other compared the "Age of Louis XIV" favorably with that of Augustus. The comparison ran the gamut of man's activities: science, literature, philosophy, art, and architecture. It called attention to the fact that perhaps changes in one direction or another (progress?) could occur. At the end of the century, Bishop Fénelon, looking back to the reign of Henry IV, was astonished to find that there were changes in life styles, manners, and behavior codes as well as in artistic and literary modes. The doctrine of progress was ready to be born.

Skepticism found in the works of Greek philosophers, in Cartesian thought, and in the rising historical criticism also invaded other areas. European men in the late sixteenth and early seventeenth centuries believed in various levels of superstitions. Some believed in werewolves, gremlins, and fairies; others gave credence to witches and wizards; others believed in portents from the skies. The ignorant were to be found in the pulpits, on the law benches, and in the universities—as well as in the streets. The burning of witches was common in Protestant countries in the early seventeenth century; it was less common in Catholic lands where the Inquisition knew more about evidence, but there were witches burned throughout the century all over Europe. However, there were also skeptics who doubted the witchcraft stories, and in the second half of the century a trickle, at first, and then a flow of books attacked the magic world of demons, witches, and portents. The English judge who dismissed a case because he found no law against riding on a broomstick was akin to Fontenelle when the latter proved that, contrary to Saint Augustine and other Christian writers, the Oracles did not go out of business with the birth of Christ nor were their prophecies credible either before or after the year 1 A.D. In the early 1680's when a great comet (named by Halley) streaked across the sky, the ignorant assured each other that this was a sign from God. Their pronouncements provoked Pierre Bayle to write about comets— and other things. Indeed, he wrote several books on comets in which he peeled off layer after layer of falsehood from the superstitions of his fellow men until, like an onion stripped of its layers, nothing remained. Bayle was only one, but a most impressive figure, in the company of men who attacked superstitions of all kinds and stripped the magic from the world in which men lived.

There were other forces at work to undermine traditional beliefs of all kinds. The vituperative literature of the Reformation protagonists did much to make many men shrug their shoulders and refuse to believe either side, but even more important was the fact that after the mid-sixteenth century the presses of Europe reproduced edition after edition of the works of the great authors of classical antiquity: Seneca, Epicurus, Cicero, Horace, Tacitus, Vergil, Livy—to mention only a few of the most famous. These works became available to and were read by many people. These men spoke of a world that was becoming skeptical of the gods of the Greek or Roman pantheon and sought explanations for men's lives in human reason and human values. They seemed more reasonable than the violent men who urged the destruction of their religious enemies, and their voices were more serene than those of the saints of both the Calvinist faith and the Counter-Reformation Catholic church. How many men were "corrupted" by their words? We do not know, for in the seventeenth century it was not popular, or easy, for a man to write in terms that would betray disbelief in the Christian traditions, and yet there were so many men who must be classed as "libertines," that is, unbelievers who demanded liberty of belief or action, that the movement cannot be ignored. In the eighteenth century, when deism and nonbelief flourished in the elite classes of society, the libertine tradition surfaced as an important phenomenon, but even in the seventeenth century, disbelief in the traditional religious patterns of Christianity, probably inspired by the books of Latin and Greek men of letters, was not unknown.

TEXTUAL CRITICISM

The humanist scholars of the fifteenth and sixteenth centuries recovered the works of Latin and Greek authors and developed the critical tools for editing and purifying the texts. This was a massive task requiring knowledge of the historical evolution of the language in which the book was written and skill in the detection of errors that had crept into the text as a result of either careless copying or actual intention of earlier scribes to give new interpretations. Some of the texts had been so jumbled that the problem was to find the proper sequences; others had been carelessly or ignorantly copied with the result that inserted words often changed the meaning. This great labor of editing texts continued throughout the sixteenth and seventeenth centuries. When there were no more literary texts to edit, scholars attacked the books on mathematics, war, and commerce as well as the inscriptions on monuments. Indeed, every kind of ancient document became grist for their mills. In the latter half of the seventeenth century, a priest of the Oratory, Richard Simon, armed with a knowledge of Latin, Greek, and Hebrew, turned his attention to the Bible as a text that might also need editing. It was inevitable that this should happen; it was also inevitable that it would cause a scandal.

Simon, of course, had no intention of scandalizing his fellow priests or his society. He was a scholar, and he discovered that there were textual problems in both the Old and New Testaments that could be cleared up by the application of his knowledge of languages. It seemed to him to be a laudable enterprise, in part because it would show the world how foolish the Protestants were to rely entirely upon the Bible for their doctrine rather than also to accept the Church's living tradition as a source for religious teachings. Simon's first book, *A Critical History of the Old Testament,* appeared in 1678. His was not the first work to call attention to the fact that there were problems in the Holy Book; Spinoza, Grotius, and others had been there before him. But Simon was the first to be armed with the linguistic skills necessary for textual criticism. He pointed out that ignorant men in both the pulpit and the theological schools had twisted and interpreted the Biblical texts to suit their fancies and had built upon their interpretations large doctrines and weighty propositions. But, he added, what they really needed to know if they were to understand the Biblical message was, first, whether the passage in question had been altered in the course of its transmission by the carelessness of copiers or by interpositions intended to buttress dogmas, and, secondly, whether the grammar used actually conveyed exactly what the text really meant. Both conditions were unacceptable to a large body of men representing both Catholic and Protestant positions. To equate theology with grammar seemed outrageous. And to insist that a preacher should be restrained in interpretation of texts suggested that much of the writing about religious belief was nonsense. In spite of the storm that his research raised around him, Richard Simon continued his work. *A Critical History of the Text of the New Testament* appeared in 1689, *A Critical History of the Versions of the New Testament* came out in 1690, and *A Critical History of the Commentaries on the New Testament* was published in 1693. Finally, in 1702 he produced *The New Testament of Our Lord Christ, Translated from the Ancient Latin Edition with Notes.* In this last book, Simon reiterated his belief that the literal meaning of the text must be the source of doctrine; interpretations were merely the compounding of errors. But even more than this, he argued, the meanings of words must be understood in proper context, and the text must be purified so that not even an "or" or an "and" could be out of place.

Simon's works were condemned, but he lived out his life as a scholar and a priest of the Oratory serene in his conviction that he was right. However, to the theologian it was a monstrous idea that a doctrine based upon a scriptural passage could be found false by a mere grammarian. Even worse was the fact that textual criticism supported the ideas of men who did not want to believe in the Christian tradition. There had been enough questioning about the "myths" of Arabian, Persian, Egyptian, and other Near Eastern peoples who often had stories similar to those in the Bible. The anonymous essay by an Oxford Master of Arts, published in 1695, in which all these myths, the Hebrew included, were treated as "romantic hypotheses" was only one of many such books that were to scandalize the conservatives and support the ideas of the deists, who were already proposing a belief based upon Nature rather than upon Scripture.

POLITICAL PHILOSOPHY: HOBBES, BOSSUET, AND LOCKE

The seventeenth century produced a galaxy of political philosophers who attempted to justify either the rule of the king or the right of his subjects to overthrow him. The English revolutions of the 1640's and again of 1688 required political justification for rebellion; and kings like James I of England and Louis XIV of France wanted justification for their power. Of the men who stepped into the breach to provide such arguments, we shall consider only three, all of whom happened to be philosophers as well as political theorists.

Thomas Hobbes was undoubtedly the *bête noir* of the seventeenth-century theorists because of his atheistic materialism and his brutal explanation of man's psychology. Dissatisfied with the philosophy taught him at the university, Hobbes visited Italy, met Galileo, became acquainted with the skepticism of Montaigne, and reached the conclusion that everything was material: the earth, the bodies of men, the corporation of the state. He lived in an era when it would have been rash to expose overtly anti-Christian ideas, but he suggested that religion came as a result of man's inability to distinguish dreams from experience when awake. His reader is left to draw further conclusions. Hobbes explained that men are naturally suspicious of others because they know themselves to be capable of evil. They lock their gates, their houses, their desks, because they know that no one can be trusted—not even members of their family. This conception of man became the basis for Hobbes' ideas about society prior to the emergence of the state: In this society the law of the jungle prevailed, with every man's hand against his neighbor, and man's life was "short, nasty, and brutish." Men escaped from the evils of the state of nature only by combining in political society, by creating the Leviathan, the state. In Hobbes' book, this meant that the people, in making a contract with the sovereign, surrendered their will in return for protection. After that surrender there was only one justification for not accepting the rule of the sovereign: self-preservation. It would follow that a man has no duty to a sovereign who could not protect him. Thus, only when society collapses, when the state of nature prevails so that each must preserve his own life, does the subject have the right to rebel.

Hobbes' *Leviathan* was a strong indictment of the revolution in mid-seventeenth-century England. His contract theory justified the king against the revolutionaries. But his materialism, his failure to find a place for God, his psychology so uncomplimentary to man all made him hated and feared by many; his reputation required that every political philosopher who followed him had to confront the Hobbesian conceptions of man and the state.

Bishop Bossuet made a nice foil for Hobbes. In a way, he represented the most intelligent and reasonable approach to the problems of politics and philosophy that could be made using the traditional Christian arguments. Bossuet believed in Aristotle, in Saint Thomas, and above all in the Christian Bible. His political theory was a justification of the rule of the king based upon Holy Scripture and Christian tradition. Bossuet maintained that all power and authority ultimately rested in God and that God invested kings with the power to govern, retaining to Himself the authority to rule. This contract was between God and the king; God granted the king power in return for the obligation to rule justly and well. Since Bossuet believed in free will, this meant that if the king did not govern justly, the fault was not God's for the king had freedom of choice, but it also meant that God would hold the king responsible for his actions, that God would judge a king more severely than ordinary men since He had endowed him with so much responsibility. This doctrine forbade subjects to revolt even against a bad king. They could storm heaven with their prayers and their tears, but they had no other recourse against a ruler given to them by God. Bossuet's argument is largely taken from quotations from the Bible. He was one of the greatest Biblical scholars as well as one of the important historians of his day. But his whole point of view is based upon static absolutes drawn from Saint Thomas, the Bible, Aristotle, and his own superb intelligence. Like Hobbes, he defends the right of the king to rule, but for different reasons. His work contrasts even better with that of the eighteenth-century philosophers who followed him because Hobbes' world, like his own, was static, absolute, and fixed, while theirs is in motion, is relative, and is changing.

The English Revolution of 1688 produced a political philosopher capable of rationalizing the dethronement of James II and the government of William and Mary. However, John Locke was not the first philosopher to justify rebellion. Indeed, Locke, as well as Bossuet, could point to Saint Thomas Aquinas as an intellectual predecessor. Saint Thomas wrote: "A king who is unfaithful to his duty forfeits his claim to obedience." Locke could also find a large company of other philosophers contemporary with and after Saint Thomas who gave reasons for rebellion against an unjust king who did not obey the law. The Huguenot rebellion in France had produced theorists, like the one in the *Vindiciae contra Tyrannos* (1579), who developed a contract theory but justified rebellion only when it was led by great noblemen or town governments. Locke went a step further and produced an idea that was to have important consequences for the entire Western world. Contrary to Hobbes, Locke believed that in the state of nature men were good and happy, that they had organized political society for their own benefit. In its simplest form, the contract between men and their kings ran something like this: The people gave to the king the *power* to govern, but retained the *right* to govern themselves. Thus, as long as the king obeyed the law, governed justly and wisely, the people submitted to his rule; but if the king failed to obey the law, that is, became a tyrant, the people could depose him and place another on the throne. Locke's argument amply supported the action of the Whig party that drove James from the English throne, and it became a tool in the hands of the revolutionary politicians, statesmen, propagandists, and philosophers who directed the revolutions in America and France in the late eighteenth century.

MUSIC

Sixteenth-century music was largely written for use in the churches. The Catholic Reformation spirit is strongly present in the polyphony of Palestrina (1525–1594), as is the Protestant cause in the hymns of Luther. Much of the secular music of this century consisted of popular traditional tunes arranged to please the ear of the rich, and to serve the formalized dance that was becoming the thing to do at court.

The demand for church music played an important role in seventeenth-century music, as did the development of the organ. The great developments, however, came as the ballet, opera, and orchestra moved from the courts to the cities. The ballet began to be performed by professional dancers rather than courtiers; vocal stars, often castrati, were the object of diplomatic negotiations; and composers and librettists turned out operas with about the facility and quality of Hollywood scenario writers. Part of this "music industry," too, was the addition of woodwinds and horns to the king's violins, and the direction of performances of the expanded orchestra by a maestro. Chamber music, like the ballet, continued as a mélange of amateur and professional artists: Emperor Leopold I and his sons composed and performed it; and the compositions of the Hapsburg emperors are even played today. Historians of music have borrowed the word "baroque" to characterize seventeenth- and early eighteenth-century music.

The eighteenth was the century of Handel, Bach, Haydn, Mozart, and Beethoven, to mention a few of the most famous. It was a time when extended musical education and a demand for musicians attracted young men to the profession; when improvements in keyboard and string instruments produced the virtuoso; when the court of Vienna, a babel of Italian, German, Hungarian, French, Spanish, and several Slavic tongues, where the dramatic arts could never flourish, became a center for the universal language of music. The works of eighteenth-century composers still command our attention in their own right. In addition, they have been models and inspiration to all composers since their era.

EIGHTEENTH-CENTURY SCIENCE

The great scientists of the early seventeenth century worked alone or with a small company of fellows or disciples; sometimes they were favored by patrons who gave them money or other assistance, but much of their work was supported by their own efforts as professors or from their private income. By the opening of the eighteenth century, kings and noblemen, city governments, and foundations of one kind or another had come forth with support for scientific societies and botanical gardens, pensions and gratification for individual scientists, and funds to finance experiments or even expeditions to distant lands. Naval officers and their ships were often placed at the disposal of science, the "king's physicians" and royal governors located in colonies collected biological specimens from beyond the seas while royal cabinets of curiosities (museums), royal libraries, and royal patronage for schools and academies supported the efforts of scientists in Europe. The support was not yet as munificent as it was to become in the nineteenth and twentieth centuries, but the time had arrived when public and private support for the scientists and their activities assured the progressive development and expansion of knowledge about the world.

The expeditions that "proved" a part of Newtonian theory by empirical evidence provide us with a nice illustration. Newton argued that the force of gravitation exerted upon the earth would have the effect of shaping the earth more like a pear than a globe; the earth, he felt, must be somewhat flatter at the north pole than at the equator, and thus a degree of latitude should be greater at the pole than at the equator. Since the new astronomical and surveying instruments made it possible to take an accurate measurement, this theory could be tested empirically. The French government sent two expeditions: Maupertuis led one to Lapland, La Condamine and Bouger another to Peru. Maupertuis returned first and reported that he had found a degree of latitude to be 57,438 toises. The expedition to Peru had more trouble surveying, but when the work was finished it discovered that the degree of latitude at the equator was 56,753 toises. Newton was correct.

The law of gravitation supplanted the plenum theory in the eighteenth century. In 1688 Newton left it open whether or not the universe was empty space or filled with some subtle material, a plenum, such as posited by both Aristotle and Descartes. In the eighteenth century the plenum idea was discarded. There were some who objected that the gravity theory was too fragile an explanation, fraught with mysticism, but as the astronomers, with better telescopes, proved that the planets also attracted each other when their orbits brought them into a proximity, the idea of gravity took on more credence. The plenum theory no longer seemed necessary after Herschel (1781) discovered the new planet Uranus, beyond the orbit of Jupiter by positing Kepler's third law and Newton's law of gravitation. Other astronomers studying the universe beyond our solar system posited the idea that our sun was a star in the Milky Way, and, with more exact telescopes, they began to make measurements in outer space. By the end of the eighteenth century when Laplace published his *Exposition du system du monde,* a daring synthesis of the Newtonian universe, he and his readers assumed that the secrets of the skies were fully exposed, the vast time-space machine of the universe fully understood. They could not know that the next century would end with an even more daring hypothesis of an expanding universe that no longer was a simple time-space machine.

While the astronomers with more powerful telescopes were proving the Newtonian conception of the universe, other scientists were opening new areas for investigation. Newton's great prestige gave his theory of light so much weight that Huygens' particle theory had to wait until the twentieth century for consideration. (Perhaps the equipment available for experiment in the eighteenth century would not have facilitated any further development anyway.) The great excitement in physics came with the discovery of electricity. The phenomenon of sparks emanating from a cat's fur or a woolen rug was long known but not understood; by the opening of the eighteenth century, however, it was seen that sparks could be generated by rubbing a glass tube or globe with the bare hand. Then the cylinder and later the disk replaced the globe, and the bare hand gave way to a piece of leather covered with an amalgam of tin. The first discoveries concerned the fact that there were good and bad conductors and that there were positive and negative charges, obviously related to the magnet, when paper fragments were brought in contact. The Leyden bottle, which permitted the experimenter to create a pile of electricity that could be discharged at will, was an exciting experience. It was used at one time to shock 180 French guards holding hands; another time, three thousand monks were jolted so sharply by a single release that they all jumped into the air. Franklin demonstrated that the electrical charge and the lightning bolt were both electricity; it was fortunate for him that his kite proved the relationship without killing the experimenter. Toward the end of the century, experiments showed that electricity could also be in the form of a current as well as a pile. Of the many experimenters who contributed to the understanding of electricity, Volta was one who gave his name to a characteristic of the electrical charge.

Knowledge about heat came with the development of a proper thermometer. In the seventeenth century, several scales were proposed, but none of them achieved anything like universal recognition. Thus, it was difficult for one experimenter to reproduce the work of another. A new scale, developed by a Dane, Fahrenheit, and widely used in the United States, came into being in 1724. In 1742 a Swedish professor scaled a thermometer with 0° for the boiling point of water and 100° for the freezing point; in 1750 Strömer launched the present centigrade thermometer by reversing this scale. These new instruments allowed men to study heat and the problems of vaporization. It was left for men of the next century, however, to work out the laws and the significance of thermodynamics.

At the end of the seventeenth century, a group of statesmen-bureaucrats in Emperor Leopold's court at Vienna developed the theory that a subtle substance, phlogiston, was responsible for the processes of burning and calcination; using the symbol ø, they were able to formulate an equation to demonstrate the existence of this substance. Certain things like oil, wood, etc. were rich in phlogiston; others like glass had none. It was a blind alley, and yet it also was the first attempt to isolate the causes of rusting, burning, etc. In the course of the eighteenth century, chemists in France, England, and Scotland made important discoveries that laid the foundations for the nineteenth-century chemical breakthroughs. The first was the discovery that air was in fact made up of several "airs," some "vital," others "inert." The discovery of oxygen gave the first clue to the nature of the structure of matter; this would be expanded in the next century with the formulation of the atomic table. Like the physicist, the chemist also studied heat and its relationship to the problems of matter.

Perhaps the most important work of the eighteenth-century chemists was the development of a proper nomenclature for chemical substances. As long as chemists used curious names, such as "butter of arsenic" or "vinegar of wine," in describing their experiments, no one could check on their findings. Indeed, recipes used by chemists were more like lists of ingredients for cooking than formulas for the compounding of chemical substances. Lavoisier divided the elements into four categories: (1) the gases oxygen, nitrogen, hydrogen, and "imponderables"; (2) elements which upon oxidation yield acids: sulphur, phosphorus, and carbon; (3) metals—of which he names seventeen; and (4) earths: lime, magnesia, baryta, alumina, and silica. Lavoisier recognized twenty-three elements in the modern sense, but his own list, which included compounds, was much longer. Modern chemists hail him as the founder of modern chemistry, but like most "founders," he stood on the shoulders of others; Cavendish, Black, Priestley and Scheele were all important in the development of the conception of matter that freed the chemist from the idea that "air, fire, earth, water, and sulphur" were the prime elements in nature.

The biologists also made progress; indeed, they not only worked out scientific methods for taxonomy of both fauna and flora, but they also came close to proclaiming the theory of evolution. Once animals and plants were classified so that every known species had a position assigned to it involving the grouping of the species into genera, the genera into orders, and the orders into classes, it became possible to visualize the problem of their origins. The system that finally prevailed was one developed by Karl Linnaeus; it left much for future biologists to do, but the binomial nomenclature—using two Latin names for each species—offered a simple way of fixing the species in its genera, thus providing an international nomenclature for all species of plants and animals. Linnaeus believed that the species were constant and invariable, that they were just as they had been created by God. Buffon, who also attempted to find a suitable method for nomenclature, grouped the species together and added a notion of environmental influence upon the species; thus, he decided, for example, that a donkey was a horse that had developed in an unfavorable environment. He also was the first to place man in the classification of the apes, recognizing, of course, that man was the highest of all and that the baboon was a degenerated man. At the end of the century, Lamarck, Buffon's son-in-law, developed the doctrine of "use and disuse." A giraffe thus became a deer-like creature that had developed a long neck because it was necessary for it to find food on the trees. Conversely, an animal that did not fully use some organ, eyes for example, would, like the blind mole, cause the organ to degenerate. Acquired characteristics were passed on from generation to generation. Both Buffon and Lamarck labored under the impression that the world had been created a relatively short time before. They were not, however, bound to the Biblical thesis: Buffon assumed that the world was at least 75,000 years old, time enough for a species to degenerate in a bad environment. (It would not be time enough for the process explained in the next century by Darwin.)

While theological geologists posited Noah's flood as the cataclysm that explained strange phenomena like clam shells on high mountains and fossil plants in limestone quarries, Bishop Steno, a Dane living in Italy, developed a theory of the earth from the stratification in Tuscany; but one had to wait for Buffon, in the mid-eighteenth century, to produce a history of the earth which began with matter torn from the sun by a passing comet. Buffon's earth was molten hot for 3000 years. In the next 35,000 years its crust gradually formed the metallic ores. Then the following 15,000 to 20,000 years saw the emergence of atmosphere, followed by 5000 years of intense volcanic activity. Finally, calm ensued and huge terrestrial animals and plants appeared in the polar regions and gradually migrated toward the equator as the earth became cooler. Then came man and his supremacy. Buffon thought that this last period would last until the cooling process made it impossible for animals to live on the earth. Buffon's was the first effective attempt to relate the stratifications to the history of the earth. But this ingenious theory seemed too violent for many scholars; they were more attracted to Werner's "Neptunist" hypothesis. Werner, a teacher in the school of mines at Freiburg, assumed that his native land was typical of the rest of earth; its strata were obviously the result of aquatic action, so he decided that water, rather than fire, was the formative agent in the history of the earth. Goethe liked this Neptune thesis because it suited his sense of classic form: No one knew how to prove or disprove it.

It would be interesting to speculate on the processes of scientific discovery. The seventeenth century produced a Galileo, a Kepler, and a Newton as well as a galaxy of lights, only slightly less bright, who broke new ground in physics and astronomy. No such figures appeared in the eighteenth century. The chemists and physicists did prepare the ground for the great nineteenth-century discoveries in electricity and chemistry, and the biologists and geologists established the classifications upon which their nineteenth-century successors erected monumental conceptions of the earth and its inhabitants. Why these eighteenth-century workers did not develop breakthroughs comparable to those of their predecessors and successors in the seventeenth and nineteenth centuries is an interesting question for which answers must be only tentative. We do not understand clearly either the problem of genius or the processes of discovery, but both present fascinating questions.

SOCIETY AND MAN

Eighteenth-century students of the human condition and the problems of man attempted to apply Cartesian methodology and the mechanical model of the world to the problems of man and man's society. The conception of environmental impact and inherited characteristics that Buffon and Lamarck used to explain the various species within a genera allowed Buffon to assert the unity of the human species. Differences in color of skin, texture of hair, and the like could be explained by environment. The fact that all men, no matter what their color, had the ability to think, Buffon insisted, distinguished them from the other animals. This "spiritual characteristic" gave man his most important mark of distinction; the other characteristic differences among the races were the result of the environment. Thus, anthropology as well as astronomy seemed susceptible to mechanical analysis, but it proved impossible to do much with this environmental thesis.

An Italian scholar, Vico (1668–1744), developed a general theory for understanding social phenomena. He recognized that God directed the flow of history for His own purposes, but even though God was the primary cause, there also were secondary causes that could be studied as the natural laws of history. Vico investigated languages, mythologies, poetry, primitive laws, and other things that would give him insight into the psychology and society of earlier peoples. In his *Principles for a New Science,* he, like Buffon, also developed the idea of the unity of man and explained the similarities in man's social development from place to place. He believed that men moved through "stages," from hunters to inhabitants of agricultural villages, from builders of city-states to creators of empires. He thus established a law of evolution of society that fitted the mechanistic Cartesian conception of the world. Vico was often confused and obscure, but he had an important impact upon men like Montesquieu and, when his complete works were finally available, upon the social scientists of the nineteenth century. The idea that different societies were simply at different stages of development provided a mechanistic framework for the explanation of laws, morals, and constitutions; this framework meshed with the idea that differences in climate, soil, or geography could explain differences in color, skin, and hair texture.

Montesquieu, a distinguished member of the nobility of the robe and one of the brightest lights of the century, produced a synthesis that was destined to have great influence on the course of subsequent political history; the men who made both the Constitution of the United States of America and successive constitutions in France following 1789 had studied and absorbed his teachings. Montesquieu approached the study of social and political thought as a lawyer and as a perceptive student of human affairs. His first effective sally into print came with a series of letters, presumably written by a Persian visitor, discussing the society of Western men and making comparisons with that of Persia. The *Persian Letters* were well within the framework of the late seventeenth-century literary ventures that used travel experiences to make invidious comparisons between European and other, more exotic cultures. Montesquieu next undertook to study the great problem of the decline and decay of Roman civilization. In his *Considerations of the Greatness of the Romans and Their Decadence,* Montesquieu tried to fathom the social dynamics of change. He discussed the theories of determinism and relativity. His most important book, *The Spirit of the Laws,* fully developed his thesis of social relativity by analysis of the differences in constitutions and customs of the peoples scattered about the earth both in space and in time. Their political development was conditioned and determined by climate, soil, geography, and history. (These determinative forces were of the same order as the ones astronomers and physicists were discovering in the natural world.) Thus, if man could come to understand the dynamics and the statics of social and political life, he could become free by conforming to the natural laws. It was a grandiose conception founded on beliefs in Cartesian methodology and the mechanistic world.

While Montesquieu tried to grasp the total picture of society, other thinkers were satisfied to analyze smaller segments. Several French philosophers who sought to understand the problems of economics have been grouped together under the title "physiocrats." Quesnay (1694–1774) was the first of this group to insist that all wealth was the gift of God. It was His action in the creation of the sun, the soil, and the winds and weather that made agriculture possible. The net product in any society was the result of agriculture and, perhaps, fishing and mining. All other workers, craftsmen, merchants, and transporters of commodities could create nothing; they only changed the form or the location of the wealth created by God. Armed with this conception, the physiocrats advocated the end of all restrictions on the economy imposed by government in the forms of tariffs, tolls, and taxes, for these only added to costs and did nothing to add to wealth. They felt all taxes should be collected from the "net product," that is, from the source of wealth which God freely gives to man—the land. The physiocratic doctrine of *laisser faire, laisser passer* became a slogan for those who wished to free the manufacture and exchange of goods from state controls.

The physiocrats, however, were not the founders of economic science. Adam Smith, author of *The Wealth of Nations,* provided the intellectual underpinnings for the science of economics taught by both liberals and socialists in the nineteenth century.

Smith was confronted with the bullionist doctrines of wealth of the preceding century, doctrines which taught that gold, silver, and jewels were real wealth and all trade and all economic legislation should be directed toward supplying the kingdom with these commodities. In Smith's view, this was nonsense; it overlooked the true source of wealth and, indeed, would impoverish the kingdom. Smith emphasized the doctrine that wealth was the result of human labor. Even the pear that one plucks from the tree cannot be consumed before it is picked. Smith also understood the importance of the divison of labor. One of his most eloquent passages deals with the manufacture of pins. In this section, he shows how a single pinmaker cannot compete with the efforts of a team of pinmakers when each of the team is specialized to carry out one operation in the manufacturing process. From this idea, Smith went on to show that the territorial division of labor also produced greater quantities of wealth. Each territory or state, he felt, should produce those items that it is most fitted to produce and trade with other territories for the items that they most effectively produce. From this evidence, Smith easily drew the conclusion that it was folly for a state to impose tariffs upon commerce and rates upon manufactures; such acts would only force its people to produce goods uneconomically.

Smith's studies convinced him of the existence of the "economic man"; that is, he posited man as a creature who, if left free to act, would further his own best economic interests. This in turn would further the best interests of the entire community. Thus, the slogan *laisser faire, laisser passer* fitted his economic teachings as much as it did those of the physiocrats.

While Smith and the physiocratic philosophers sought to explain the economic system in terms that fitted the Cartesian mechanistic thought of the era, Jean Jacques Rousseau developed a political theory that attempted to demonstrate the idea that human political institutions were the result of the processes of development not of mechanics. His first important book was an attack on Adam Smith and all the other philosophers who praised the development of urban, commercial civilization. He titled it *An Inquiry into the Causes of the Poverty of Nations* and argued, in effect, that as men moved further from the state of nature, they became brutalized and impoverished. Voltaire called Rousseau's work a book against the human race. But Rousseau did not stop there. In his most important political treatise, the *Social Contract,* he developed a dynamic theory about political processes. Like Hobbes and Locke, he started with the state of nature, which he believed to be a good and happy condition. But from there, he developed the idea that each individual is bound to the sum total of the society in which he lives by a mysterious social contract that holds his individual will in union with the "general will." This general will is the true source for law, custom, morality, government: It is, in effect, the result of men's living together through time, and its character is formed by the history of the society. It followed that the magistrate, e.g., the king or the government, was also bound by this general will, and the magistrate's government was legitimate only as long as it carried out and conformed to the general will. Rousseau not only presented an important political concept that could be developed into democratic conceptions of society, but also, by his insistence upon processes, he became one of the sources of the romantic movement of the nineteenth century. Rousseau's conception of man discards the Cartesian mechanical model and substitutes the idea that man is the result of the process of human history, that his words for "good and evil" are the result of evolution in the society and his tie with the general will is complete because he is, in effect, himself the creature of the development of the general will of the society into which he was born.

Montesquieu, Smith, and the physiocrats presented an ideal of society in which guarantees should be created to protect the individual from the power of the state and thereby assure the perfect functioning of the "machine" of government and economics. In effect, they suggested that human welfare and prosperity would depend upon constitutional laws prohibiting state or church or family from interfering with the freedom of the individual. Rousseau, on the other hand, assured his readers that "the people will not harm itself" and therefore that the general will of the people is the sole guarantee of the freedom necessary in society. Rousseau even insisted that society had the right to force the individual to be free, that is, to force him to conform with the general will. Since this general will is a mysterious force, it could easily be confused with the will of the majority, even though Rousseau specifically rejects that notion. Thus, we see that eighteenth-century political thinkers prepared the groundwork for the two contradictory doctrines that emerged in the nineteenth century: the ideal of liberalism, which demanded freedom for the individual from state controls; and democracy, which demanded popular sovereignty, popular control over policy, and even popular control over economic and social organization—all of which might deny individual liberty.

While political and economic thinkers struggled to find a methodology and a conception of man and society that would liberate the forces of human progress, eighteenth-century historians also sought answers to the human condition. Moreover, they reflected the desire to understand the world and man in mundane terms rather than in theocentric conceptions. The eighteenth-century historians were not the first to insist upon historical causation as a problem dealing strictly with the actions of men and the forms of human institutions, but they did have a greater impact upon both contemporary and later thinking than their predecessors had enjoyed. Perhaps the greatest of their number, certainly the most important historian of the day, was Edward Gibbon who, in casting about for a suitable topic for his talents, suddenly realized that the city of Rome posed the greatest historical problem of the era. He spent much of the rest of his life writing *The Decline and Fall of the Roman Empire.* Gibbon's canvas was a large one extending from Arabia to England, from the great days of Roman power to the conquest of Constantinople by the Ottoman Turks. His style, with its balanced sentences loaded with wisdom, polite skepticism, and occasional flashes of wit, has been the delight of civilized readers for two hundred years and surely will be read for many more yet to come. Gibbon sought to write history as a story of the past, a story of human events undirected by God, fate, or destiny. He did not find immutable laws such as some of his contemporaries hoped to discover, but he did believe that history could deepen experience and thus provide wisdom and understanding. He could not, of course, escape his own preconceptions; he was a skeptic and a deist, and his dislike for Christianity led him to believe that it was the basic cause for the disruption of the institution of the Roman Empire. He rarely veiled his hostility toward the men who were responsible for both the propagation of "superstitions" that served the needs of corrupt and tyrannical politicians and for the development of social and economic patterns that he believed to be unfortunate.

There were other historians whose works should be mentioned. Hume wrote on the history of the English islands; his biases are not less evident than Gibbon's, but, like Gibbon, he tried to write from the evidence and in terms of human action. Montesquieu also wrote a history of the fall of the Roman empire, but his scholarship was unequal to his task.

While historians were exploring the written records of the past, a German scholar, Winkelmann, prepared the foundation for the science of archeology by his excavations at Pompeii and Herculaneum. His book on *The History of Art in Antiquity* demonstrated that art shared the processes of change with the other activities of men. Interestingly, German scholars, artists, and architects of the latter eighteenth century adopted Winkelmann's Roman styles as an alternative to the Rococo French modes of the era. Winkelmann provided a flag for the nascent German nationalism.

Another German scholar, Herder, provided an even more significant underpinning for the emerging German consciousness of national identity. He sought the source of cultural differences among the several European communities and found his answers in the mysterious past of the different peoples, their respective village cultures—their identity of self in folklore, song, and custom. It was this village culture concept that gave distinctive form to the idea of "national" culture and allowed each people to make a distinctive contribution to the world community. Herder himself believed that all the differences would be resolved in a new concept of cosmopolitan society, but he gave to the Germans a sense of their uniqueness and meaning that was later to be turned into nationalist slogans and ideals.

Throughout the century, historians and philosophers as well as moralists and scientists came more and more to believe in the idea of progress. Vico, Montesquieu, Voltaire, and many others either explicitly or implicitly proposed that if men would only understand the laws governing human society and systematically use them for human betterment, progress, that is, knowledge, and humanitarian (a new word) respect for human personality and men's institutions, would yield a better world. At the end of the eighteenth century, Condorcet produced a book that developed this optimistic point of view into a law. His *Sketch of the Historical Tableau of the Progress of the Human Spirit* (1794) was almost a bible for the men who wished to believe in a new and better world. Condorcet explained that man's capacity for improvement *(perfectibilité)* is practically unlimited. He did not say that man could reach perfection, but simply that man and society could move in stages, each of which would be an improvement on the conditions of life found in the previous stage. Condorcet identified the process by dividing the history of man into ten stages: (1) tribal society, (2) the pastoral period, (3) agricultural society before the invention of writing, (4) Greek society, which was characterized by progress of the human mind, (5) the age of science before Christianity, (6) the period of decadence caused by Christianity, (7) the age of recovery of learning and the invention of the art of printing, (8) the period from the rise of the art of printing to the early seventeenth century when science freed itself from authority, (9) the period from Descartes to the French Revolution, and finally (10) the age of the future progress of the human spirit. In a sense, Condorcet summed up the beliefs of his generation of philosophers by insisting that once men come to understand the past they can avoid the pitfalls of prejudice, obscuratism, and stupidity. It was an alluring idea. Knowledge would banish the superstition and obscuratism that caused interruptions in the onward march of mankind toward a better civilization. Condorcet the prophet took the pulpit to proclaim what he believed that Condorcet the scholar and historian had discovered about the world of men.

EIGHTEENTH-CENTURY PHILOSOPHY: EMPIRICISM

Galileo and Kepler overthrew Aristotle's physics and Ptolemy's astronomy, but it was left to Locke and his successors to make a direct assault upon metaphysics, and establish a new epistemology. Locke taught that we cannot know anything except through the sensations of sight, smell, taste, sound, and touch, and that any systems to explain the world based upon deductive reasoning would only compound error. Locke did not push these ideas to their logical conclusions, but Berkeley and Hume, who followed him in the eighteenth century, did so without hesitation.

The problem that they faced was simply this: How does man know anything about the world? Berkeley pointed out that our knowledge of the world is limited to our perception of it. Thus the world that we can know exists only in our minds. The real world is therefore problematical: Perhaps if God did not exist to keep it always in view, all material objects would lead a jerky existence, coming into being when someone looked at them, ceasing to exist when no one was about. This is a simplification of his idea, but Berkeley did drive his reader to accept the conclusion that he cannot really know anything outside of himself. This theory was damaging to deductive metaphysics. Hume, however, carried it even further by attacking the idea of causality. All metaphysics of the past rested upon the proposition that if we find that A follows B at all times, we can assume that A is a cause of B. But Hume, with remorseless logic, pointed out that there is no possible way to prove that this is true: there is a *probable* relationship but not an inevitable one. For example Hume agreed that one could say that the sun probably will come up tomorrow, but it is not inevitable. In other words the idea that the future will resemble the past is derived from habit rather than from conclusive argument. Hume forces his reader to admit that truth simply cannot be discovered by deduction of any kind. His arguments were as devastating to earlier philosophers' systems as Galileo's physics had been to those of earlier physicists.

Rousseau tried to solve the problem by admitting that the human mind could not deduce truth, but he insisted that the human heart, the emotional life of man could establish a solid basis for human existence. This idea freed the romantic movement of the first half of the nineteenth century from the cold grasp of Hume's empiricism. Immanuel Kant also admitted that our knowledge of the world cannot transcend our experience with it, but he insisted that we still can know many things. For example we may not able to prove the existence of God, but we can know, *a priori,* that justice is good, that moral values do exist. Kant's idealism allowed nineteenth century thinkers to return to theology with new vigor, nineteenth-century literary figures to develop their romantic movement, and the idealist philosophers (Hegel et al.) to propound their systems. Like other thinkers whose influence went far beyond their own era, Kant cannot be reduced to a few simple ideas. All that this account can do is to point to his importance.

THE CENTURY OF LIGHT

A familiar motif for painters and engravers of the eighteenth century was that of the brilliant sun high in the skies banishing clouds of darkness that always seem about to depart at the sides of the picture. This symbol of optimism represented a great contrast to the attitude of earlier men. Most seventeenth-century writers and thinkers had regarded the world with the pessimistic outlook characteristic of much of Christian thought. Their world was a vale of tears, a period of existence in which not much could be hoped for; any expectations of retribution or righting of injustices had to be postponed for the life beyond the grave. In heaven there would be justice and happiness, but no such things should be expected from life on earth. The evils of the religious and civil wars, the brutal systems of law and justice, the inequalities and humiliations of the world all underlined this pessimism. Men spoke of the future softly, sometimes skeptically or fearfully, for there was no good reason to expect too much from it; it would only repeat the past. In his *Philosophical Dictionary,* Pierre Bayle (1647–1706) almost completely reflects this pessimism; his book tells of the superstitions, brutalities, intolerance, prejudices, and bigotry of the world. The *philosophes* of the eighteenth century read Bayle, yet most of them adopted a positive, optimistic view of the world. Voltaire's *Candide,* which ends an account of the terrible things that happen in the world with the admonition: "Go cultivate your garden," was almost out of tune with the optimism of men who hoped for progress in human affairs and believed that men could achieve happiness on this earth.

There were several reasons for this optimism. The Cartesian philosophy that permeated so much of the thinking of the era painted the world as a machine obeying natural laws. God was its creator, to be sure, but the lawful universe did not require His constant attention. Gradually, whether Descartes would have wished it or not, God ceased to be the governor of the universe who ruled and controlled events on earth; he became, instead, a constitutional monarch who reigned but did not control or govern. Since it was the middle of the eighteenth century before the writers for the important Jesuit journal *Les Mémoires de Trévoux* came to realize how much this philosophy had undermined traditional Christianity, we can understand how widespread this notion had become. Of course, there were many men who recognized that such a cosmology really meant that they could, or perhaps must, develop a new conception of God. By the end of the seventeenth century there was a handful of men who called themselves deists. In general they rejected the Christian tradition and the religion revealed by the Bible in favor of a belief in a god revealed by nature and in a lawful universe being discovered by the scientists. During the eighteenth century, this little company grew to include a large part of the intellectual community; usually, the men who regarded themselves as *philosophes* were also deists. They could not, however, formulate a doctrine or develop a cult. The Masonic Order came close to institutionalizing deism, but its mysticism and rites were only for a few. Indeed, if one takes a look at the religious convictions of the *philosophes,* it soon becomes evident that they represented a fan of opinion ranging from near or absolute atheism to a doctrine, such as Thomas Paine presented in the *Age of Reason,* in which God is discovered in the lawful universe, but he turns out to be much like the

Christian God who in an afterlife rewards and punishes the actions of men. Most of the deists also believed that God was friendly, that the rule of law in the universe was somehow favorable to men; this allowed them to be optimistic.

There were other factors involved in this new optimistic view of the world. The historians and social philosophers discovered and proclaimed the idea of progress. This was a comforting idea, for it allowed men to believe that the future could be better than the past, that man could modify the conditions of his life to obtain a good life on earth. This idea helped to spawn the many secular "isms" of the late eighteenth and nineteenth centuries. These were the secular doctrines for the achievement of happiness on earth through progress, and one could almost say that they became the doctrines of salvation in a future heaven. Society was rapidly becoming secularized.

Finally, it has been pointed out that in the first half of the eighteenth century, social and political thinkers came to understand that the evils of the world around them might be corrected; in the second half of the century, these thinkers became propagandists demanding change. We see the elder Voltaire thundering against religious intolerance and bigotry, while others demanded reforms of the laws, of prisons, of care for the insane, of economic regulations, and of a host of other things that obviously needed reform. This belief that reform could really change the conditions of life for man, could lead to a better system, became the oasis for the "isms" of the next century. It was necessary for an optimistic view of the world. Thus, it was one of the reasons that eighteenth-century men so often spoke in a major key.

Optimism is probably always a bit naïve, but as this optimistic attitude filtered down in the society to the people who had learned to read, it became almost a simplistic formula announcing that man had finally conquered the problems of knowledge and therefore would soon be able to solve all things. These people, however, wanted to acquire this knowledge as easily and as quickly as possible. Perhaps their attitude is not unusual; they "like to know things, but they want to learn quickly, and they do not like hard work. That no doubt accounts for the new methods that come out every day, and for all the short cuts to knowledge we see about." This quotation from the *Journal des Savants,* November 1749, is representative of the proliferation of popular accounts, abridgments of serious works, and digests of important ideas that purported to provide readers with the understanding of the world that philosophers, scientists, and scholars of the era had finally achieved. This also was the time for "handbooks" of all kinds. Some furnished their readers with whole libraries of data; others explained "fully" the arts, commerce and trade, geography, or science. The creators of these materials were not very interested in probing into the nature or the processes of things; it was enough to supply "facts" that would assure their readers of knowledge without raising any disturbing questions. Booksellers and intellectuals were quick to take advantage of this "desire to know"; a steady stream of these compendiums of knowledge flowed from the presses to enlighten the European world.

The most impressive of these was the great *Encyclopedia* edited by

169

Diderot and d'Alembert. The first volume, which appeared in 1751, announced a grandiose plan to provide its readers with a compendium of all knowledge. Its publishers assured prospective buyers that this *Encyclopedia* would, in fact, give them access to the truths of the age and supplant ancient texts. "In these days," it announced "when philosophy is advancing with giant strides, subduing to her uses everything she needs, when she speaks in such commanding tones, and we are beginning to cast off the yoke of precedent and example and obey the dictates of reason, we can scarcely discover a single elementary work which can be regarded as wholly satisfactory. . . . Even Aristotle and Plato are looked on a little doubtfully, and the time has come when works that still enjoy the highest reputation will soon be shedding some of their glory or even be falling into complete neglect, so rapidly is reason progressing."

It was no small matter to insist that the new *Encyclopedia* would fill the gap. Its editors and contributors wished to prepare a book that, "should all the libraries of the world be destroyed, this work alone would preserve everything essential so that human knowledge would not be impaired by the catastrophe." And, indeed, these men actually attempted to achieve that goal. They proposed to lay before their readers a rational outline of all human knowledge, knowledge of the world and of man, of the arts and letters, of divine science. But the prime considerations were man and his achievements. The outline divided all knowledge into three broad areas: Memory, Imagination, and Reason. Memory was the basis for human and natural history, for understanding the functioning of the world. Imagination was fundamental to man's artistic achievements in letters, architecture, and the fine arts. From Reason came philosophy and theology, man's rationalization of the world and his being. The *Encyclopedia* also promised to provide its readers with an understanding of the arts and crafts; it was to include discussions and pictures that would explain how things were made—all things, from glass to cannon, from flour to ships or paper. It was a prodigious task.

The secular, homocentric orientation, the skeptical tones of some of the first articles, the vaguely revolutionary attitudes struck by the editors very early alerted the conservatives to the dangers to traditional Christian doctrines inherent in this new *Summa.* There were objections to its publication, but these were eventually overcome in one way or another so that the whole project did finally become available to anyone who could afford a great monetary outlay. The *Encyclopedia* in its final form had seventeen large quarto volumes of text and eleven volumes of illustrative plates. Today, it is still a monument to the eighteenth century; in it we find the civilization of western Europe of that period spread out before us in pictures and words in great detail.

Diderot and d'Alembert were its editors and they wrote a large number of the articles, but the *Encyclopedia* was, in fact, the work of a generation of intellectuals. Over a hundred and thirty men were involved: lawyers, doctors, professors, priests, officials, industrialists, engineers, men of commerce, writers, and scientists—in short, the elite of the bourgeois society of the century. Like Laplace, who at the end of the century produced a great astronomical treatise that "completely" explained the universe for its readers, these men believed that they were giving their readers the final word on a myriad of subjects. The *Encyclopedia* defined man as "a sentient, thinking, intelligent being, moving freely over the earth. He is above all the other animals and exercises dominion over them; gregarious in his habits, he has invented various arts and sciences, and has virtues and vices peculiar to his species. He has appointed rulers and made laws for himself. . . . " Such a creature could "know all that can be known" and rationally could manage his own affairs. No one should derogate either the importance of the *Encyclopedia* or the sincerity and integrity of its editors and authors; it is at once a monument to the achievements of the Enlightenment and a warning to later generations not to assume a simplistic attitude toward the world and its questions.

SUGGESTED READING

Two books by Paul Hazard provide a stimulating survey of European thought in the late seventeenth and eighteenth centuries: *The European Mind, 1680–1715* (1963) and *European Thought in the Eighteenth Century* (1963). The best statement of the history of science is A. R. Hall, *The Scientific Revolution, 1500–1800* (1954), but the thoughtful student should also consult E. A. Burtt, *The Metaphysical Foundations of Modern Science* (1955) and A. W. Whitehead, *Science and the Modern World* (1948). Stuart Hampshire (ed.), *The Age of Reason* (1956), and Isaiah Berlin, *The Age of the Enlightenment* (1956) are useful as illustration of the thought of the era. R. H. Popkin (ed.) and Pierre Bayle, *Historical and Critical Dictionary, Selections* (1965) is important both for the items from Bayle and for the introductory essay. A. Wolf, *A History of Science, Technology, and Philosophy in the Sixteenth and Seventeenth Centuries* (1961) is more like an encyclopedia than a history, but it is still valuable. R. R. Palmer, *Catholics and Unbelievers in Eighteenth Century France,* (1966) is provocative. The volumes in the *Rise of Modern Europe* series (see bibliography for chapters II, III, and V) by Friedrich, Nussbaum, Wolf, Roberts, Dorn, and Gershoy each have interesting chapters on intellectual history. Ernst Cassirer, *The Philosophy of the Enlightenment* (1955), Frank Manuel, *The Eighteenth Century Confronts the Gods* (1967), and Peter Gay, *The Party of Humanity, Essays in the French Enlightenment* (1964) present interesting interpretations. Carl Becker, *The Heavenly City of the Eighteenth Century Philosophers* (1959) may not coincide with much of modern scholarship, but it is a superb and charming essay.

ROBERT HOOKE (1635–1703)

Robert Hooke was born at Freshwater on the Isle of Wight, where his father was a minister of the parish. After working for a short time for the famous painter Sir Peter Lely, he went to Westminster School and then on to Christ Church, Oxford, where he worked his way through the university as a servant. After 1655 he became associated with the chemist Robert Boyle and attracted enough attention to himself by his clever mechanical inventions to be appointed curator of experiments to the Royal Society; in 1663 he was elected to that important company of scientists and learned men. Like so many men of humble origins who had to struggle for recognition in a society where ancestry often counted much more than ability, Hooke tended to be difficult, cantankerous, and at times quite rude. All his life, he felt that his merits were not adequately recognized, and he was sure that others received credit for things that he did simply because they had powerful connections. He never married, but his niece, Mrs. Grace Hooke, lived with him for many years, and her death in 1687 caused him deep affliction.

This was a man with immense ingenuity and many varied interests. He wrote importantly about astronomy, watchmaking, physics, music, glass manufacture, the barometer and climatology, the microscope and the microanimals to be seen through it, mechanics, heat (he set the zero on the thermometer at the freezing point of water), navigation, and many other things. In 1665 he was on the verge of proclaiming the theory of gravitation propounded by Newton. Further, his experiments with air led him to the verge of discovering oxygen, and a posthumously published paper suggested that rock formations and fossil remains were actually a calendar of the earth's history. Perhaps no one of his contemporaries had as many different interests or developed as many different experiments. He even proposed a plan for the rebuilding of London after the great fire; it won much approval, but Wren's project was eventually preferred.

Hooke was unattractive in appearance; hunch-backed, excessively thin, usually sickly—he made a sorry picture even in an age when bad teeth, rickets, malnutrition, goiters, and other evils marred many people. He spent most of his life as a professor of geometry at Gresham College, but he also occasionally took employment as a surveyor. He became involved in a serious lawsuit to recover his professional salary, and yet on his death he left a long-unopened iron chest containing several thousand pounds, perhaps income from his surveying. In spite of his reputation as a difficult person, his colleagues in the Royal Society honored him for his achievements, and he was made doctor of medicine at the Doctors Commons (1691). Even so, Robert Hooke always felt that others were preferred before him, that others were honored for discoveries that he had made first, and that life had not given him what he deserved. ■

Chapter 5

The Eighteenth Century: Unity or Diversity as the Source of European Power

ECONOMIC STABILITY AND CHANGE

The traveler in eighteenth-century Europe would have found more in common with life in the fifteenth century than with life in the twentieth. The vast majority of the people still lived in small villages, usually in the vicinity of a lord's manor house or château; their agricultural methods were hardly changed from those of the preceding three or four hundred years. The *Encyclopedia* (see Chapter Four) might show us plates on which relatively complex agricultural machinery of all kinds were portrayed, but the traveler would have had great difficulty finding such machinery in the countryside.

The land was still owned by landlords who were either the descendants of the military nobility of past centuries or wealthy townsmen who had bought the estates in hopes of someday seeing their families become members of the nobility of the sword. These landlords still possessed feudal rights over the villagers who used the mill, the wine press, the bakeovens; however, they often commuted the corvée (labor) duties to money payments. In the west where most of the peasants were free, the lord collected a *sens,* or quit-rent owed by the land rather than by the peasant—but, of course, paid by the peasant. In the east, the peasants were more likely to be serfs, bound to the land by a servile contract. The peasants were still allowed to pasture their animals on the common lands and on the fields after the harvest, and they had the right to cut wood, collect wild honey, forage, and do other things relative to the traditions of the place. But the landlord reserved the right to hunt the wild animals, and he meted out a rough sort of justice and provided whatever police service existed. Moreover, the landlord usually reserved for himself large tracts of his land, which he had farmed by an overseer and hired labor.

Some differences from fifteenth-century life were evident, however. In parts of eighteenth-century England and the Netherlands, more advanced agricultural methods were in use. In some cases, the landlords themselves, anxious to increase their incomes, experimented with new methods or

EUROPEAN TRADE ROUTES—EARLY 18TH CENTURY

ATLANTIC

OCEAN

NORTH
SEA

BALTIC
SEA

BLACK SEA

CASPIAN
SEA

MEDITERRANEAN SEA

To China
to India, East Indies and China
to East Africa, India, East Indies and China

Caravan routes to Timbuktu,
To African slave coasts
to colonies in North and South America

Perm
Kazan
Astrakhan
St. Petersburg
Moscow
Smolensk
Kiev
Odessa
Riga
Königsberg
Warsaw
Christiana
Stockholm
Copenhagen
Hamburg
Berlin
Leipzig
Breslau
Cracow
Prague
Vienna
Augsberg
Buda
Pest
Venice
Belgrade
Edinburgh
Dublin
Liverpool
Bristol
London
La Havre
Amsterdam
Cologne
Paris
Geneva
Milan
Lyons
Genoa
Marseilles
Barcelona
Le Rochelle
Bordeaux
Madrid
Toledo
Seville
Lisbon
Tangier
Sijimasa
Algiers
Tunis
Tripoli
Bengasi
Rome
Naples
Constantinople
Trebizond
Teheran
Baghdad
Basra
Aleppo
Damascus
Cairo
Alexandria

174

machinery; in others, the land was rented to farmers who exploited it as capitalist entrepreneurs. In England, too, the practice of enclosing the common lands for the use of the lord forced many of the peasants to sell their holdings since they could not make a living without the use of the common land and the right to pasture in the fields after harvest. Much of this land was then given over to the raising of sheep. Nonetheless, the traveler in eighteenth-century Europe would have been struck by the forces that resisted change; he could not have seen how many of the old families had been forced to sell to the new ones; he would merely have sensed that century-old patterns of rural life were relatively unchanged and unchanging.

This apparent stability, however, was in part an illusion. Sometime after about 1730, the population in nearly every one of the European states began to increase. After almost two centuries during which the total population of the continent had unquestionably been in decline, and, in some places, in precipitous decline, the trend was reversed. It was not so apparent at first, but after 1760 no one could miss the fact that the villages no longer could support all the children that managed to survive and that the old cities of Europe were beginning to fill up and new ones were coming into existence. If modern estimates are nearly correct, by the end of the century the population of England, France, and Germany had increased almost 50 percent over that of 1730. It was no accident that at the opening of the nineteenth century, Malthus proposed his melancholy laws about population and food supplies.[1]

This change in the population had many obvious, and many more hidden, implications for European society. The amount of land under cultivation did not appreciably increase; the cities grew in size and spread out into suburbs; the walls were pulled down and often made into boulevards; and the value of urban property went up rapidly. There was an abundant supply of cheap labor for the work that had to be done, and, as Malthus was to predict, the workers lived largely on a subsistence level while the capitalist entrepreneurs and the landlords became rich. All accounts of late eighteenth-century Europe tell of the swarms of mendicants both in the country and in the cities. Europe's poor looked something like the poor in the underdeveloped countries of our twentieth-century world, where population explosions have outpaced the means of producing the necessities of life.

Another extremely important factor for change was the explosive increase in the amount of commerce in European cities. Most striking was the commerce of England, but, in a way, all the port cities from Seville to Riga or the new Russian capital of St. Petersburg burgeoned with the new commerce. One of the most important of the "new" commodities that flooded the market was sugar. It had been known for more than a century, but the great burst of economic activity in the Caribbean islands—whence most of

---

[1]Malthus explained that population increases at a geometric ratio (2, 4, 8, 16, etc.) while food production can increase only at an arithmetic ratio (2, 4, 6, 8, etc.). This fact seemed to condemn the human race to a melancholy, indeed disastrous, future. The importation of food from oversea lands saved nineteenth century Europe from experiencing Malthus' predictions.

the supply originated—came after 1713. All Europe wanted sugar; it was the exciting new taste. The production of sugar, however, was dependent upon a supply of cheap labor—slaves. The native Indians did not make good slaves, so black men were imported from Africa where there seemed to be an endless supply of poor wretches captured in war or by raids and brought to the coast to be sold by Negroes or Arabs. The commodity most in demand in exchange for human flesh was rum, and rum was a by-product of the sugar industry: When the molasses was shipped to Europe from the islands, it was made into rum and sugar. The slaves needed to be fed and clothed, but cheap food was available in the form of the poorest grade of cod caught off the Newfoundland banks, and corn from North America, and cheap cloth came from Europe. This commerce powered by the European demand for sugar resulted in the establishment of refineries in many of the coast towns of Europe. It also led to the involuntary migration of black men to the Caribbean and to South America where their descendants still live.

Two other "new" commodities were almost equally important in the new commerce: tea and coffee. In the eighteenth century, these beverages became popular throughout much of Europe; they were expensive, exotic, fashionable. Tea and coffee houses became centers for conversation; everywhere stores sprang up to sell "colonial" goods: tea, coffee, sugar, cocoa, and spices. Most of these items came from Asia, and in the eighteenth century the Asiatic trade was in the hands of the great India companies of England, France, and the Netherlands. Their ships, armed with cannons and powered by sail, plowed the oceans and dominated the ports of India and the East Indies. Men could go to the Orient for a few years and return to Europe laden with personal wealth. After the mid-century, conflicts severely limited the role played by the French; the English and their satellites, the Dutch, who operated by English sufferance, largely controlled the trade in spices, coffee, and tea.

Chinese art objects and silks also loomed large in the commerce with Asia. The eighteenth century was a period when the rich became fabulously wealthy, and the luxury trade expanded like mushrooms in a wet summer. The new rage in architecture and art in Europe was the French Rococo, and to the joy of the importers, this style evoked a taste for things Chinese: *le goût chinois*. Chinese vases, brasses, screens, pictures, sculpture, and, of course, tableware of all kinds became the fashion. European manufacturers attempted to imitate both the designs and the materials of Chinese pottery and porcelains, but one has only to visit a museum showing both their reproductions and the Chinese originals to see the artistic gap between the two. This taste for things Chinese led to another problem. There were not many European commodities that could be sold on the Chinese market. For instance, the English were the first to discover that the Chinese would buy opium raised in India; at the end of the century this became the basis for a profitable three-cornered trade among Europe, India, and China. This trade lasted until the nineteenth-century Chinese reformers decided that opium was a dangerous drug. But that is another story; it did not alter the exchanges of the eighteenth century.

HUDSON
BAY

HUDSON'S BAY CO.
1670 Br.

CANADA
Fr., 1763 Br.

NEWFOUNDLAND

NOVA SCOTIA

LOUSIANA
Fr., 1763 Sp.,
1800 Fr.

UNITED

STATES

THIRTEEN COLONIES
Br., 1783 U.S.

ATLANTIC

OCEAN

FLORIDA
Sp., 1763 Br., 1783 Sp.

NEW

SPAIN

BAHAMA IS.
Br.

CUBA

BR. HONDURAS
1786

JAMAICA
Br.

HAITI

PUERTO
RICO

Sp., 1665 Fr.   Sp., 1795 Fr.

MARTINIQUE
Fr.

CARIBBEAN   SEA

Neth., 1796 Br.

Neth., 1799 Br.

GUIANA   Fr.

PACIFIC

NEW

GRANADA

OCEAN

B R A Z I L
Portugal

**COLONIAL EMPIRES IN THE NEW WORLD
AT THE END OF THE 18TH CENTURY**

P
E
R
U

LA PLATA

Portugal

Spain

Great Britain

France

DRAKE STRAIT

177

While mentioning sugar, tea, and opium as items of commerce, we should not forget that much of the trade was in the many other items that crowded the docks of London, Liverpool, Amsterdam, Bremen, and the other ports of Europe. Coal from Newcastle, tin from Cornwall, iron from Sweden, cloth from all parts of Europe—but particularly from Flanders, Italy, and England—perfumes, cutlery, jewels, iron pots, bullets, dried and pickled fish, wheat, hammers, saws, cannon (from Sweden and Germany), whale oil, lemons, and oranges would constitute only a partial list. In the eighteenth century, the English played the role that the Dutch had had a hundred years before. English ships controlled a lion's share of the carrying trade and the deep sea commerce of Europe, but other countries also sent their men and their ships to sea to share in the expanding commercial opportunities of the era.

In England this commerce touched, in one way or another, nearly everyone who was important in the society. Merchants and sea captains of the port cities, merchants and manufacturers in the interior, people with money to invest in the India Company or other commercial ventures, noblemen and squires whose sons were in the royal navy or who themselves held commissions in the army or went out to India or America as company officials or political officers—all these people were involved in England's commercial ventures. In France, despite a class "feeling" that presumably prevented the nobles from sharing in the profits of trade, the situation was almost the same; noble as well as bourgeois money was invested in commerce, and noblemen as well as bourgeois figures found employment in the colonial and commercial ventures. The same could be said of the United Netherlands—with the additional observation that so much Dutch money was invested in English ventures and in English state obligations that the vital interests of the wealthy in the United Netherlands were deeply involved in English enterprises all over the world.

This eighteenth-century commercial expansion was unquestionably the most important political, economic, and social force operating in European society. The rapid development of cities, the ever larger numbers of poor people, the extended demands for Oriental and Western goods, the development of huge fortunes, the inevitable rivalries among trading nations that led to great wars—all operated to alter the structure of European life. The countryside may have seemed unchanged and unchanging, but the impulses from population growth and expanding commercial activity were transforming Europe.

A EUROPEAN NATION, A UNIFIED EUROPEAN CULTURE, OR EUROPEAN DIVERSITY?

The word "cosmopolitan" was first coined in the eighteenth century. German philosophers assured their students that they lived in the world of Europe, not just in Germany. French *philosophes* who believed that there was a European community that transcended their homeland could hail Frederick the Great's victory over French armies because he, too, was a *philosophe* who spoke their language and shared their culture. Jean Jacques Rousseau announced: "Today, there are no longer Frenchmen, Germans, Spanish, or even English; there are only Europeans." The cosmopolitan spirits of the eighteenth century were ready to see the world around them as a republic made up of various states in one or another form of development.

The illusion of European unity and cosmopolitan society was partially the result of the seemingly all-pervasive influence of French culture and the French language. What the philosophers did not understand was the fact that the influence of this cosmopolitan culture was limited to the elite of the society: the men of letters, the wealthy nobles and bourgeois, and the courts. The mass of men lived as they had always lived and spoke the dialects that their fathers and mothers had taught them.

There were many reasons for the extraordinary conquest made by French culture in the eighteenth century. In the first place, the French language emerged as a facile vehicle for expression; with the possible exception of English, it had achieved a stable literary form before the other European languages. The seventeenth-century French playwrights, philosophers, essayists, and other men of letters, aided by the labors of the French Academy, stabilized the language and gave it elegance. Eighteenth-century French was a language that could be learned relatively easily by men whose mother tongue was another language; this was not as true of the other languages of Europe. They would have to wait until literary men with a sense of style could give them elegance and precision.

But precision and clarity alone could never account for the empire won by the French language. The court of Louis XIV undoubtedly was an important factor. Men from all Europe marvelled at the splendor and elegance of Versailles, and the sophisticated sought to imitate it. In the eighteenth century, princesses of the French and Spanish Bourbon families married into many of the other courts in Europe, bringing with them French retainers and French ways. The expulsion of the Huguenot community in the late seventeenth century also contributed to the exportation of the French language, for the exiled communities kept their native tongue and supplied Europe with French language teachers. When the Revolution of 1789 sent another large body of Frenchmen into exile, they were surprised to find excellent French spoken in Berlin, Vienna, Munich, and elsewhere in Germany.

Whatever the reasons, French became the first language for many Europeans and the second for all educated ones. German, Spanish, and Italian scholars and men of letters either wrote in French or had their materials translated into French. Rulers like Frederick the Great spoke and wrote only French; to him German was a peasant's language. Lessing, Goethe, and Schiller, who were to make German into a literary vehicle, considered writing in French, and all spoke the language fluently. Leibniz wrote in French, the publications of the Berlin Academy were in French, a treaty between Turkey and Russia was written in French, and Maria

Theresa of Austria and her numerous children corresponded with each other in French. A German nobleman remarked: "I speak French like Diderot, German like my nurse." Of Tolstoy's characters in *War and Peace,* only the peasants habitually used Russian; the upper class spoke French. But for all its international usage, French was spoken only by the elite of the society: princes and their ministers, diplomats, men of the court, nobles, and scholars and men of letters. In the eighteenth century, these were the people who counted, and, in a way, they really did form a European culture that was general and cosmopolitan in nature. Before the century was over, however, a rebellion against this empire of the French language was underway, particularly in Germany where the university community was beginning to form a German culture strong enough to contest the French.

Accompanying the expansion of the French language were many other aspects of French civilization. Again, Versailles was the model. All over Europe princes built châteaux in the mode of Versailles, and noblemen and wealthy bourgeois figures built châteaux in the mode of the châteaux built by their peers in France and furnished them *à la mode française.* Even as far away as Washington, D.C., Versailles' great parks and formal vistas became the model for the city planners.

The places and the boulevards built under Louis xiv, and also under Louis xv and xvi when the walls of the city of Paris were razed, became models for all Europe. Modern Paris, one of the most beautiful cities in the world, began to take shape; throughout the eighteenth century, as today, it was a mecca for tourists, wealthy landlords, and commercial entrepreneurs who came from all over Europe and the Americas and took back with them "French taste" and a desire to imitate French city planning.

Even in the seventeenth century, French styles of clothing had invaded neighboring lands—particularly women's dress, hair styles, and make-up. In the eighteenth century, the exaggerations in men's dress of the earlier period tended to disappear in France; men's wigs became smaller and the cane replaced the sword; Europe followed suit. Women, however, reserved the right to change: Toward the end of the century, French women piled their hair so high that the hair was about one third the height of the woman: Europe followed suit. In men's costume, however, the English style became modish after England's great victories in the Seven Years' War.

French cooking and serving also became the mode and has remained so ever since. French manners and, critics insisted, French morals, also invaded all Europe. The French salon as a literary or political institution or merely a social gathering set the style for all Europe. Toward the end of the century, the English "tea" was merged with the French salon, but the basic pattern remained French. It was small wonder that the Italian Marquis Carraccioli could write a book with the title *Paris, the Model for Foreign Nations, or French Europe.* What was even more interesting, however, was the fact that this French cultural conquest came during the century when French military power was proving no match for the English and the Germans, rather than at the period when Louis xiv seemed to dominate all Europe.

Eighteenth-century noblemen all over Europe regarded themselves as near sovereign, or at least as relatively independent of their ruler in their personal lives. They did not hesitate to take service in another kingdom, even when that service meant they would have to fight against their rightful king. Eugene of Savoy governed the emperor's war council, and after waging war against Louis XIV, his rightful king, he made war on the Turks and pushed the Hapsburg empire to its furthest limits. Marshal Saxe, a natural son of August, king of Poland and elector of Saxony, served Louis XV so splendidly that the grateful king presented him with the Château of Chambord, a royal gift if ever there was one. The princes of Savoy and Saxony were only the most renowned of the men who served where they wished; many other noblemen occupied lesser posts in the service of princes other than their own. The great noblemen, whether they happened to be French or Spanish grandees, Polish or Hungarian magnates, German barons or princes, or English lords, tended to see themselves as a community and tended to regard the bourgeois class with contempt. The noblemen had more in common with each other than with their more humble fellow subjects. It was even true that royal officials of relatively humble birth were regarded contemptuously by the great nobles, notwithstanding the fact that the officials often exercised real power while the noblemen's power was being eroded. In England, where younger sons became "commoners" and the squires and country gentry very often were the children of retired merchants, it was not uncommon for bourgeois figures to rise easily to social position; men of great wealth, the nabobs, for example, who had made fortunes in India, could and did mix on equal terms with the lords. But on the continent, a bourgeois family that managed to purchase a patent of nobility usually had to wait two or three generations before being accepted as equal by neighboring nobility. In Germany and farther east, where the number of wealthy commoners was much smaller, their social plight was even more insecure.

The bourgeois class, below the nobility and usually regarded contemptuously by them, was less influenced by French culture than the social elite had been. In Germany, there were patrician bourgeois families in the commercial cities whose sons went to the universities and returned to manage the family businesses or joined the bureaucracy of one or another of the princes. As the commercial expansion reached into central Europe, these families tended to increase in number. Their culture was German, and they were educated in German universities where their professors, also men of bourgeois origin, lectured in German and tended to be resentful of the French language hegemony. These German universities were interesting institutions. With so many princes to patronize them, Germany had more universities per capita than any other part of Europe, and the prestige of these schools grew rapidly in the eighteenth century as the professors freed themselves from clerical control and established norms of academic freedom. The men of the German enlightenment—Herder, Winkelmann, Goethe, Lessing, Schiller, and a host of lesser lights—were all, at one time or another, university professors. This was in sharp contrast to the situation in either France or England, where practically none of the intellectuals who made the century bright were university professors. The German professors at first thought of themselves as cosmopolitan because there was no German fatherland, but they were the men who sharpened the German language and prepared the German bourgeois and lesser nobility to take a place in society. Toward the end of the eighteenth century, these men also developed intellectual tools to resist the "Frenchification" of their culture. They were responsible for the excellent translation of Shakespeare into German and for the use of Winkelmann's excavation (see Chapter Four) to popularize English and Latin, rather than French, culture.

Similar moods developed in both Italy and Spain where there were men who remembered that the Italian Renaissance and, later, Spanish Baroque cultures had once had prestige comparable to that of eighteenth-century French civilization. Critics pointed out the faults of the French: frivolous, sexually irregular, blabbermouthed, untrustworthy, dishonest, etc. Such faults were obviously shared by a considerable segment of the human race, but now they were attributed solely to the French. The critics also decried the invasion of French words into German, Italian, and Spanish speech.

However, the greatest resistance to the hegemony of French culture came from the people themselves. The bourgeoisie throughout Europe carried on the culture they had received from their parents, and there were few indeed whose genealogy did not include at least one peasant as a grandfather. The words for good and evil that had been common in the past continued to be honored by most of these people, and this was a bulwark against the encroaching French modes, manners, and language. As the economy expanded, this class also expanded—much more rapidly than the elite. It was soon to demand recognition of its own national status and the rejection of foreign ways.

Europe, then, was only superficially a united community with a European culture. The language and religion of both the pre- and post-Christian eras, the history, and the vagaries of geography and climate had divided the European peoples into a number of subcultures in which the differences were too great to be smoothed out by the French language and the civilization of Paris and Versailles.

VARIETY AND DIVERSITY IN EIGHTEENTH-CENTURY EUROPE

It has often been said that the eighteenth-century traveler who visited central and eastern Europe moved eastward in space and backward in time. This generalization, like the one about a "European nation," is subject to some criticism. The peoples of central and eastern Europe did live far from the market economy that was changing so much of the society of the western part of the continent, and yet the same generalization could have applied also to many of the hinterland villages of England or France. The

European peoples shared in the market economy to different degrees, but this alone was not the basis for the variations among European societies. History, geography, and climate as well must share, with the market, as factors creating the differences that the traveler encountered crossing the continent.

The United Kingdom. The Act of Union of 1707 united the kingdoms of England and Scotland into a single state with a population of about six million; by the end of the eighteenth century, that population was over nine million with about one-fourth of the total living in and around the port of London. There were, in fact, two societies living on the island: the urban commercial people who inhabited the port cities and the areas from which the sea could be reached by river transportation, and the rural men who lived on the land, rarely saw anything of the market beyond a peddler's pack, and spent their whole lives within a few miles of the places where they were born.

The city of London was the political and commercial capital of the kingdom. The other port cities that traded with London, and to a lesser degree with the colonies and the outside world, were tied to the capital city by water transportation and the bonds that make a commercial society. London was the center. There were the shipowners and sea captains, the bankers, the brokers of insurance, stocks, and commodities, the headquarters of the great trading companies that ranged from India to the Levant, Hudson's bay, and Archangel, the merchant manufacturers whose connections involved the labors of peasant spinners, weavers, dyers, nail makers, and other domestic industrial tasks; there were also the hundreds of shops that made everything from watches to hammers, from pins to cheap jewelry, from soap to beer. London was the home of the lawyers, the publicists, the journalists, and the political jobbers as well as of the thieves, beggars, and carriers of burdens. It was a dynamic society bent on the rapid accumulation of wealth, and the declining interest rate that dropped from 5 percent in 1700 to 3 percent in 1750 is eloquent evidence of success.

The wealth of this commercial England was unevenly divided. There were a few very rich whose control over the shipyards, warehouses, and commercial enterprises yielded huge profits. There were a few others who were in the process of joining this select group, for it was possible for an enterprising man to make his fortune. But the great mass of the people in this commercial society were dreadfully poor, exploited, and, if the evidence of the day is correct, often driven to despair. In the eighteenth century, these little people did not count; they were ignorant and inarticulate; their occasional riots were easily suppressed. This was an era for the rich. The articulated goals of society were theirs; they controlled the political as well as the economic levers of power, and they exhibited a callous disregard for the "rabble" that made up the mass of men.

Rural England was also a society in which the rich were the ones who counted. At the apex of the rural society were the titled lords who owned large tracts of land and whose holdings increased considerably during the eighteenth century. Their titles often enough were relatively new, of seventeenth-century origin, and their Whig politics led them to make alliances with the urban politicians against the squires who were their rivals for power in the countryside. This latter group, the country gentry, was the ruling class in the country and had considerable influence in Parliament. Some of the squires were as well educated as the great lords and owned lands almost as extensive as any in the country; others were ignorant "gentlemen" with a few hundred acres and much pretension to quality. The great lords were often appointed as lords lieutenant in the country; the squires were the justices of the peace, the sheriffs, the overseers of the poor, the forests, etc. The squires were usually in close alliance with the clergy of the established church to control the activities of the peasants below them. The third group in the country was made up of yeomen farmers—who either owned their own land or rented land from a neighboring lord—copyholders with small plots, or landless peasants deprived of their living and forced to sell what land they had because of enclosures by great noblemen who turned the land from agriculture to sheep raising. Some historians have insisted that these were the people who migrated to the American mainland colonies in the eighteenth century as indentured servants of one kind or another.

The country gentlemen stood for king and church and could be counted on to be Tory in their politics, but the vast majority of them were not seduced by the efforts of the Stuart pretender to return to England. In 1715, and again in the 1740's, when the Stuart "king" attempted to return, country gentlemen watched the process from their manor houses rather than from the ranks of the Stuart army. They may have been dissatisfied with the way the country was managed, yet they allowed the Whig ministers to buy their votes with offices and favors. They ruled the countryside and allowed the Whigs to rule the kingdom.

The role of the established church in English life was very important. The lower clergy tended to be members of the gentry class and usually identified with it. They profited from the Test and Corporation Acts that kept non-Anglicans from political office. The upper clergy tended to be Whigs for they received their sees from the crown; thus, the spiritual lords could be counted upon to support the government. The dissenter churches had a very different position. In the rural communities where they existed, they were regarded as possibly traitorous groups; in the urban centers they were tolerated, but if their members wished to hold office they had to take communion in the established church. Thus, dissenters were second-class citizens, but they were usually better educated in their private schools than the rank and file of the established church, and their commercial activity gave them wealth that made them attractive allies for the great landed proprietors against the squirarchy.

The eighteenth century in England began with the death of Queen Anne in 1714. George I, elector of Hanover and great grandson of James I, mounted the throne. The new king had been Marlborough's companion in arms in the recent war, and he understood that the Whig politicians had assured his right to the throne. Though the Tories did not support the

Pretender's effort to unseat George I in 1715, their hostility to his Hanoverian advisors and his friendship with the Whig chiefs both helped to exclude them from power. In 1714 the king of England was the executive authority in the kingdom; he had the right to appoint his ministers and to seek advice wherever he wished. In theory, he held a veto over legislation of Parliament; in practice, that power was not used. Since the first two Hanoverian kings understood that they could govern England best if they called to their service men who had firm positions in the House of Commons, their "royal command" became, in effect, an invitation to exercise power in the direction that suited the minister and his friends in Parliament. Thus, George I and George II were constitutional monarchs whose interpretation of the revolution of 1688 caused them to call on the leaders of the dominant party in the House of Commons to be their ministers. The Tory theorists argued that the constitutional forms of William III better suited the meaning of that revolution; William had called on nonparty ministers or men from both parties to make the executive independent of the Parliament. George III, who came to the throne in 1760, tried to govern in the Tory sense—only to find that it could no longer be done.

The practice of appointing ministers who could deliver a majority in Parliament had some interesting results for the unwritten constitution of England. In the first place, when elections were close, the ministers had the opportunity to corrupt voters who controlled boroughs that no longer really represented any considerable number of the electorate. Some of these boroughs had become the property of great lords; others were controlled by a tight oligarchy; in short, corruption was easy. Of course, if any great majority of the electors disapproved of their policy, the ministers would be unable to corrupt so large a number. Secondly, appointment of ministers led to an effort to impose a solidarity upon them and to force the king to consult only with them. By law, the king governed the country, but in fact he had to keep his programs within the limits approved by a majority of Parliament and draw his ministers from the narrow body of men with influence in the Parliament. This did not mean that he shared his power with the people of England; he shared it only with a few thousand of the most important men in the kingdom.

George III, the grandson of George II, became king in 1760. He was the first of the Hanoverians to consider himself more of an Englishman than a German, and from childhood he was destined to be king. His personal friends were Tories, and he was resolved to revert to the political solutions of William III, that is, to call to his ministry whomever he wished without regard for party. This pleased many who objected to the system of corruption that had characterized the governments of previous parliamentary leaders from Walpole through Newcastle, but it was not easy for the king to place himself in the position of a "crowned Lord Newcastle." The Revolution of 1688 and the events of the years following had effectively altered the position of the king so that a return to earlier modes of action, unless done more subtly than George III was able to do it, simply could not work. Unhappily for George III, his personality and character provoked a major crisis for his system and he had the misfortune to become involved in a dispute with the colonists in America at the same time that he attempted to revise the role of the king at home. By the end of the century, Parliament again reasserted itself in directing the conflict with revolutionary France.

The second half of the eighteenth century also witnessed an important development in the economic life of the kingdom that was to assure England's economic primacy for the next century. After several false starts that produced machines too inefficient to be useful, the Watt and Bolton steam engine came into being. At first used primarily to pump water, it gradually replaced the wind-and-water power that had traditionally provided motive force for many sorts of manufacturing. This engine came on the scene at almost exactly the same time as new machinery for spinning and weaving cloth came into being. Since the steam engine could provide power not dependent upon unpredictable wind or water, it was not long before many manufacturing processes were modified to make use of steam power.

Perhaps equally important was the Darby process for making iron that blossomed in the second half of the century. The English iron industry had flourished in the early seventeenth century only to be blighted by the lack of wood for charcoal. By the opening of the eighteenth century, most of the iron used in England came from Sweden. However, when the process of forging iron with coke and limestone was developed, the iron ore in England could again be used, for there was an abundance of coal on the island, and iron industries could give up their peripatetic behavior and settle down at the heads of the coal pits to develop the first real heavy industry. After 1760, a cheap iron was available for all sorts of things that formerly had been made of wood: Everything from ships to coffins, from bridges to lathes was now made of cast iron. Along with the new steam power, the revitalization of the iron industry proclaimed the coming of a new era in which England's commercial supremacy would be reinforced by industrial power.

Bourbon France. Louis XIV died in 1715 leaving his great grandson, a child of five years, a throne and a political system that had placed the kingdom of France at the summit of European affairs; in two wars the kingdom had been humbled, but only as a result of the efforts of practically all the rest of the European states. This regime was solidly based upon the idea of divine right, and it was equipped with a system of councils, ministerial bureaucracies, and provincial administrations under intendants, all responsible to and directed by the king. It was true that many overlapping jurisdictions of the Church, the *parlements,* and the seignorial and town administrations created friction for the machine so that it might be possible for the king to command but not always possible for him to be obeyed. However, despite this, Louix XIV left his great-grandson an army, a ministry of marine that could build a navy, a system of tax collection and administration that provided revenues that would be adequate for any peacetime government, and a police and administrative machine that provided a measure of public tranquility as well as considerable control over the economy of the kingdom. Moreover, Louis left a Church under royal control that was an instrument of the royal administration.

He also left the boy-king, Louis xv, a host of critics who objected to Louis xiv's system. Most of these men were noblemen who were hostile to any government by professional royal officials that excluded them from power and influence. Also, the critics included members of the high robe, that is, magistrates of the king's sovereign courts who had been rigorously excluded from political decisions; still other critics were men of affairs who disliked the rigid controls, the system of privileges granted by the crown, and the extension of royal power into the economic community that had prevailed under Louis xiv. Finally, there were those who were shocked at the distress and poverty in the country that had resulted from the king's wars and the cumbersome fiscal machinery that allowed the rich to avoid paying taxes while placing great burdens on the poor. The handsome child who was to be called Louis the Well Beloved was thus the heir to a functioning system of power, but it was a system also confronted with serious problems.

Perhaps the most important problem was one that no one saw in 1715—Louis xiv's system conceived of the political world as a static machine. There was no place built into its organization and institutions to provide for change to accommodate new social and political constellations. But the child-king's reign spanned the period when commerce and population expansion as well as revolutionary intellectual currents demanded change.

The scene in *Parlement* on the morrow of Louis xiv's death was symbolic of some of the problems to come. The duke of Orleans went before the *parlement* even before the funeral obsequies were completed, to ask for parliamentary recognition of his regency government and suppression of Louis xiv's will. The king's bastard sons were deprived of the place that their father had hoped to assure for them, Orleans became regent, and the *parlement's* right to remonstrance that Louis xiv had taken from it, was reaffirmed. The nobles of the high robe and the great nobles of the sword, both of whom had been excluded from political decisions, returned to power. Orleans set up a government in which six councils of ten members each, governed foreign affairs, war, navy, finance, commerce, and home affairs; the councils were manned by great nobles and royal officials. This system of *polysynodie* was probably doomed from the first, for the great nobles proved to be incompetent and the financial problems of the regime were enormous because of the burden of debt inherited from the recent war.

But the sociopolitical problem represented by the return to power of the nobles of the high robe, members of *Parlement,* and the great nobles of the sword was one that eighteenth-century France did not solve. At the opening of the preceding century, there had been an obvious conflict between the high robe nobility and the great nobles of the sword, a conflict that had rendered the Estates General of 1614 inoperative; by the eighteenth century this had changed. The nobilities of the robe and the sword had intermarried and had recognized that they had common interests to defend and that the system of Louis xiv was politically fatal to both of them. Finally, the great nobles of the sword had come to see that the better-educated magistrates were effective spokesmen for the interests of both groups. With the recognition of their right to remonstrance, the nobles of the high robe were again in a position to attempt to exercise the right of judicial review over acts of the king's government. Unfortunately for the Bourbon regime, neither the nobles of the high robe nor the great nobles of the sword had any program other than the defense of their own prerogatives and economic interests. Their intervention into the political arena was nearly always on the side of reaction; the high robe nobles allied with a noble cabal which can be credited with the overthrow of Turgot in 1776, the only leader who might have paved the way for rational change.

While the system of *polysynodie* broke down quickly and the secretaries of state reoccupied their places of power, the nobility nonetheless did succeed in establishing a near monopoly as officers of the army, and the best appointments in the Church. This had serious results for both institutions. The French army developed the highest ratio of officers to men of any army in Europe, eleven soldiers to one officer, but it also had the highest officerial absentee record. But the problem did not stop there. It was easy enough for a poor nobleman to secure a lieutenant's commission, but to become a captain or a colonel cost money, for these ranks were venal, and it was practically impossible for anyone not of the very highest nobility to become a lieutenant general or marshal of France. A nonnobleman with money might be able to buy a commission, but his "status" in the army was conditioned more by his social status than by the office that he purchased. What this really meant was that a military career was often not open to people whose only asset was talent. Napoleon himself and many of the marshals of the revolutionary and imperial armies would never have been able to rise to the top in the eighteenth-century French army.

The Church also suffered from the fact that the nobility was able to insist that the important benefices and all the offices of the upper clergy should be filled by noblemen. This meant in effect that the intelligent, educated cleric with bourgeois background found the doors to high office closed to him. Indeed, the same can be said for men from the lesser nobility. But the most unfortunate thing was the decline in the morals and religious influence of the upper clergy. Bishops who did not reside in their sees, who lived more like noblemen than clerics, and whose educations left much to be desired brought no prestige to the Church at the very time when the inroads of the deist philosophers were eroding respect for Christianity itself.

The offices of the magistrates in *Parlement* as well as a host of other offices in the country were all venal, and it was practically impossible for newcomers to buy them. The high robe had many men in its ranks who were learned, conscientious judges, but there was also a considerable number whose tenure was simply a matter of heredity. Moreover, the composition of the sovereign courts was uniformly conservative, even reactionary; these men looked backward into the past for inspiration and took little note of the stresses that were building in a society that was so rigid in institutions but so fluid in structure.

A serious problem emerged because of this rigidity. In the eighteenth century, the French, like the English, also experienced a boom in commercial activity—with the result that commerce in sugar, coffee, wine, cloth, and other items enriched men in Nantes, Le Havre, Toulon, Marseilles, and other port towns. These people did not have the English ideal for reinvestment of their profits; in France the whole society more or less accepted the nobleman's *mystique* that proclaimed trade to be ignoble. Thus, the rich bourgeois merchant wanted to end his career as a merchant as soon as possible and purchase either an office of a patent of nobility, or government *rentes* (interest from loans) so that he could live "nobly." But offices were largely closed to him; if he were able to buy a patent of nobility, his grandchildren might be accepted, but his generation probably would not. Even an opportunity as a tax farmer was not usually available since a closed corporation, tightly held by a few families controlled most of the tax collections. The way to get into this corporation was to be a son or nephew—hardly possible for the newly rich merchant.

The fact that outsiders had great difficulty entering the Church, the army, the government service, the *parlement,* even the tax farmer's bureau because the nobility of the robe and the sword monopolized these positions did not mean that there was real solidarity in the ranks of the noble class. The "people of quality," that is, the great nobles, lived a different life from that of the country nobles who never went to court; in turn, these country nobles could be anything from very wealthy and cultured men to poor, ignorant, petty noblemen whose lands were no greater than their peasant neighbors and whose positions were simply miserable relics handed down from an ancestor who had fought for the king. These people had little in common with the wealthy of their class. Nor was the robe nobility more united. The high robe nobility in *Parlement* looked with contempt upon their fellows who occupied lesser posts. The royal officials who administered the king's government may have originally come from robe families, but by the eighteenth century there was bad blood between them and the *parlement* because of differences in their personal interests.

The clergy was no more united in feeling or in interests. As we have noted, the best posts in the Church were occupied by nobility; the town and village priests, as abbés and curés, were usually recruited from the bourgeois class. They did enjoy a greater freedom from episcopal control than was true in the following century since they could not be removed, but they also were frustrated by lack of opportunity for advancement and angered when the bishops shifted most of the burden of the "gift" to the king on them. Even more of a problem was the fact that in this century, when the philosophers were undermining the foundations of the Church, too many of the clergy lived lives that brought no credit to themselves or their Church.

The lower clergy, backed by a few of the bishops, provided the leadership for the Jansenist and Richardist movements of the century. The former became more of a contest between the clergy and the state than a heretical movement involving controversy over "grace"; the latter was an effort by the lower clergy to force recognition of a sort of democratic control over the

Church and its teachings, with the parish priests sharing the powers of the bishops and the pope. Both movements provided evidence that the institution that should have been the prop of divine right monarchy, the Church, was troubled by dissatisfactions and contests for power.

The so-called third estate in France included everyone from the rich wine merchant in Bordeaux and the dealer in slaves in Nantes to the poorest peasant in Auvergne. Of course, it was a myth that these diverse people had any political aims or ideas in common. But it was a fact that there were many changes taking place within the ranks of those lumped together as the "third estate." Most important for the emerging history of France was the fact that, as elsewhere in the Atlantic community, there was a growing number of wealthy families whose sons were educated and whose ambitions for upward social mobility grew with their wealth. These people organized literary and philosophic societies, established clubs with libraries and reading rooms, and patronized the *philosophes,* but they were frustrated by the *mystiques* and facts of French society that taught them that trade was ignoble and prevented them from achieving "respectability."

At the other end of the scale, where we find poverty stricken peasants and the poor of the towns and cities, population increases combined with the structure of landholding, caused great distress. Fluctuations in the price of bread brought these people to the brink of starvation at a time when the institutions to relieve their distress were quite inadequate. Although they were not very articulate, these poor were nonetheless potentially dangerous to the state.

No short discussion of the class structure in eighteenth-century France can possibly explain its complexity. In the peasant villages there were a few "cocks of the village"—owners of land and animals whose wealth increased with the demands of the cities for food—but the majority of the peasants were much less fortunate. Few could live from their own holdings without taking service from the wealthy peasants or landlords. Some were landless; some held copyholds or leaseholds owing dues to a lord; a few were freeholders.

Great variations also existed in the towns and cities. The guilds had hardened so that there was a rift between the masters who owned the shops where goods were manufactured and the craftsmen who worked at the benches. Some of the artisans were organized into *compagnonnages,* labor unions of a sort, which gave them a little protection; most were not. The shopowners and the petty shopkeepers who sold colonial wares and other imported things were becoming a petty bourgeois class standing between the artisans and the upper bourgeois merchants, bankers, and professional men. They, too, had their troubles in a society that did not provide opportunities to protest their problems or many outlets for their ambitions for upward mobility. Since the tensions increased as the century progressed, it is not surprising that at its end the bourgeois classes were ready to throw in their lot with the men who overthrew the divine right monarchy in favor of a regime which proclaimed liberty of the individual and, above all, equality of opportunity for service and advancement before the law and the tax collector.

Any discussion of the class structure in France must also indicate the gross injustices and inequalities in the tax burden imposed upon the king's subjects. The nobles and the clergy, the officers of the crown, the municipal officials and magistrates in the courts of law all evaded the direct tax, the *taille,* which was the most important source of the king's income. This tax fell most heavily upon the people least able to pay, the peasants and poorer classes in the towns. There were, of course excise taxes on wine, cards, candles, and many other such items that were paid by everyone who bought them. The excise was the best way to force the privileged class to pay into the king's treasury. There also were hidden taxes in the form of tariff dues on commodities of both internal and international commerce. The clergy presented the king with a "free gift" each year that was only a token in terms of the tax burdens of others; the nobility had to pay fines and fees of one kind or another, and, presumably, a "blood tax" in the king's armies; but they did not really support the treasury in proportion to their wealth.

This statement of tax inequalities based upon class does hardly more than scratch the surface of the problem of taxation. The *taille* was not the same from province to province; some of the king's subjects bore much heavier burdens than others simply because they lived in this or that province. The tax laws for the excise taxes were also different from place to place—both in the methods of collection and the amount to be collected. The salt tax in one province could be almost ten times as high as it was in another simply because of the differences in the charters, traditional laws or customs. There were several attempts to impose taxes upon all classes somewhat in relation to their ability to pay, but these efforts were never successful because the privileged classes insisted on their privileges. These inequalities and obvious injustices were the source of much complaint; the revolutionary slogan "Equality" proclaimed by the men of 1789 took much of its meaning from the tax structures of the regime.

After the failure of the experiment with *polysynodie,* the government of France returned to the patterns set by Louis xiv. From 1726 to 1743 Louis xv entrusted his government to his teacher, Cardinal Fleury, who ruled much as Richelieu and Mazarin had in the preceding century. In other words, Fleury acted as a first minister who governed while the king's role was simply to review policy. Fleury managed to pilot the regime through difficult times with considerable wisdom, and France prospered under his government because he realized that the way for Bourbon France to maintain a sound regime was to avoid serious wars. Before he died, however, Fleury saw his control over the king slip into other hands which in spite of his efforts involved France in the War of the Austrian Succession.

Upon Fleury's death, Louis xv announced that he would henceforth be his own first minister. This turned out to be a great misfortune for France. The king was well intentioned, handsome, even cultured, but he was also indolent, self-indulgent, and hopelessly unable to make a decision. His two interests, women and the hunt, occupied much of his time; his political actions were conditioned by favorites, by his suspicion of his ministers, and by sheer unwillingness to assume responsibility. He conspired against his ministers, maintained a shadow diplomatic service, and allowed court cliques, cabals, and intrigues to have great influence on the policies of state. His regime was just what Louis xiv most feared, and it was disastrous to the monarchy.

Louis xv did not want to become involved in war, but his regime fought two great wars that drained the treasury, cost the kingdom most of its colonies in America and Asia, and lowered French prestige in Europe. When he neared the end of his life, Louis xv was said to have remarked: "After me, the deluge." Thus, this king, who began his career as Louis the Well Beloved, left his grandson a kingdom in deep distress.

Louis xvi wanted to become an enlightened ruler in the mode of Frederick ii of Prussia or, indeed, of his own seventeenth-century ancestors. He called to his government Turgot, a reformer who had a program to rehabilitate the monarchy. But Turgot's program quickly succeeded in making enemies of the whole "power structure" of privilege and favoritism. Turgot might have weathered the storm of intrigue that his program aroused if the king had not also returned the *parlement* to its former position in the state at the same time that he appointed Turgot as minister. The *parlements* had been exiled in the last years of Louis xv's reign for obstructionist tactics. The judges returned to Paris with a determination to protect their interests, and Turgot's reform projects soon became their target. After Turgot was dismissed, Louis xvi called a Swiss banker, Necker, to help him govern France, but at the same time he became involved in a costly war with England, the War of American Independence, that placed impossible strains upon his treasury. By the time that war ended, it was clear that the privileged classes would have to pay their share of the taxes if the king's government were to survive.

After several fruitless experiments, Louis xvi called an Assembly of Notables to advise him on ways of solving the fiscal crisis. The notables were the privileged ones who did not pay taxes commensurate with their wealth. They refused to tax themselves; instead they proposed that the king should call the Estates General to solve the crisis. The Estates General had never been called by a major Bourbon king. In previous centuries, it had often shown revolutionary tendencies, and in the late sixteenth century, under control of the Catholic League, it had threatened to set the duke of Guise on the throne claimed by Henry of Bourbon. Marie de Medicis, as regent, had called the Estates General in 1614; it had been unable to act constructively because of conflicts of the robe members in the Third Estate with both the nobility and the Gallican clergy in the First and Second Estates. The Estates General had not met for over a century and a half. Who knew what it would do, how it should be organized, what its function should be? The Assembly of Notables, however, assured the king that an Estates General would be friendly to him and his government and demanded that it be called. This revolt or refusal of the privileged ones to accept responsibility was the first step in the French Revolution.

192

United Netherlands. The War of the Spanish Succession was too great an effort for the United Netherlands; it emerged from the conflict with crushing debts and taxes to find that England and then France had usurped the economic and political place that it had occupied in the mid-seventeenth century. Amsterdam remained an important commercial city, and the Dutch, on British sufferance, continued their rule over the East Indies; but the former position of power and importance was gone forever. Wealthy Dutchmen invested their money in British bonds and commercial ventures to a point where the interests of the men who governed the United Netherlands were closely entwined with British interests. The English government accepted this situation by practically making the United Netherlands an economic vassal of the United Kingdom.

The patrician regent class in the United Netherlands had two opportunities to establish their oligarchic control over the government. The first came when William III died in 1702 without a direct heir. Heinsius, William's friend and confidant, continued to direct policy until his death in 1720. The following years saw a contest for power between the regents, mostly centered in Amsterdam, and the Orange faction, in the rural and northern provinces. The latter were successful in 1747 when William IV, the grandson of William III's cousin, was proclaimed hereditary Stadtholder. But he died in 1751 leaving a child as his heir. When William V came of age (1766), he proved to be weak and ineffective, but the regent class was also too weak to take advantage of his lack of ability. He was deposed from office by the French Revolution, but his son became William I, king of the Netherlands, after the defeat of Napoleon.

DESPOTS, ENLIGHTENED AND OTHERWISE

The Europe of the western and central Mediterranean basin, like the Europe east of the Rhine, had not experienced royal reforming efforts on the scale that the seventeenth-century enlightened kings of France had provided for that kingdom. On the contrary, in both the Iberian and the Italian peninsulas, the seventeenth-century rulers had been backward and without vision, with the result that the governments of those lands as well as the economies suffered by comparison with France, the United Netherlands, or England. In the eighteenth century when the princes deliberately made efforts to provide more rational government and to bring reforms that the *philosophes* considered important, they were hailed as enlightened despots. Thus, Charles III of Spain, Frederick II of Prussia, Joseph II of Austria and his brother Leopold of Tuscany, and Catherine II of Russia, whose work was to bring the administrative and economic reforms of Richelieu, Mazarin, Colbert, and Louis XIV up to date in the milieu of the eighteenth century, were the "enlightened despots" whose labors introduced a measure of order into the administration of justice and taxation and the organization of economic life in their lands.

Spain. At the opening of the eighteenth century, reform was long overdue in the kingdom of Spain. When Charles II died at the turn of the century, the kingdom had lost at least one-third of its population in the preceding hundred years. Its economy was in ruins, the kingdom could hardly support an army or a navy, and general depression had settled over the land. A fantastic amount of the "gross product" of the kingdom was spent supporting a large population of monks, nuns, and secular clergy and beautifying churches and monasteries. Valladolid, a town of 20,000, supported fourteen parish churches and forty-six monastic institutions; Olemedo, with a population of 2000, supported seven churches and seven convents. What extra money was available was spent for religious processions, vestments, furniture, relics, and other noneconomic religious purposes. The Spanish seemed so bent upon salvation that they cared little or nothing about the affairs of the world. Agricultural activity was crippled by the fact that most of the great estates were held in entail, that is the incumbent could not sell or mortgage his property, so he exploited it for all it was worth—with no regard for the future. The land was deforested by peasant woodcutters and by sheepherders who set fire to the forests so that the flocks—perhaps two and a half million sheep—that came down from the mountains to the lowlands would have pasture. The sheep walks necessary for these migrations further destroyed the agricultural potential of the land. A sales tax of 14 percent and the *mystique* of the noblemen whereby any manual work was considered "vile" had wrecked industry. These few facts only partly explain the decay of Spain: bad administration, debased coinage, ruined markets, savage taxation burdens on the poor, all these joined to cause disorder. When Philip V arrived in Spain, the army had less than 20,000 men; the navy had twenty ships that could not put to sea. In short, Charles II had not left the "splendid gift" that Philip believed his crown would be.

The recovery of Spain began with the arrival of the Bourbon prince on the throne, but Philip V should not be given much personal credit for this. Indeed, Louis XIV was the first reformer of Spain: He sent ministers from France and placed advisors beside the young king who began the reorganization of the finances and of the administration. Their work was so well done that the king of Spain had an army and a treasury at a time when his grandfather's kingdom was reeling in defeat. Archduke Karl failed to capture Spain, and the Spanish gained confidence in their own powers. The issue of the war in Spain allowed the reformers to "Castilize" all of Spain: that is, to impose the royal controls in Aragon and Granada that had so long been common in Castile.

In the years after Utrecht, the driving force in Spain was Philip's second wife, Elizabeth Farnese, who was anxious to find thrones in Italy for her sons. She supported ministers who could provide ships and soldiers and skillful diplomacy, and in the end she did succeed in establishing Don Carlos as king of Naples and Sicily and Don Philip as duke of Parma. To do this, she supported strong ministers who managed to reform the Spanish tax structure, increase the commerce of the kingdom, and enlarge the king's income from the Americas.

When Philip V died in 1746, the throne went to his melancholy son Ferdinand IV whose wife, a Portuguese princess, was sick and childless. Ferdinand left the government of the kingdom to one of his ministers, Caravajal, who ably continued the work of his predecessors by encouraging the development of industry and a pacific foreign policy. The reform movement under Philip V and Ferdinand IV paid some dividends, but the important impulses for the recovery of Spain came with the arrival of Don Carlos III to the throne in 1759.

Carlos III had already learned his trade as king in Naples and Sicily, where he had become aware of the reforming spirit of the Enlightenment and the need to remake institutions and practices that blocked both justice and social welfare for the people and financial security for the king. His reforms struck out in all directions—from restriction of the privileges of sheep ranchers to liberation of industrial enterprises from guild control. He fought the extra-religious privileges of the Church, introduced secular and humanistic education, and reorganized the lines of political power in the kingdom. As might be expected, such reforms infuriated many people; at one point, a rebellion in Madrid forced the king to flee his capital. But Carlos III persisted, and by the end of the century travelers in Spain were astonished at the machine industry in Barcelona and elsewhere in the kingdom and at Spain's general prosperity. The population also increased more rapidly in Spain than was the norm for Europe. In 1700 it was under six million; by 1789 it was almost ten million. Perhaps more important, the Spanish people seemed to have recovered some of their respect and vigor. When Napoleon drove the Bourbons from the throne, Spain became the "running sore" of the Napoleonic empire; the Spanish people arose against their invaders and helped to drive them out.

Portugal. Spanish reforms in the late eighteenth century paralleled those in Portugal. During the first half of the century, that kingdom was somnolent, priest-ridden, commercially controlled by England, and in decay. It sank to the status of a fourth-rate power. In 1750, Joseph I came to the throne and entrusted power to his minister, the Marquis of Pombal, who began reforms in the kingdom. Pombal was a brutal, tyrannical, strong-minded dictator who struck out at one institution after another. He reorganized the government, the military forces, and the economic structure of the kingdom; he forced reforms on the religious orders and the Church, expelled the Jesuits, and brought the grandees to heel by a framed charge that they had plotted to kill the king. Pombal's Portugal was a police state; when he fell from power, out of some 9000 people that he had arbitrarily sent to prison about 4000 were still alive to tell of the horrors of their lot. In line with his firm conviction that only the state could direct the kingdom's economy, Pombal did renovate Portugal and institute important reforms, but he was unable to restore it to its sixteenth-century prosperity. After the death of Joseph I (1777), Pombal fell from office, and some of his enterprises, such as the Opporto wine company and the Brazil trading company monopolies, were abolished and the arbitrary powers of the police were restricted. What remained was a restored monarchical power and

195

reduced powers and privileges of both the grandees and the Church.

Italy. The European traveler making his grand tour saw Italy as the land of sunshine, song, and orange blossoms. Goethe, like many others, was lyrical over the beauty of the land. It was a land where skilled artisans made silk, stockings, gauzes, and hundreds of other things; where artists, opera stars, and musicians abounded; where schools taught the arts and where universities taught medicine and law as well as theology. The cities of Venice, Florence, and above all Rome, were magnets for tourists; their churches, palaces, and public squares were models for architects and municipal planners elsewhere in Europe. Seen from the eyes of the traveler, who contrasted its brilliant skies and seemingly happy people who sat in the sun and sang with the fog and cold of England or northern Germany or even Paris, Italy was indeed an extraordinarily attractive place. Even in the century when French culture made its great conquests, the Italians were still able to pose as the schoolmasters for Europe, the makers of standards for music and art, and competitors with both the French and the Chinese for the luxury trade. Italy was also a land in which a majority of the people were agricultural workers, and yet the cities imported grain from abroad. It was a land of extremes of wealth and poverty, of arbitrary and often ruthless exercise of power at all levels of society. It was a land burdened by the necessity of supporting an enormous clerical establishment. Naples is an example. With a population of about five million, it supported some 50,000 monks and nuns, another 50,000 priests, 165 bishops, and twenty-one archbishops. The church was the richest institution in the land; its high clergy lived in luxury unmatched elsewhere in Europe, while the common people lived in squalor. Some Italians may have been abreast of the culture of the Enlightenment, but most were sunk in superstition and ignorance. Princes from the houses of Bourbon and Hapsburg may have attempted to bring enlightened despotism to their lands, but there were large tracts of the Italian countryside where the government was exercised by local lords or bandits rather than by the king's officers.

The treaties of 1713–1714 that provided for the partition of the Spanish inheritance awarded Spanish Italy to the Austrian Hapsburgs and the duke of Savoy, entirely excluding the Spanish Bourbons. But in the course of the first half of the century, as we have noted, two Spanish Bourbon princes found thrones in Italy. The peninsula was ruled by the Bourbon kingdoms of Naples and Sicily, the Papal States, the Duchy of Tuscany that, on the death of the last Medici, was awarded to a Hapsburg prince, the Duchy of Savoy-Sardinia, the Duchy of Milan (a Hapsburg province after 1713), and the Republic of Venice. There were several petty states between Milan and Tuscany. The preponderant political influence continued to be Austrian and Spanish. Certain princes attempted to bring enlightened rule to Italy: Carlos of Naples-Sicily, and Leopold of Tuscany, but their efforts could not raise their lands to any position of power or influence in Europe as a whole. Italy continued, as it had been during the sixteenth and seventeenth centuries, a congeries of states whose destiny and existence were governed by forces outside of the peninsula.

196

The Germanies. Eighteenth-century German history witnessed the emergence of the dualism between the Hapsburg Danubian monarchy and Hohenzollern Prussia-Brandenburg: it also was the period when the German princes flourished while the authority of the Holy Roman Empire declined. Like the situations in Spain and Italy, German political life lagged behind the developments in England and France; Germany had few seventeenth-century "enlightened kings" like Louis XIII and Louis XIV, so the eighteenth century had to produce "enlightened despots" to clear away the abuses and anachronisms inherited from the past.

The Hapsburg monarchy was the largest and the most powerful state in Germany at the opening of the century. The work of Leopold I had gone far to consolidate the government of the three areas: Bohemia, Hungary, and the German *Erbländer.* There was, however, no possibility of doing the same for the territories in Italy and the Netherlands that had come under Hapsburg rule with the settlements of 1713–1714. The Danubian monarchy was governed by complex political machinery that reflected the diverse origins of the several communities that made up this curious state. The diets and *Landtage* still met in most of the kingdoms and provinces, but, although their committees did manage both military and fiscal affairs, they had largely lost their administrative and fiscal control over the monarchy. The chancelleries for Hungary, Bohemia, and the *Erbländer,* aided by a complex of treasury officials, concentrated power in Vienna. The royal privy council, the war council, and the court chamber tended to give a sense of unity to the government of the whole area. Even so, the Danubian monarchy was a cumbersome political machine that reflected its origins in the need of the Hungarian, Bohemian, and German peoples for protection against the Turks.

It is difficult to generalize about the social structure of a society as complex as the Hapsburg monarchy. Nonetheless, in general, it was true that this was a society of rural noble landlords who dominated the peasants who worked their lands. Some of these noble families owned huge estates with many dependents; in contrast to noblemen elsewhere, others operated mines, textile mills, or metallurgical enterprises, although in parts of the empire, the nobleman's *mystique* branded such trades as vile. In the German lands, the noblemen were usually of German origin; in Bohemia, perhaps a majority of the landlords were of German, Italian, or other than Bohemian (Czech) origins. In Hungary, many of the old families had been dispossessed from their lands by the events of the war of 1683–1698, but in many cases other Hungarians had purchased the confiscated estates. The population of the kingdom of Hungary was much less than it had been in the fifteenth century; Turkish occupation and wars had sent large numbers of Hungarians into exile or had simply depopulated the countryside. In the eighteenth century, however, Hungary practically tripled its population— in part by natural increase, but more as a result of immigration.

The towns and cities of the Hapsburg monarchy were few and far between and the bourgeois population weak. As early as the first half of the century, the government did try to extend commerce by building a road to connect Vienna with Trieste, constructing a fleet on the Adriatic, and opening commercial contacts with both the Near East and western Europe, but the results were at best mediocre. Nonetheless, it was enough to attract the hostility of the sea powers. The major difficulty with the Austrian economy rested in the fact that there was no considerable internal trade upon which to base a tax structure to support the military power. Unlike Brandenburg-Prussia, the Danubian monarchy did not create an internal economy capable of sustaining any considerable military effort; indeed, the government was always on the verge of bankruptcy.

Charles VI (Karl; see pp. 118–122) ascended the throne on his brother's death in 1711, but it was difficult for him to accept the fact that he could not be king of Spain. He surrounded himself with Spaniards and affected Spanish modes. However, by 1720 he came to realize that there was a problem with the thrones he occupied in central Europe. When he succeeded his brother, the line of succession was fixed in his male heirs; but should he have none, his nieces, the daughters of Joseph I, were next in line. One of these girls had married the duke of Saxony, the other the duke of Bavaria. By 1720, it became apparent that Charles VI probably would not have a male heir, and the king realized that in such a case the Hungarian Diet would regain its right to elect a king. Charles' father, Leopold I, had long before declared the crowns of the Danubian monarchy indivisible, but the failure to produce a male heir could create a serious problem that might disrupt that Hapsburg state.

Consequently, Charles VI spent much time and effort to secure the acceptance of the Pragmatic Sanction which was, in effect, a constitutional document declaring the indivisibility of the Danubian monarchy and assuring the succession for Charles' eldest daughter, Maria Theresa. It was not too difficult to secure the assent of the diets and *Landtage* of the monarchy, but Charles realized that he must also have the consent of the German princes and the states of Europe. Critics have pointed out that had he spent as much time and energy building fortifications and a military establishment, his daughter could have mounted the thrones without question. This may or may not have been true, but in fact when Charles died in 1740, his neighbors invaded and laid claim to a large part of Maria Theresa's inheritance. As we shall see, she proved to be more resourceful than anyone expected, and the political constitution of Europe in the form of the balance of power asserted itself to assure her most of her father's lands.

Brandenburg-Prussia. The Hohenzollern state complex that stretched across northern Germany from the Rhine to the Vistula was the creation of a military institution that began humbly enough toward the end of the Thirty Years' War and blossomed luxuriantly in the decades following the treaties of 1713–1714. We have already met Frederick William, the Great Elector (1640–1686), who was in a sense the founding father of this Hohenzollern state. It was his conviction that a German prince must either subsidize a powerful neighbor to protect his lands or provide military power of his own for that purpose. With that principle in mind, he built an army that alternately required subsidies from the United Netherlands, France, and the emperor to a degree that made him look like a condottiere soldier rather than a German elector. But this army also forced him to develop institutions to collect revenues from taxes and the royal estates, as well as to superintend the organization of the army itself. When he died, he had already established the tradition that the nobles of his lands should send their sons to be officers in his army and administration.

The Great Elector's son, Frederick III (I)[1] (1686–1713), did only two things to enhance the power of his house. First, he set aside his father's will, which would have divided the Hohenzollern territories among several sons so that children of the second bed would also become sovereign. Secondly, he secured European recognition of his title as king in Prussia by supporting Leopold I in the War of the Spanish Succession. He also beautified Berlin with a bridge, a schloss, and an armory, held magnificent celebrations and pageants for any occasion, and, with Leibniz' help, founded the Berlin Academy. Frederick III (I) did not maintain discipline in his government nor effectiveness in his army; his court was expensive and his regime lax. Had his successor been of the same mold, the Hohenzollern lands would not have evolved much differently from those of the other princely houses in the Holy Roman Empire.

Frederick William I (1713–1740) was the true founder of the power of the Hohenzollern lands. When his father died, he ordered a magnificent funeral such as Frederick III (I) would have wanted, and then he introduced a regime of economy in his court and government. During his reign, about 80 percent of the revenue of the state was devoted to the army; of the remaining 20 percent, a part was packed away in kegs and put in the cellar of the schloss as a war chest. Under Frederick William I, the Prussian army grew far out of proportion to the population of his lands. While in 1740 the kingdom of France, with about twenty million inhabitants, had about 160,000 soldiers, Brandenburg-Prussia, with a little over two million, maintained a field army of 72,000. Nor was it simply a matter of numbers; the Prussian army had the best trained officer corps in Europe, its troops were better drilled and better equipped than any other army, and behind it stood a bureaucracy with less graft or corruption and more efficiency than any in Europe. While this development of the military establishment was within the mold started by his grandfather, nonetheless, Frederick William I was the true founder of the Prussian military state.

The Prussian rise in power is all the more surprising if we remember that the Hohenzollern lands were largely agrarian and poorly endowed. Sandy soils, lake and forest culture, and sparse population characterized much of Hohenzollern empire. Frederick William, the Great Elector, and his successors encouraged immigration into their lands: French Huguenots, displaced Protestants from the Catholic Rhineland and southern Germany, and large numbers of mercenary soldiers recruited into the Prussian army were encouraged to marry and settle in the Hohenzollern territories. Likewise, the Hohenzollern princes, and particularly Frederick William I,

[1]He was Frederick III (Elector) I (King) in the Hohenzollern time.

encouraged the development of industry and crafts—both by their own subjects and by foreigners who were given special favors in return for bringing their skills to the Hohenzollern lands. Frederick William encouraged the development of internal as well as foreign commerce; both types contributed to the revenue collected through his excise taxes. Frederick William I believed in work for everybody because he saw that by work men created wealth that could be taxed to support his army. The story, probably apocryphal, that he objected to women gossiping unless they knitted at the same time, is in the spirit of this king who felt he had to wring everything possible from his limited kingdom.

Frederick William reorganized the government of his realm by combining tax collecting, the administrative (police) function, and the superintendence of the military in a general directory under four ministers assisted by a number of financial privy councillors. This bureaucracy was staffed by career men whose advancement depended upon their performance of duty and a primitive sort of civil service examination. Under his supervision, Brandenburg-Prussia thus developed the first civil service system in Europe to govern both the king's general directory and the towns and cities of the kingdom. In the eighteenth century, when most kingdoms were managed by men swimming in a sea of corruption and inefficiency, "working for the king of Prussia" became a saying meaning working for low pay, long hours, and no bribery. His government was not the only bureaucratic regime in Germany, but it was the best organized and in time became the model for other states.

Frederick William was interested primarily in developing a state that could support his army; he did little toward the reorganization of the courts or the codes of law. He was uninterested in education except that which could strengthen his army. Curiously enough, he also was uninterested in political adventures that might lead to war; his soldiers were much too valuable to be placed in jeopardy. His successor, Frederick II, had no such qualms; he found that his father had indeed created a military institution that, in the hands of a brilliant prince like himself, could secure for its king the sobriquet "Great."

As we shall see below, the death of Charles VI provided Frederick II the opportunity to invade Silesia and precipitated the war over the Austrian succession. Frederick alone gained considerably from that war, but even for him it was not an unmixed success. His rape of Silesia led directly to the Seven Years' War (1756–1763) in which Brandenburg-Prussia and its king suffered severely from invasions. During the two wars and the period of peace between them, the new monarchs, Frederick II of Prussia and Maria Theresa of the Danubian monarchy, developed their particular styles of enlightened despotism. Frederick had the advantage because his father's reforms had already set a pattern for efficient, effective (by eighteenth-century standards) government, while Maria Theresa not only inherited a much less effectively governed regime, but also, in order to secure the support of the Hungarians for her war to maintain her crown, she had granted them a special and favored position in the Danubian monarchy.

Thus, while her ministers were able to bring reforms to Bohemia and the German *Erbländer,* Hungary remained apart except in as much as she was able to entice Hungarian magnets to her court and marry their children to those of her German and Bohemian nobility.

Maria Theresa called to her service able men who directed her government: Von Haugwitz, von Kaunitz, and Bartstein were responsible for the reorganization of the bureaucratic structure of the Austro-Bohemian lands into a form of government best described as "bureaucratic despotism"; it was a form that became common throughout the German lands during the hundred years that preceded the Bismarckian unification of Germany. Under their reforms, the army was reorganized and given a regular base for drawing recruits; the fiscal system was systematized so that all classes—nobility, clergy, and commoners—paid taxes; and a supreme court of justice came into being (1748) that took appellate jurisdiction from the legislative bodies and the bureaucratic administrative agencies. (There is no evidence, however, that Montesquieu's *Spirit of the Laws* was the inspiration of this move.) They also created a universal directory for commerce and a council of state as a "watch dog" and "brain trust," respectively, committees of "wise men" whose duties were simply to advise the empress. The Theresian reforms went far to coordinate local, provincial, and central administration, and they provided machinery for the six high offices of the state: defense, foreign affairs, justice, interior, finance, and commerce.

Maria Theresa's reign introduced the cultural influences (schools, libraries, hospitals, etc.) that became Austria's contribution to central and southeastern Europe. It has been called German Christian civilization, for along with the bureaucratic reforms that provided more rational administration came educational reforms that extended from the University in Vienna to the development of primary schools, *Gymnasia,* and *Realschulen* for secondary education, and normal schools to train teachers for village and town primary schools. Maria Theresa's government cut down the number of religious holidays and disestablished some of the monastic churches, despite protests from Rome. Protestants in her realm were transferred to Transylvania where their religious practices were tolerated, and the Jesuits lost control over university and court life.

When her husband died in 1765, Maria Theresa's eldest son, Joseph II, became co-regent in the Danubian monarchy and emperor of the Holy Roman Empire. He and his mother had many conflicts for he wanted to move faster and more drastically than she in the direction of rational government. He greatly admired Frederick II, who had caused his mother so much grief. After her death, Joseph II had the opportunity to try out his reforms only to discover that drastic changes in land tenure, the status of peasants, and commercial organization led to great protests and even to open rebellion.

Joseph II was a rationalist. He issued an Edict of Toleration (1781) that allowed all religions to practice their cults and granted non-Catholics full rights as subjects. Joseph also established civil marriage and the possibility of divorce, and he attempted to simplify Catholic services. Even the Jew benefited from his toleration. Theresian and Josephian reforms were paternalistic in their nature and bureaucratically administered; however, for all of Joseph's hopes for reforms, not dissimilar to those made by the French Revolution, his efforts were frustrated by the multistate and multinational structure of his realm. Hungarians, Bohemians, Netherlanders, Italians, and, after 1775, Poles—all with their own backgrounds of language, customs, laws, and political institutions—could not be transformed into citizens of one state by royal decree.

Frederick's Prussia was a simpler problem, at least until the annexation of Polish provinces introduced large elements foreign to the German cultural and political patterns. Frederick II could build upon his father's work; he had only to extend the state's influence in the developing economy of the kingdom, sharpen the efficiency of the bureaucracy, and enlarge and strengthen the army in the characteristic forms set by Frederick William I. He did reform the law and the legal institutions to provide Prussia with judges who were both well trained and above venality. During Frederick's reign, about 60,000 families migrated into his lands; vast marsh tracts were drained and put into agricultural production, canals were built, rivers dredged, harbors brought into being. Frederick might well have earned the title "Great," for his domestic programs even if he had not won it on the battlefield. His encouragement of commerce and introduction of new industries could not make Prussia a rich land, but it did greatly increase the amount of tax revenue available to the king, and it did much to transform a poor country into one of the most flourishing in Germany. All Germany looked to Frederick for inspiration. Both the success of his arms and the effectiveness of his government encouraged imitation.

Frederick did not consider education to be an integral part of the state's activities. There were a good number of schools established in the towns and villages, but except in the Catholic area where there were Catholic orders to provide teachers, there was a conspicuous lack of qualified instructors. Frederick, with his French orientation, did not believe that more than a very few should be educated except to a level that would allow them to fulfill their occupational tasks. He failed to grasp the meaning of the unfolding civilization in Germany—perhaps because he despised everything not French and assumed that civilization was a static phenomenon, one essentially the same in all ages except when submerged by barbarism. He was tolerant of all ideas and voices, so long as they did not criticize his government, but he did little to raise or expand purely German civilization since he believed that the civilization that had reappeared under Louis XIV was the model for civilized man, a reincarnation of the Augustan civilization of Rome. A skeptic himself, Frederick was happy to tolerate all religious sects. Even the Jesuits, expelled from Catholic kingdoms, could find refuge in Prussia. Indeed, the king was said to have remarked: "I do not care how my subjects go to hell, so long as they pay their taxes."

Frederick ruled Prussia much as a personal enterprise. His ministers corresponded with him; they did not meet together. The king made long inspection trips accompanied by his secretaries who kept him current on the affairs of the kingdom and dispatched his orders to his subordinates. This was a personal despotism that required a talented ruler willing to spend hours at his desk and in the saddle to manage its affairs. When Frederick died, a system more like the Austrian bureaucratic despotism developed to fill the void left by the removal of the king.

Germany beyond Austria and Prussia, by far the larger percentage of the population of the country, was a congeries of states and free cities and smaller political entities. The reforms that were made in Vienna and Berlin brought those states up to the stage reached by Louis xv's France; very few of the petty states had rulers enlightened enough to follow their patterns. The ruler in Germany was more apt to be a petty tyrant, a ruler without education, imagination, or vision whose personal appetite wasted the wealth of his people. Some of these rulers sold their subjects as soldiers to England or the Netherlands for wars with which they were unconcerned. Here and there, we find a bright spot where a ruler subsidized either a university or musicians or artists, but even in this area it was Maria Theresa's Vienna that led the way in patronizing the arts.

Russia. Peter the Great introduced many changes into Russian society, changes largely designed to provide the state with an army and a navy that could compete with the armed forces of his European neighbors. In the process, he developed an army of 100,000 men with a recruiting system that imposed the burden of military service upon the peasants, and he created a navy largely officered by non-Russians that, by 1720, was the strongest in the Baltic Sea. He reorganized the government several times; indeed, between 1701 and 1721, one reorganization followed another in an effort to increase the effectiveness of tax collections and expenditure supervision. Russia was divided into "governments" in an attempt to decentralize administration so that this vast land could be more carefully controlled. The central authority was organized into "colleges" on the Swedish model, and a large number of foreigners, especially Czechs who could easily learn Russian, were invited to help administer the bureaucracies. Peter also encouraged the development of industries that would further his war efforts. Iron production was increased to a point where, by 1720, there was an exportable surplus, and the needs of the army for guns and cannon and the navy for guns, anchors, and other equipment were satisfied by home production. He was not equally successful in freeing Russia from the need to import cloth to uniform the army, but the amount of such imports did drop significantly.

By opening a port on the Baltic Sea and building a canal that linked the Neva and Volga rivers, Peter greatly expanded Russian commerce with the West. In 1690, about sixty vessels called yearly at Archangel; by 1720 over six hundred called in the Gulf of Finland, and Russian exports of furs, timber, turpentine, grain, flax, and other commodities produced a sizable surplus of exports over imports. In the course of the eighteenth century this trend continued, particularly after the wars with the Ottoman Empire established Russian commerce on the Black Sea and thereby allowed the river systems of Russia to carry the commodities from the plains to the world market. Peter's successors were able to wipe out many internal trade barriers and to further develop the transportation systems so that Russia could and did take a place in the commercial activity of Europe.

Peter's reforms did much for every class in Russia except the peasants— who comprised 93–94 percent of the total population. His need for soldiers and money led to a head tax that weighed heavily upon the peasants and a system of recruitment that fell exclusively upon them. To assure the collection of taxes and soldiers and the support of the nobility who owned the land, Peter's system reinforced the legal bonds that held the peasantry to the status of serfs bound to the land, disposable by sale, or transferable to mining or industrial enterprises of either the state or private entrepreneurs. The eighteenth century, in which the nobility further consolidated its hold upon the land and the peasants who worked it, saw the peasants' conditions of life deteriorate even further. Many fled the land to join the Don Cassocks in the south as brigands, cattle growers, or wandering peoples; others fled into Siberia or the north where agriculture was difficult or almost impossible, but where they could be comparably free of the exactions of the landlords and the state—at least until organized government caught up with them. The peasants' plight was largely responsible for one of the most extensive peasant uprisings in modern history, the Pugachev rebellion of 1774–1775, in which the rebels captured Kazan, Nizhni-Novgorod, and threatened Moscow. The slogan "seize, execute, and hang the landlords" suited the feelings of a peasantry that could see no way to escape its tragic plight.

The nobility ultimately benefited most from Peter's program because his successors were unable to govern without them. Peter wiped out the differences between the landed nobility and the service nobility by making all of them serve the state, but there was a great difference between the status of the great princely families who owned vast tracts of land with hundreds of "souls" and that of the petty squires who squatted on their property. The former could count upon positions at court and in the diplomatic service; the latter were supposed to fill the ranks of the officer corps in the army and navy. After Peter's death, the term of service was limited to twenty-five years, starting at age ten when a young nobleman entered school; at fifteen he joined the guard regiments as a private, entered one of the bureaus, or, if he were backward, the navy. By twenty he was promoted to the rank of an officer in the army or to a similar level in the governmental service. Later in the century, nobles were able to enter their children at birth so that by twenty-five, they had completed their term of service; with so many years of service seniority, however, such a young man might even be a general. There were several attempts to abolish the system of compulsory service entirely, but until the end of the century the needs of the army were too great to allow it. In return for their service, the noblemen were given extensive control over the lives of their serfs and allowed to exploit them completely; they determined who would be recruited into the army so that disturbing elements were sent away before they could cause trouble. Under Catherine II, the nobles also came to control the administration of the government's programs in the countryside, so that their interests were well cared for. Moreover, as we shall see, the nobles were also important in the palace revolutions that characterized Russian political life in the eighteenth century.

Peter also "neglected" to appoint a patriarch and in the latter's place established the Holy Synod, a board of governors, to rule the Church. In earlier years, the patriarch had played a role quite comparable to that of the czar himself and the Church had had important political powers. It was significant, however, that the Church played practically no part at all in the palace revolutions of the eighteenth century. Earlier, the priests and nuns had composed about 2 percent of the total population, but since Peter had considered the monastic institutions to be parasitic, their number was reduced and the weaker institutions closed. The Church did begin to open schools for "young persons of every class" in the towns, but they made very little impact on the massive ignorance of the country.

The bourgeois merchant class also amounted to about 2 percent of the population of Russia. Peter encouraged its members to start manufacturing enterprises, and in the course of the century they did greatly expand the production of cloth, hardware, iron, and leather goods, but their factories were usually small, and they had no motive power. They never were able to keep up with the rising demand for manufactured goods. Catherine II's reforms gave the merchant classes some control over the administration of the towns, but they had no real political power. However, Peter's system, which established grades in the bureaucracy and the armed services and promoted to the status of "nobleman" anyone who reached a rank eight from the top, allowed the sons of the bourgeoisie a chance for upward mobility.

When Peter died (1725), there were two candidates for the throne: his wife, Catherine, and his grandson, whose father had died in prison, perhaps at Peter's orders. The old aristocratic families, anxious to reverse Peter's reforms, wanted Peter Alexseyevich, but Menchikov, one of Peter's creatures who commanded the army, succeeded in placing Catherine I on the throne. Like Menchikov, she was of humble origins, a product of the Petrine revolution. When she died (1727), Peter II (Alexseyevich) came to the throne, and Menchikov soon lost his power. Peter II wanted to return to earlier patterns of government. The court moved from St. Petersburg to Moscow, and had he lived, Peter II might well have reversed the trends his grandfather started. However, he contracted smallpox and died in 1730 just before his marriage. The supreme privy council asked Duchess Anna Ivanovna, the daughter of Peter the Great's dimwitted half brother, to assume the throne under conditions that would have limited the autocracy. But when she came to Moscow to assume office, the nobility indicated that a majority of the noble rank, including the officers of the guard regiments, did not want her authority limited by the old aristocratic families. She tore up the "conditions" that she had signed, and arrested and either executed or exiled the men who had tried to limit her power.

Czarina Anna ruled for ten years with the assistance of German favorites. She revoked Peter's entail law that prevented the nobility from dividing their lands among their children; she created the cadet corps for young nobles rather than send them to guard regiments as privates. There was one serious attempt to overthrow the "German clique," but it ended in the execution of the principal plotter. When Anna died in 1740, there was again a crisis over the succession. She had named Ivan, the son of her niece Anna, wife of the duke of Brunswick, as her heir, but Ivan VI had only a year on the throne when he was overthrown and imprisoned in a plot inspired by the French ambassador and a noble clique which named Elizabeth, daughter of Catherine I and Peter the Great, to the throne. The Russians were used to government by czarinas. Elizabeth, however, did not break with Austria as the French had hoped she would. Elizabeth's rule coincided with the periods of the great wars of the mid-century, and her armies came very near to giving Frederick the Great a disastrous defeat. Indeed, her death was the miracle needed to save Prussia since her successor, Peter III, son of her sister Anna and the duke of Holstein, was an admirer of Frederick the Great and desired to go in person to Pomerania to place the Russian army under the Prussian king's command.

At this point in Russia's history, the true successor to Peter the Great appeared on the scene. Catherine II, born Princess Sophia Augusta von Anhalt-Zerbst, took her Russian name when she entered the Russian Orthodox church and married Peter, duke of Holstein. She was involved, but her part was not discovered, in a plot against Elizabeth, but most of her life in Russia before she mounted the throne was spent becoming more Russian than the Russians themselves. She and Peter III lived parallel lives. Her lovers included the future king of Poland, the commander of the guards, and several other dashing men of the court. It was obvious from the moment that Peter III took the throne that he could not retain it as he was weak and uncomprehending; a plot formed almost immediately, and Catherine was hailed as empress while her husband went to prison, where he died shortly afterward from "hemorrhoidal colic." As d'Alembert remarked, "Hemorrhoids are terribly dangerous in Russia." Catherine apparently thought of marrying one of her lovers, but finally decided that it would be best to "marry Russia" instead. This German princess, who came to be known as Catherine the Great, continued the process of Russianization of Western modes of politics, economics, and society that remained characteristic of Russia until the revolutions of the twentieth century.

Catherine carefully courted such Western philosophers as Voltaire, Diderot, d'Alembert, and others with flattery and Russian gold to assure a good "press" in Europe. The "liberal, enlightened despot," Catherine II, was something of an illusion created by publicity and a carefully planned "dust in the eyes." However, her reign was important. Catherine strengthened the power of the throne but she also continued the process that brought the serfs completely under the authority of the landlords. Further, by administrative reforms she succeeded in making the squires into unpaid servants of the crown and at the same time deprived them of the ability to affect political decisions. The Pugachev revolt broke out during her reign; Catherine's answer was simply repression. However, alliances with the great nobles and the wealthy bourgeoisie and trade policies more liberal than any in Europe allowed Catherine to greatly extend Russian commerce. The recovery of Courland gave Russia an ice-free port on the Baltic Sea. Catherine's foreign policy supported territorial expansion. By war with the Ottoman Empire, Russia became a Black Sea power, and St. Petersburg established control over the wild Cossack populations of the Don and Crimean areas; extended Russian serfdom throughout the Ukraine; and built new towns on the rivers leading to the Black Sea to exploit the commercial opportunities that breaking into the Mediterranean basin evoked. Catherine's regime also pushed Russian influence and power across high Asia and on to Alaska.

Although this expansion of commercial capitalism was largely confined to the assembly and export of raw materials and agricultural products, Catherine did expand manufacturing by encouraging both nobles and bourgeoisie to enter the economy and by allowing serfs to be bound to merchant enterprises for the manufacture of iron, cloth, and a few other craft products. A distinguished historian sums up Catherine's career thus: "Wily and calculating, the tsarina of the nobility was a patriot queen, like Elizabeth of England, brooding over the destinies of her country. She was almost all things to all men, except to the peasantry, who constituted a mere 94 percent of the population. To them, she was a blight and a calamity,"[1]

Russia's rise to power in the eighteenth century pressed heavily upon its neighbors to the west and south. In the seventeenth century Russian expansion had been confined to the east where it encountered only loosely organized, more or less nomadic peoples; but after Peter the Great's reforms of the military institutions, Sweden, Poland, and the Ottoman Empire came under the shadow of Russian power. Unhappily for all three of these states, they were in no way prepared to stand against Russian expansion.

Sweden. After the death of Charles XII, the Swedish nobility reasserted its right to power in the king's government, but Sweden did not regain its former position. There were two political factions in post 1720 Sweden, the "Caps" who proposed to follow a neutralist policy and the "Hats" who were more aggressive. In 1738 Count Gyllenborg came to power, allied Sweden with France, and soon afterward provoked a war with Russia. The war was a disaster, and by the treaty of Abö Sweden was forced to surrender territory on the Gulf of Finland. She was in full decline. In the 1770's king Gustavus III, fearful that Russia and Prussia were planning partition of his kingdom, seized power by a coup d'etat and set out as an enlightened despot to reform the kingdom. In 1788 he became involved in a war with Catherine II's Russia, only to lose Finland and Carelia. Sweden's "period of strength" ended with the death of Charles XII; the eighteenth century was one of weakness and decline for that nation.

Poland. The story of Poland is even more dismal. After the devastations of the northern war, Charles XII and August I used the kingdom as a

---

[1]Gershoy, *From Despotism to Revolution, 1763–1789* (New York: Harper & Row, Publishers; 1944), p. 126.

battlefield and Charles XII manipulated the Polish Diet to suit his purposes. When August II died, Russia and Austria agreed upon the election of his son, August III. The French backed the candidacy of Stanislas Lesczynski, who was to become Louis XV's father-in-law. The war that followed was indecisive; it ended with a compromise that gave August III the throne in Poland and Lesczynski one in Lorraine, with the understanding that the province would revert to France on his death.

The problem of Poland was twofold. Its internal political organization made impossible the development of a strong royal authority. The so-called Liberum Veto that gave each member of the Diet the ability to check any action created absolute deadlock, and so Poland did not develop a bureaucratic police and military establishment. The other problem concerned Poland's frontiers, where Russia, Prussia, and the Danubian monarchy stood ready to interfere with money or with troops to control the course of events in Poland. There was a long tradition of foreign powers using money to bribe Polish magnates at election time, but in the eighteenth century, Russian and Prussian bayonets were added to the bribes. Catherine placed one of her lovers on the throne with the threat of bayonets. When Catherine's war against the Ottoman Empire was obviously about to increase Russian territory greatly, Prussia and Austria found ways to obtain compensatory territory for themselves by joining Russia in the first partition of Poland (1772). When the French Revolution extended the frontiers of France, the rest of Poland fell to its neighbors as compensation via the second and third partitions of that kingdom (1793 and 1795).

The Ottoman Empire. The Ottoman Empire, the third state on the Russian frontiers, was a natural target for Russian aggression. How could it be otherwise? Turkish military power was in rapid decline, and the Turkish empire stood athwart the water outlet for much of Russian commerce. Russia's most important rivers went into either the Caspian or the Black seas; their courses naturally beckoned to Russian statesmen, merchants, and soldiers. Peter's march southward was checked by his defeat of 1711 and the treaty of Pruth, but this check could not last long for Russia was a growing power. However, she was not the only power on the Turkish frontier. After two centuries of standing on the defensive, the Danubian monarchy turned on the Ottomans with aggressive intentions. Leopold I recaptured Hungary and Transylvania at the end of the eighteenth century. After the War of the Spanish Succession, Eugene of Savoy led the Austrians, in support of the Venetians, in a new aggressive conflict that forced the Turks to surrender Serbian territories below the Danube that had never belonged to the Hapsburgs or to their predecessors on the Hungarian throne (Treaty of Passarowitz, 1718).

By 1720, many observers believed that the long awaited day had come when the Turkish government could be expelled from Europe. But in the hour of his extremity several factors came to the aid of the sultan. First, the Greek population of his empire, led by a large number of wealthy and well-educated merchants and professional people in its ranks, reached the conclusion that it would be better to support the sultan than to accept the overlordship of the Venetian merchants and the Jesuit Roman Catholic priests. Commercial competition and religious antagonism combined to rally Greek intellectuals to the sultan's government, where they acted as much-needed diplomats and bureaucrats in support of the regime. The same forces began to work in Serbia. The Orthodox Serbs did not like the Roman Catholic German-Hungarian government. Some of their number even made an effort to attract the attention of the Orthodox emperor in Russia a generation before Russia was ready to pose as the defender of the Orthodox church. All this worked heavily against the Austrians. There were two further factors, namely, French influence and French renegades who joined the sultan's armies to teach Western military tactics. By 1736 the Ottoman Empire was again at war with its neighbors, and in 1739 Emperor Charles VI surrendered Eugene's gains beyond the Danube when he saw his own armies checked and a Russian army making headway in a spectacular battle at Jassy. Deserted by their allies, the Russians also made peace with the sultan, giving him three more decades of peace on his frontiers with the European powers.

But the onward press of Russia against the Ottoman Empire was only temporarily slowed up; when Catherine became empress, commercial and military interests demanded Russian expansion into the Black Sea and beyond. In 1768 war broke out, and the overwhelming victories of Russian arms made it clear to the world that the Ottoman Empire was no longer a match for Western military power. However, if the Turks were unable to stop the Russians, jealousy and fears on the part of Russia's other neighbors, which were to last until 1919, could check encroachments on the Ottoman territory. The men at Vienna realized that Russian power in the Balkans and Black Sea might be less advantageous to them than Turkish. The crisis was averted in 1772 by the intervention of Frederick the Great, whose own policy after the Seven Years' War was based upon agreement with Russia. He arranged for the first partition of Poland so that Prussia and Austria as well as Russia would gain territory as a result of the decline of the Turkish empire.

The treaty signed at Kuckuk Kainardji between Russia and the Ottoman Empire (1774) was an important landmark in the disintegration of the Ottoman Empire. By this treaty, Russia acquired further territory on the northern coast of the Black Sea, but more importantly, Russia also obtained the right to free navigation for her commercial ships in all Turkish waters and the right to protect the Orthodox Christians in the Turkish state. Heretofore, the French kingdom had been the "protector" of the Christians; henceforth, Russian claims in this area were to expand Russian interests and ambitions throughout the Ottoman Empire, with fateful consequences. The destinies of this decadent empire were no longer decided in Constantinople: for the next hundred and fifty years, decisions made in Vienna, St. Petersburg, London, Paris, and, finally, Berlin were the decisive factors in the history of the empire on the Bosporus and Dardanelles.

209

Eighteenth-century statesmen understood that the problems of high politics concerned the adjustment of the political, military, and economic realities of the day to the given institutions and *mystiques*. After 1715, there were two divergent assumptions about sovereignty. One was the traditional belief that God invested kings with power to govern but retained the authority for himself; the second, emerging from the English Revolution of 1688, invested the power and authority to govern in a mystical assumption about the people that really meant the people with money, who invested their rulers with the power to act but retained the authority themselves. Thus, if the ruler failed to govern according to the law, he could be put aside. Neither of these conceptions, however, could provide for the predatory patterns of politics, for the shifting balances of war, or for the changing economic structures in the larger world beyond Europe. This non-European world was becoming open for European conquest as eighteenth-century shipbuilders, cannon manufacturers, and soldiers were perfecting their techniques to the point where no people on the planet could hope to hold their harbors and perhaps even their hinterlands against European power. The only question that remained was: Which European power would inherit the earth?

These same forces were active in Europe itself. As we have noted, there was a vast difference between the economically and militarily developed kingdoms and those that remained more or less in the traditional patterns of earlier centuries. How long could a powerful neighbor refrain from dominating and finally annexing a weaker state on its frontiers? This became a problem in central and eastern Europe with the rise of Prussian and Russian power. But by what right could Frederick II annex Silesia, Russia take Finland, and Prussia, Austria, and Russia partition Poland? Neither the "divine right of kings" nor the English doctrine of sovereignty could justify such action. And since neither the philosophy of popular sovereignty nor the *mystique* of nationalism had yet come into being to justify aggressive political action, there was nothing left but *raison d'état,* and many eighteenth-century theorists enthroned this doctrine with its most brutal consequences. They refused to recognize justice, morality, honesty, equity, or any private virtues as having validity for the behavior of states. This left only the law of the jungle as the law between states. What was called "international law" was simply a set of rules imposed by the stronger powers upon the weaker ones.

The rule of the jungle was modified, however, by the development of the concept of the balance of power. In the preceding half-century, European rulers had leagued together in 1668, 1672–1678, 1688–1697, and 1701–1713 to check the aggressions of Louis XIV. In the course of these years, they had learned coalition warfare, and, more or less, to adjust their divergent aims to a common action. In general, the structure of politics of the War of the Spanish Succession formed the backbone of the European balance of power:

England, the United Netherlands and the German empire and the emperor on the one side; France and Spain on the other. The French attempted to use Poland, the Ottoman Empire, and Sweden to balance the empire in the east; the Anglo-Imperials used Portugal and Savoy in the west and in the Mediterranean basin. But the term "balance of power" was a mechanistic conception with only limited application to a political situation that was inevitably in flux. The decay of Sweden, Poland, and the Ottoman Empire; the rising power of Russia; the recovery of Spain under the Bourbons; shifts in the political constellations of Italy; and, perhaps most dramatic of all, the rise of Brandenburg-Prussia from a third-rate to a first-rate power—all these made permanence in international political structures impossible.

Nor was it solely such ponderable political factors that affected the ongoing processes of high politics. In each of the states of Europe, there were divergent interests that translated themselves into action in high politics. Political theorists might argue that states' interests were paramount in the organization and direction of foreign policy. And yet, there were eighteenth-century wars for the Polish, the Austrian, and the Bavarian successions that seemed to have dynastic origins; Spanish policy during thirty-odd years after 1714 was much concerned with the ambitious programs of the queen, Philip v's second wife, who sought thrones for her sons; the last twenty years of Charles vi's reign in the Danubian monarchy were concerned with the acceptance of the Pragmatic Sanction regulating the succession to his crowns. On the other hand, Frederick's invasion of Silesia, and the partitions of Poland, Sweden, and the Ottoman Empire were obviously acts of aggression based on reasons of state. Likewise, the English preoccupation with attempts to destroy commercial rivals made economic interests predominate in high politics. The French effort to secure a throne for Stanislas Lesczynski in Lorraine was motivated by the French desire for secure frontiers, because upon the death of the ex-king of Poland, Lorraine was to pass to his daughter, the queen of France, and to her heirs.

On another level, we find policy made because the king happened to be ruler of another territory as well. For example, the Hanoverian kings of England tied that kingdom to the electorate of Hanover; and the Witten kings of Poland were also dukes of Saxony. These facts made a difference in high policy. The family relations of the house of Romanov in Russia affected the behavior of the Russian empire as well as that of the petty German principalities and the kingdom of Sweden, where relatives of the Russian royal family had interests. After 1740, the neighbors of Frederick the Great's Prussia had reason to orient their policies around the fact that Prussia had become a revolutionary force in central Europe. And all Europe after the mid-century had to consider the meaning of the sensational rise in military power of the Russian empire.

High Politics Following the Treaties of 1713–1714. In 1715, even though it had suffered a serious setback, the kingdom of France was still potentially the most powerful state in Europe. Its population of twenty million made it the most populous state on the continent, and its rich agricultural lands and prosperous commercial harbors made it the wealthiest kingdom in Europe.

As a result of the War of the Spanish Succession, though, France found herself surrounded by enemies that would not soon forget the fact that they must unite to keep France from dominating them. The counterweight to French power was the United Kingdom of England and Scotland, which had the wealth necessary to subsidize the emperor as well as the princes in Rhineland, Italy, Portugal, and the Dutch Republic so that France could be contained. In the years after 1715, however, other factors made the fear of France unnecessary. Indeed, the French government also wished to associate itself with the English power to secure protection from the aggressive dynastic policies of the Spanish Bourbons. Even though he had renounced that throne, Philip v did not really give up his hope of becoming king of France until after Louis xv married and sired a son. And Philip's second wife, Elizabeth of Parma, drove her husband and his Spanish statesmen to secure thrones in Italy for her children—since they presumably would have no chance to become kings in Spain, where sons from the earlier marriage were first in line. The regent duke of Orleans and the governments that followed him in France until about 1731 cooperated with England to hold this Spanish policy in check.

Until the death of Peter the Great in 1725, the Baltic also was the scene of Anglo-French cooperation in high politics, for England as well as France had reason to worry about Russian policy in Germany. The rise of the Russian Baltic fleet and the powerful Russian army that reached into Mecklenberg to promote interests of relatives of the Russian emperor could not be ignored by either Anglo-Hanoverian or French statesmen. On the other frontier of central Europe, Eugene's war with the Ottoman Empire (1716–1718) did not provoke intervention from the west because the government of France was exhausted from its recent war and preoccupied with the problems of the regency and the succession. Thus, the Hapsburg monarchy was able to annex Serbia and the Banat without arousing opposition from the Western states.

However, French policy could not be bridled for long. When August ii of Poland died in 1733, a flood of French money and propaganda against foreign interference in Polish politics persuaded the Diet to elect Stanislas Lesczynski to the throne. The Russian and Austrian governments, however, had another candidate, August III, son of the late king, and the Russians supported their choice with a huge army that drove Stanislas out of Poland. Cardinal Fleury used this as a pretext for war, but he carefully managed the conflict so that it was fought in Italy and in the upper Rhineland where neither England nor the United Netherlands would take offense. The English stood aside; indeed, an English minister boasted that although 50,000 men were killed in battle, not one of them was an Englishman. The treaty of peace gave the Polish throne to August III; Stanislas Lesczynski became duke of Lorraine; and Charles of Lorraine became duke of Tuscany while Don Carlos, son of Philip v of Spain, was given the throne in Naples. It was very satisfactory for Stanislas' daughter became his heir and thus assured that Lorraine would be French, and Elizabeth Farnese, Philip v's wife, had the satisfaction of seeing her son properly endowed with a throne.

212

While the war over the Polish succession and the subsequent division of Italy occupied the attention of Vienna, Paris, and Madrid, a situation was building up in the Caribbean that was to result in a war between Spain and England. Neither power wanted war, but the situation in Spanish America became explosive as the Spanish governors there attempted to control the English smuggling trade by commissioning private sea captains to act as coast guards and giving them the right to confiscate offending foreign ships. There was a long, unsuccessful discussion about compensations for losses before the ear of a Captain Jenkins was cut off in a fight with the Spanish. The government of England was quite unprepared for war, but Parliament, in a buoyant mood, declared war on Spain anyway. In the preceding decade or so, the British admiralty had allowed its navy to deteriorate just at the time when the government of Spain had much improved the Spanish navy. But what was more ominous for England was the fact that in these same years, Cardinal Fleury had also been rebuilding the French navy to match the explosive expansion of French commerce. However, the cardinal, almost ninety years old, was about to launch a blow at England for the expansion of French overseas trade when events in central Europe offered the opportunity to crush forever the Hapsburg monarchy that had so long been the enemy of France. Fleury would have preferred to allow central Europe to solve its own problems while France redressed the balance against England, but the young hotheads, who succeeded in getting the ear of the king, maneuvered French policy in Germany so that French resources were used for land warfare and could not be channelled into a maritime war. This problem of land versus sea warfare was to be the fate of French policy in every war with England from 1740 to 1815 except the war for the American independence. It also was the fate of twentieth-century Germany, which also fought two major wars with England on the land.

The Austrian Succession. As we have noted above, the conflict in central Europe concerned the Austrian succession. Charles vi's failure to sire a male heir to the thrones of the Danubian monarchy made it necessary for him to secure the consent of both the estates of his own lands and the rulers of Europe for the Pragmatic Sanction which provided that his daughter Maria Theresa would succeed him. Charles died in October 1740. In spite of their previous acceptance of the Pragmatic Sanction, there were a number of princes who believed that they had claims to Charles' crowns as good or better than Maria Theresa's. However, the prince who first challenged her right to a part of her inheritance was the one with the poorest case. Frederick ii of Brandenburg-Prussia did not really care that his claim was a shaky one; he saw the opportunity to enlarge his own kingdom and lightheartedly, or recklessly, decided to take it. His invasion of Silesia in 1740 became the axis of Prussian policy for the next twenty-three years. Silesia enriched his kingdom, but later it also brought Russian and Austrian armies into Berlin, caused ravage of war that desolated much of his kingdom, and, without the "miracle" of 1762, undoubtedly would have reduced Brandenburg-Prussia to the status of a third-rate power.

Frederick's act of piracy encouraged other princes to dust off their claims to segments of the Austrian inheritance. Charles Albert of Bavaria, August III of Saxony, Charles Emmanuel of Sardinia-Savoy, and even Philip V of Spain each found that they had "rights." None of these princes could have challenged the Hapsburg monarchy alone; all needed the support of France for any hope of success. Cardinal Fleury was more interested in following a pacific policy in Germany, but Belleisle and a group of younger French officials not only rounded up enough support in the electoral college to place the imperial crown on the head of Charles Albert of Bavaria, but also succeeded in committing the French government to act as auxiliary to a Bavarian-Saxon effort to partition the Hapsburg empire. The war hawks in Versailles who dreamed of the wealth, adventure, and power that could be won in war argued that the time had finally come to end Hapsburg power in Europe. The French also made a treaty with Frederick II, but this alliance did not commit him to continue the war. Fleury was unable to check the aggressive rush of French policy, but he did prevent a declaration of war against the Danubian monarchy. At first, the effort to partition Maria Theresa's empire made rapid progress. The Bavarian-Saxon army invaded Bohemia; Charles Albert was elected emperor; and a Spanish army invaded Italy. The French army was an auxiliary force in Germany.

Maria Theresa's position was dangerous indeed, but it was not simply her inheritance that was at stake. The French also seemed about to try to use the situation in central Europe to overthrow the balance of power established by the treaties of 1713–1714 by making one of their clients, the duke of Bavaria, emperor of the Holy Roman Empire and king of Bohemia; securing an alliance with Prussia; and, with the kings of Spain and Sardinia-Savoy, reorganizing the political structure of Italy. Since Russia was unable to help redress that balance because the French had succeeded in embroiling that state in a war with Sweden, there seemed no help for either Maria Theresa or the balance of power established by Utrecht.

Maria Theresa appealed to the maritime powers for money and military aid to support the Pragmatic Sanction and to the Diet of Hungary for troops. A wag remarked that a Hapsburg could as well hope for aid from the devil as from Hungary, but the Diet listened to her requests. It was impressed by her beauty, her valor, and, perhaps most of all her promises of special treatment for Hungary, and it voted her support. The Hungarian troops were not of the best quality because of their tendency to loot rather than fight, but they were a help in the crisis. The maritime powers also responded, but not exactly as Maria Theresa had wished. The United Netherlands was in no position to give much aid, but England was both able and anxious to do so—on English terms. The problem was simple enough: The English wanted to reestablish the balance of power, but the connection between England and Hanover demanded that it be done by ending the war between Prussia and the Hapsburg monarchy. Prussia was potentially very dangerous to Hanover, and as long as Prussia was at war with the Hapsburgs, it would be impossible to reorient Germany in an anti-French coalition. Thus, the English sent subsidies to Maria Theresa and demanded that she make peace with Prussia. Such a peace was distasteful to her, but

English pressure—no peace, no subsidies—forced her to conclude first a truce (Klein-Schellendorf) and then a definite treaty (Breslau-Berlin, 1742) by which she accepted the loss of Silesia. The treaty was particularly favorable to Frederick largely because the British ambassador acted on behalf of the Hapsburg monarchy; it was easy enough for him to give Frederick Hapsburg territory! Once Frederick was out of the war, the elector of Saxony also decided that he, too, should withdraw from the conflict, for obviously the Hapsburgs, supported by an Anglo-Hanoverian army, were stronger than Charles Albert and his French auxiliaries. Indeed, the Hapsburg army not only reoccupied Bohemia but also invaded Bavaria and captured Munich.

English aid was also successful in Italy. Charles Emmanuel of Sardinia-Savoy "discovered" that English subsidies and fear that the Spaniards would take Milan were enough to make him change sides. The treaty of Worms (September 1743) allied Sardinia with England and the Hapsburg monarchy. The Sardinian army closed the passes of the Alps. At about the same time, the English Mediterranean fleet sailed into the Bay of Naples and threatened to bombard the city if King Charles did not withdraw his troops from the fighting in the north. Since the French were not officially at war with the Hapsburg monarchy, they could hardly complain that Frederick, then August of Saxony, and finally Charles Emmanuel had deserted their client, Bavaria.

When Fleury died (1743), Louis xv announced that he would not take a first minister; like Louis xiv, he would rule himself. Unhappily for France, he was not Louis xiv, and his rule turned out to be wavering, uncertain, and ambiguous. But France did make a treaty with Spain for war against England, the first "Family Compact" (October 1743), and prepared for an invasion of the Austrian Netherlands, the "natural" battlefield on which France felt she could fight England and Austria. In February 1744 France declared war on England, in April on the Hapsburg monarchy.

The French army had scarcely invaded the Austrian Netherlands when news arrived of the battle at Dettingen where the Franco-Bavarian army was roundly defeated by the Anglo-Hanoverian "pragmatic" army; within a few weeks not a single French soldier was left beyond the Rhine, and the imperial army was about to invade Alsace. The meaning of this dramatic reversal of Maria Theresa's enemies was not lost on either the French or the Prussian kings. Frederick prepared to re-enter the war, and Louis xv detached a large part of his army in the Netherlands and personally led it toward Alsace. Frederick's invasion of Bohemia quickly resulted in the capture of Prague, but Louis xv fell ill and the French army in Alsace failed to act decisively. Frederick's position was now dangerous for him.

The year 1745 opened with the death of Charles Albert. The French, to Frederick's astonishment and anger, proposed August of Saxony for the imperial crown, only to find that he had sold out to Maria Theresa. Charles of Lorraine, Maria Theresa's husband, was elected. But the situation in the Netherlands turned abruptly against England when Marshal Saxe defeated the Anglo-Dutch armies at Fontenoy (May 1745). The English, needing imperial troops in the Netherlands, urged Maria Theresa again to make peace with Frederick. This she was unwilling to do until after Frederick had badly defeated her armies in three battles and the English had again threatened to withdraw their subsidies. A treaty was then drawn up in Hanover and signed in Dresden late in 1745; it left Frederick in possession of Silesia and secure in his new title, the Great. The war had now become what it had always really been, a struggle between France and England for overseas colonies and trade and for control over the balance of power in Europe. It continued to be fought in the Netherlands and in Italy as well as in India, the Americas, and Africa.

The last two years of this war were most confusing both for contemporaries and for historians. There was a Jacobite descent on Scotland that momentarily threatened to place the Stuart dynasty on the throne in the British Isles. Maria Theresa secretly proposed to allow France to keep much of the Austrian Netherlands in exchange for help in the recovery of Silesia. Philip v died in Spain; his son Ferdinand was quite willing to see the territory in Italy that was to be assigned to his half brother considerably reduced. Marshal Saxe continued his victorious sweep in the Austrian Netherlands, defeating the Anglo-Dutch armies at Raucoux. In the United Netherlands, William IV succeeded in forcing the regents to declare him Stadtholder and then insisted that he could not fight without a larger loan or a subsidy from England. The English, for their part, were asking why their armies were fighting in the Netherlands. They preferred to fight France in the colonies. The situation was discouraging for all parties, and by the end of 1747 there was a general willingness to end the conflict.

The Treaty of Aix-la-Chappelle (1748) settled nothing; it merely ended the hostilities. The French and English mutually returned their colonial conquests; the French evacuated the Austrian Netherlands and allowed the Dutch to return to the "barrier fortifications." In Italy, Don Philip, son of Elizabeth Farnese and son-in-law of Louis xv, became duke of Parma and Plaisance. Perhaps the most important fact of the treaty was its recognition of Frederick's conquest of Silesia, even though Frederick was not a signatory to the treaty. Both the French and the English wanted to court him or at least persuade him to subscribe to the settlement of 1748.

Diplomatic Revolution and the Seven Years' War. The treaty of 1748 solved none of the problems of the day, so it was not surprising that they soon reasserted themselves. The basic question in central Europe was, of course, Silesia. Frederick was correct when he pointed out that Prussia and France had "married two daughters of the Hapsburgs: Silesia and Alsace." It was simply a problem of keeping them. Beyond central Europe were the questions posited by the colonial interests of Spain, France, and England in Asia, Africa, and America. In Asia, the India companies, rather than the governments, faced each other, and they tried to enlist the aid of Indian princes for their interests; in Africa, slavers contested for the right to buy human flesh from Negro and Arab sellers; in the Caribbean, the trade in salt, molasses, and slaves as well as the smugglers and pirates of the Spanish Main raised questions; in North America, the conflict between the

216

English on the Atlantic coast and the French and their Indian allies in the Ohio and Great Lakes basins involved the fur trade as well as the whole problem of land ownership. There was a clash between George Washington, commanding frontier militia, and a French commander in the Ohio basin as early as 1754. By 1755, it had come to a point where the English navy stopped French ships bringing reinforcements to Quebec, and a pitched battle erupted between British and Anglo-American troops on the one side, and French and Indian forces on the other.

This colonial controversy must be seen in relation to the other unsolved problem of the 1750's: Silesia. In Vienna it was axiomatic that Silesia must be recovered. Count Kaunitz, who became Maria Theresa's minister for foreign affairs, was convinced that it could be recovered by an alliance combining the Danubian monarchy, France, and Russia. The Russian alliance seemed simple enough to secure as long as Empress Elizabeth ruled in St. Petersburg, for she was hostile to Prussia to a point that made her actions almost pathological. But when Kaunitz approached France with the proposal for an alliance in the early 1750's, he drew a blank. Kaunitz may have wished for an alliance among France, Russia, Sweden, and the Danubian monarchy for the destruction of Prussia, but he could not have achieved it without other developments. Indeed, it was not France, Russia, or the Danubian monarchy that finally cemented that alliance, but rather the blunders of Newcastle's England and, most important, those made by Frederick the Great.

The scene opened in London where statesmen, anxious about the Ohio valley and India, had also to concern themselves with the protection of their king's electorate of Hanover. Frederick's Prussia was allied with France; if France and England should actually go to war, Hanover would be open to invasion. The duke of Newcastle, whose influence on British governments extended over more than two decades, believed that a state could "buy" policy from its neighbors. At first, it seemed that the best way to secure Hanover would be to have Russia threaten Prussia in case the latter should consider action against Hanover. With this in mind, the duke negotiated a treaty providing for an English subsidy for Russian troops to operate against "the enemy." For Empress Elizabeth, this meant Prussia. When Frederick learned of it, this treaty aroused his fears, for he well understood that Russia was his most dangerous neighbor. He immediately suggested an earlier English proposal that Prussia should guarantee the neutrality of north Germany, including Hanover. Newcastle saw no problem in this since it also would assure the security of Hanover. Thus, Prussia and England negotiated the Treaty of Westminster (January 1756) which guaranteed Hanover, as well as Prussia, against invasion. Since Louis xv had rejected an earlier suggestion that Prussia should occupy Hanover to protect Franco-Prussian interests, Frederick did not think it necessary to warn Louis xv that he was making an agreement with England to assure Prussia's territory.

The Treaty of Westminster, however, came as a shock to the men at Versailles. They saw it as evidence of Frederick's "bad faith." Since it came just when the Austrians were urging a treaty between France and the Hapsburg monarchy, Louis xv ordered one of his agents to discuss such a treaty. The French, however, were not anxious to see Prussia destroyed or partitioned so that Germany could be fully under the control of the Hapsburgs; they were angry with Frederick for his perfidy, but, unlike Elizabeth of Russia, even the strongest anti-Prussian at Versailles did not want Prussia blotted out. Thus, the first Treaty of Versailles, between France and the Danubian monarchy (May 1, 1756), provided for the neutrality of Austria in the case of a Franco-English war. It affirmed an alliance, however, only in case one of the signators should be attacked by a third party. The treaty made a sensation in the courts of Europe. The hereditary enemies of more than two hundred years had become allies. After that things moved fast. On May 19 the Danubian monarchy and Russia signed a treaty for war against Prussia. Empress Elizabeth felt that the English had deserted her, and saw this treaty as a means for the annexation of Prussia to her kingdom. As this news leaked out, everyone believed that a general war would break in 1757.

It is however an open question whether or not the Hapsburg monarchy could have brought about a war against Prussia in 1757, but, Frederick did not wait to see. Many historians insist that he walked into a trap set by Kaunitz. For when he could not get a satisfactory reply about Austrian intentions, Frederick invaded Saxony (August 29, 1756). It was a simple matter to occupy Dresden, force August III to make peace, and enlist the entire Saxon army into Prussia's military establishment. But in so doing, Frederick assumed responsibility for a war in which his little state, spread over all north Germany so that it could not be defended, engaged the military forces of the three largest military powers on the continent without even the assurance of a British subsidy, let alone support from the British armed forces. If Frederick entered Silesia recklessly in 1740, his invasion of Saxony in 1756 was an invitation to disaster. Even his military genius was not enough to balance the enormous power at the disposal of his foes.

The invasion of Saxony was the first act in the so-called Seven Years' War. Its immediate consequences were a second Treaty of Versailles allying the kingdom of France and the Danubian state, a treaty between France and Russia against Prussia, and a declaration at the Diet of the empire condemning Prussia as the breaker of the peace. A French army entered Germany in 1757, forced the English commander of the Anglo-Hanoverian army to agree to neutrality, and pressed on to join the armies of the Diet and the Austrians. But 1757 was the last year that the French actively participated importantly in the conflict with Prussia. France's war was with England, and war over colonies and commerce naturally took precedence in the war plans of both countries. Thus, after 1757, the war in central Europe became a war between Prussia on the one side and the Hapsburg and Russian empires on the other. The English supplied Prussia with subsidies and in Hanover acted to keep the French from pushing into Germany; but the English, like the French, recognized that their war was primarily one of colonial empires and commercial companies. The interests of the central and eastern European powers were only intertwined with those of the Atlantic colonial and imperial states because France had frontiers with Germany and England had interests in Hanover. Thus, this Seven Years' War was in effect two wars, and it was finally ended by two treaties recognizing the diversity of the aims and interests of the combatants.

The Prussian campaign of 1757 started with an invasion of Bohemia but it proved to be impossible for Frederick to capture Prague or, indeed, to remain in the kingdom. By August 1757, Frederick was confronted with a Russian army in East Prussia, a Swedish army in Pomerania, an Austrian army of 100,000 in Bohemia, a German-French army of 30,000–50,000 coming from the Rhine, and, after the neutrality of the Anglo-Hanoverian "army of observation," another French army of 60,000–80,000. It was an improbable situation. However, the Russians, after defeating the Prussian army in West Prussia, encountered supply problems and withdrew back into Russia. Frederick maneuvered against the French and overwhelmed them at Rossbach (November 5), and then by a rapid march, met the Austrians and defeated them at Leuthen (December 5). The *philosophes* in Paris toasted him as one of their company and found satisfaction in the defeat of their own king; the Methodists in England hailed him as a "Protestant champion"; Pitt came to power in London with a war program that included subsidies for Prussia and a more vigorous use of the Anglo-Hanoverian army of observation. Frederick's military genius had momentarily saved his kingdom.

The war in Germany, however, had five more years to go. After Rossbach the French largely ignored the German war to fight their war with England, but Prussia had enough enemies in the Russians, the Austrians, the Swedes, and the army of the Diet. Frederick was at bay in the center of the circle; his forces decayed with each successive year as his young officers were killed, his soldiers deserted, and supplies became scarce. Neither British subsidies nor his own genius could have saved him had the war gone on a little longer. He did not dare attempt to annihilate his enemy; a victory would have been almost as disastrous as a defeat, since trained soldiers lost on the battlefield, or by desertion in the confusion following a battle, could not be replaced. A miracle was required to save the king of Prussia; that miracle came from Russia, where the death of Empress Elizabeth brought Peter III to the throne. He halted the Russian army and proposed to turn it over to the Prussian king. This miracle changed the history of Europe. Had Frederick been defeated, the whole story of German unification and German thrust in Europe would have been very different. A Brandenburg reduced to the size of a petty German electorate would not have been a counterweight to Austria in the German community, and Russia would not have had to wait until 1945 to annex East Prussia and give a new name to Koenigsburg.

The war at sea and in the colonies went against France. In India, Clive succeeded in curtailing the French India Company, and in establishing the base from which England and the English India Company could embark on the conquest of India as soon as the war with France ended. In the

Americas, too, the British were successful. Canada fell to the British army after the capture of Quebec, and in the Caribbean the English navy had the better of the fighting. By 1759, Louis xv and his advisors wanted peace, but they could not extricate France from the tangle of the conflict.

Like the war in Germany, this one on the larger stage also was affected by the death of rulers. Ferdinand (d. 1759) of Spain was succeeded by Don Carlos (Charles III), who had been king of Naples and was destined to give Spain an enlightened reforming government; and George III of England succeeded his father in 1760. Charles III joined the war against England in 1761 only to have the British navy capture several of Spain's important posts in the Caribbean, including Havana. George III brought Tories to his government and, most important of all, caused the fall of William Pitt. Pitt was a predatory man of war; he supported Frederick, he advocated war for the complete destruction of French power. His removal brought to the government men who did not wish to waste English wealth in Germany. George III and his Tory friends wanted peace, and by 1762, peace negotiations were far enough advanced to bring the conflict to an end.

As we noted above, the Seven Years' War was ended by two peace treaties: those of Paris and Hubertsburg. The peace treaty in Germany confirmed Frederick's hold of Silesia. Beyond that, it gave clear indication of the importance of Russia in the affairs of central Europe. Elizabeth's death had saved Frederick, for even though a palace revolution deposed Peter III and placed his wife Catherine II on the throne, the Russian army no longer fought in Germany, and Maria Theresa had to accept the fact that her forces alone could not defeat Prussia. The dualism in Germany was confirmed along with the fact that Russia had henceforth to be considered in German, indeed all central European affairs. The peace of Paris left the English in control of all of Canada, the Ohio basin, and Florida, while Louisiana went to Spain. In India, too, the English emerged as absolute victors. They did allow the French two small islands in the Gulf of the St. Lawrence where fish could be cured, three sugar islands in the Caribbean, and five trading towns in India. This was the debris left of the French overseas empire started by Henry IV, enlarged by Richelieu, Colbert and Louis XIV, and expanded into a commercial empire under Louis xv. It is hardly surprising, then, that when the treaty was ratified, the French government embarked upon a program of warship construction and introduced reforms in both the weapons systems of the army and the training of officers.

The Crisis in the East. The diplomatic revolution that allied the Danubian monarchy and Russia with the kingdom of France caused distrust and fear in the Ottoman Empire; France, the traditional friend of the Turks, was allied with their most persistent foes. But the Ottoman Empire was in no position to aid Frederick's Prussia. When the Seven Years' War was over, however, the new constellations of power in eastern and central Europe demanded that the Ottoman Empire, and, indeed, the rest of Europe, reconsider its policies and interests in the area that stretched from the Baltic to the Black and Aegean seas.

Even though Russia did not deliver the death blow to Prussia, the Russian empire emerged from the war with new prestige, and with the deposition and murder of Emperor Peter III, it acquired an empress, Catherine II, who understood how to promote and expand that prestige. Russian commerce had been growing rapidly since the opening of the century; by 1770 there was more Russian than Swedish iron on the English market, and Russia was almost independent of foreign cloth manufacturers for uniforms for its soldiers. Catherine's Russia was one in which soldiers, noblemen, and commercial entrepreneurs had a voice in the government, and they demanded the expansion of Russian military and commercial interests into the Black and Mediterranean seas. In time, this drive for commercial power beyond the Dardanelles was to change the Danubian monarchy from a foe to the protector of the Ottoman Empire; men in Vienna learned to fear Russian penetration of the Balkans.

The other state occupying this middle zone between the Hapsburg and Romanov states was the anarchic kingdom of Poland. The first Saxon king of Poland owed his throne to the influence of Austria, the second to the bayonets of Russia. In both cases, there had been defeated candidates unsuccessfully supported by the king of France. The Polish nobility was so far divided in its vision of the destiny of the kingdom and so anxious to preserve so-called Polish liberties, that it proved impossible for the Polish diet to resist foreign control. Indeed, the Polish nobility became clients of the foreigner rather than actors for the interests of Poland.

When Augustus III died in 1763, his son expected to be elected, but Catherine II had other ideas. By an agreement with Frederick of Prussia, she placed her recent lover, Stanislas Poniatowsky on the Polish throne and proceeded to demand that the Polish constitution be revised to assure religious liberty to the Orthodox church in Poland. French intriguers and Polish nobles not satisfied with the election started a civil war in which "volunteers" from abroad and foreign money played a large part. The Turkish sultan as well as the Austrian and Prussian rulers also became interested; the sultan's anxieties led him to build up his military forces on the Russian frontier. In 1768 an "incident" occurred. Cossacks in the service of Russia attacked (October 1768) and burned a small town belonging to the khan of the Crimea, a vassal of the sultan. The Russian ambassador in Constantinople was thrown into prison, and war broke out between Russia and the Ottoman Empire. Since the Turkish army had only recently received instructors from France and seemed to be under the influence of the French ambassador who had orders to bring about a Russo-Turkish war, this conflict appeared to be a French triumph that might have repercussions in Poland as well as on the coasts of the Black Sea. It did, but not exactly as French diplomats might have wished.

In Frederick's jesting words, the campaign of 1769 was a victory of the "one-eyed" man over a blind man. Aided by a flood on the Dniester, the Russians drove the Turk army back to the Danube and seemed poised for an invasion of the Balkans. This caused a wave of emotion in Vienna as well as in France. In 1770, a Russian fleet appeared in the Mediterranean and cooperated with the Greek insurrection in the Morea; the Russians defeated the Turkish navy near Khios and also captured several islands in the Aegean Sea. On land, the Russians occupied all Turkish territory to the mouth of the Danube. The French government, the traditional friend of the Ottoman Empire, and the Danubian monarchy, its traditional foe, both became alarmed. The situation in the East was moving rapidly toward a new European war that Frederick II had every reason to want to avoid.

In September 1770, Frederick II and Joseph II, who had become emperor and co-regent, with his mother, Maria Theresa, met in Neustadt, Silesia, to discuss the situation. The next move was the suggestion by the Prussian minister to Russia that Catherine II must be willing to find a solution for Austro-Russian rivalry to avoid a war with Austria and France. The Prussians suggested some "adjustments" of the Polish frontiers as compensations to Russia's neighbors for Russian territorial gains on the Black Sea. Frederick explained to Catherine that the sultan was willing to cede Serbia to the Danubian monarchy in return for military assistance: a gentle hint that she must come to an agreement.

In July 1772 the three Eastern states, the empire of Russia, the kingdom of Prussia, and the Danubian monarchy, reached an understanding that would save the balance of power. Each would annex a part of the kingdom of Poland, and the Russians would be allowed to acquire Turkish territory on the north coast of the Black Sea. This act was either international piracy or the guarantee of order and peace, depending upon the point of view one took. The annexations introduced more stable government to the annexed Polish provinces and prevented war. They also provided a precedent that boded ill for weak powers. In any case, the king of Poland and the Polish Diet could do nothing to prevent this theft of territory. With the three Eastern powers in agreement, it also was impossible for either France or England to interfere effectively.

Of the three monarchs whose territories were enlarged by this first partition of Poland, only Maria Theresa seems to have had doubts about the morality of the action. But Maria Theresa annexed all of Galicia with some two million inhabitants, while Frederick received only West Prussia with about six hundred thousand and Catherine secured White Russia with about a million and a half. Prussia's portion, however, was very important since it linked the lands of East Prussia with those of Brandenburg, and put the Polish grain trade on the Vistula under Prussian control. Nineteenth-century writers, thinking in terms of national self-determination, have condemned this partition as international piracy. Contemporary twentieth-century men will have trouble making a firm judgment in light of what happened in that part of the world after World War II.

Crisis in the British Empire. While the struggle for power led in eastern Europe to the first partition of Poland and encouraged partitions of the Ottoman Empire, the Atlantic community was shaken by a revolution that challenged the British empire. After the peace of 1763, the government in London attempted to require the colonists on the Atlantic coast of North America to help pay for the recent war. It had been very expensive; there was a huge public debt, and, in the reasoning of the king's ministers, the British colonists in America had received the greatest advantages from the war by the exclusion of the French from North America. Unhappily for this theory, there were men in the colonies who were ready to argue that Parliament could regulate commerce within the empire, but that only their own representative institutions could impose a tax upon them. This was a theory of the constitution of the British empire that would be accepted in the nineteenth century, but in the eighteenth it sounded bizarre in London. A second pertinent fact about the situation was that the "new men called Americans" had already developed a tradition of violence, of direct action, of disregard for laws that they did not like, and in the recent war they had also learned the first steps toward joint action.

Excise taxes, tea taxes, stamp taxes, attempts to control smuggling, and stationing of troops in Boston and other cities built up to a crisis in 1775 when colonial militia fought a pitched battle with British troops. In 1776, a Continental Congress composed of representatives of the thirteen colonies declared independence from Britain and undertook to drive the British soldiers from the land.

The colonists had certain advantages: Their land was very large with poor means of transportation; the coast was long and easily used by smugglers; and the British army was ineffectively led. But if the war were to be solely between the colonists and the British government in London, the outcome was a foregone conclusion. The colonists must eventually lose. Thus, the revolutionary government turned to the enemies of Britain for aid. It was not easy for them to seek aid from France, which had long been their enemy, and which was a kingdom and a land tainted by papism and by deistic disbelief, both of which were anathema to a majority of the colonists. On the other hand, while there were many Frenchmen who would be happy to settle the score with the English, France had a huge debt carried over from the last war, and the new king's (Louis xvi's) reforming ministers were anxious to put the kingdom on its feet financially; a new war would not do this. Furthermore, what if the colonists made peace with London, leaving the kingdom of France with a war on its hands? The French government provided under-the-counter assistance to the revolutionaries but refused to do more until there was evidence of probable success for the revolt. The victory at Saratoga (1778) was the signal for the French to actively enter the war, which thus became a continuation of the Anglo-French conflicts that had started in 1689 and would not really end until the nineteenth century.

The French role in the war was most important. By skillful diplomacy the French foreign minister isolated the British, brought the powers of northern Europe into a league to protect their shipping against the British navy, prodded the British into a declaration of war against the Dutch (the men in London believed that it would be easier to control Dutch trade as a belligerent than as a neutral), and finally brought Spain into the war as an ally of France (but not of the revolting colonists since Spain also had colonies). An army of French regular troops went to North America and the

French navy, supported by the Spanish, operated in the Caribbean as well as on the coast of the thirteen colonies. The defeat that forced the British to the peace table (Yorktown) was a victory won by the French navy and the French army supported by the colonial forces under Washington and Lafayette. When Cornwallis surrendered, the British realized that with France, Spain, and the United Netherlands as active foes, and the Russian, Prussian, Swedish, and Danish powers as "unneutral neutrals" who would not recognize British rules about the confiscation of contraband of war on the high seas, it would be folly to continue the fight.

The peace of 1783 took longer to negotiate than might have been expected because the French, as allies of Spain, felt that they had to support Spanish pretentions against the English both in the Mediterranean and in the Caribbean. The revolutionary government in the colonies, tempted by the offer of independence, actually made a separate peace before its allies and associates could come to an agreement, but this action did not really influence the negotiations as much as did the superior power of the British navy.

One important consideration in London in 1781 was the situation in India. At exactly the time when rebellion in North America deprived the British of control over their colonists on the Atlantic coast, British interests in India were moving toward the conquest of that vast territory, a market for English goods and an outlet for the energies and talents of the sons of English noblemen and city men. In 1783, no one could know what was to happen to North America or to India in the succeeding century, but at that time the prospect of a conquest in India was the brilliant opportunity that easily made up for the British failure in North America.

EUROPE ON THE EVE OF THE FRENCH REVOLUTION

At the end of the eighteenth century, the twin forces of ever expanding trade and growing population were still driving factors in the historical processes of European society. But equally important were the differences in the processes of development from one state to another. All were affected by the rise of new military institutions and tactics that gave form to the conflicts of the century, but the forms and the impacts varied with the different backgrounds of the people involved. Indeed, by the eighteenth century it was surely possible to say that one of the creative forces in European society as a whole was the conflict of interests and ideas that emerged as a direct result of the differences in the societies that made up this European community.

On another level, the eighteenth century witnessed the extension of predatory imperialism as a pattern of European political life. The divisions of Italy that bartered sovereignties over the several provinces, cities, states, and kingdoms with no more than pretense of legitimate rights; the Austrian

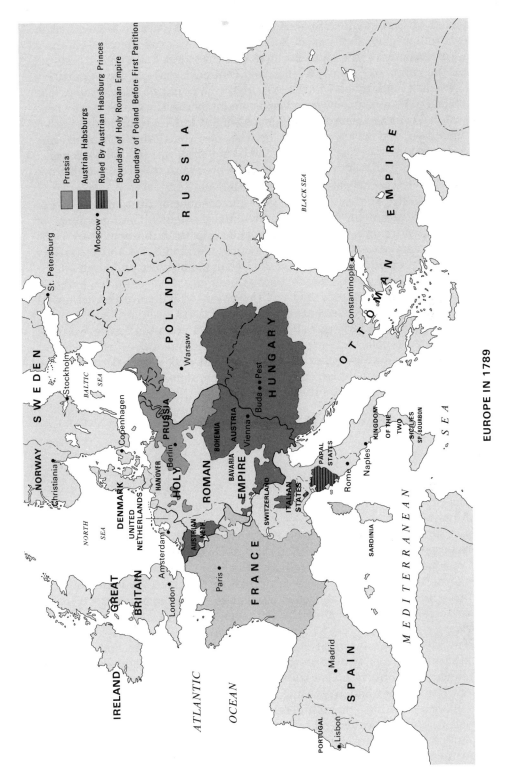

EUROPE IN 1789

Prussia

Austrian Habsburgs

Ruled By Austrian Habsburg Princes

Boundary of Holy Roman Empire

Boundary of Poland Before First Partition

Moscow •

GREAT BRITAIN
IRELAND

NORWAY
SWEDEN
St. Petersburg •

Christiania •
Stockholm •

DENMARK
Copenhagen •

RUSSIA

POLAND
Warsaw •

NORTH
SEA

BALTIC
SEA

UNITED NETHERLANDS
Amsterdam •
HANOVER
Berlin •
PRUSSIA
HOLY
ROMAN
EMPIRE
BOHEMIA
Vienna •
AUSTRIA
Buda • • Pest
HUNGARY

BLACK SEA

Constantinople •

OTTOMAN EMPIRE

London •
ATLANTIC
OCEAN

Paris •
FRANCE

AUSTRIAN NETH.
BAVARIA
SWITZERLAND
ITALIAN STATES
PAPAL STATES
Rome •

SARDINIA

KINGDOM OF THE TWO SICILIES
Naples •
SP. BOURBON

SEA

SPAIN
Madrid •

PORTUGAL
Lisbon •

MEDITERRANEAN SEA

225

conquest of Serbia after Eugene's war; the invasion and annexation of Silesia followed by partitions of Poland and the Ottoman Empire—all these were extensions of the international morality that had been introduced when the rulers of Saxony, Russia, and Denmark had decided to partition the Swedish empire of Charles XII at the opening of the century. The extension of European power and government overseas, excused by the need for control over the commerce in slaves, sugar, tea, and hundreds of other commodities and made possible by the new battleships, cannon, and infantry tactics based on the flintlock and bayonet, was further evidence of the European predatory policies that influenced both the peoples of Europe and those beyond the seas.

And, finally, the much-envisioned European constitution for an all-European government, that is, the establishment of a lasting balance of power, was developing into a system of five great military powers, each anxious to extend itself at the expense of smaller neighbors and each ready to make war, an endemic disease of European society. The philosophers, the churchmen, and some of the men of business might condemn the habitual recourse to arms, but they had not the power to influence the actions of princes. At the end of the century, the advice that Cardinal Fleury gave to the Abbé de Saint Pierre, who had a program for perpetual peace, was still valid: "Go good abbé, enlist a band of missionaries to convert the hearts of princes." Cardinal Fleury realized that the will to power was strong in the ethics of European political men, and that moral considerations could not control their predatory ambitions.

SUMMARY

Recent studies of early modern Europe seem to suggest that the social and intellectual aspects of Europe's development at this time are the most important. This may be a matter of corrective emphasis: earlier historians were largely uninterested in or ignorant of social and intellectual processes. While conceding the importance particularly of the scientific revolution of the seventeenth century, we have argued in this book that the political, military and economic evolution of western society must be given a primary place in any consideration of the influence of this era upon our present world.

The political evolution of Europe between the sixteenth and the eighteenth century has two important themes. The first is the rise of the bureaucratic, military police state. Whereas in the sixteenth century one ruler after another had to give up his projects because his government could not finance them; by the eighteenth century, while still not "absolute" in power, rulers could command the obedience and levy the taxes to support an army, navy, and bureaucratic personnel to supervise them and to administer a powerful government; thus this was an age of extensive wars, elaborate projects for economic benefits, and expensive palaces.

Another consequence of the bureaucratic and military state was that western armies and navies developed weapons that gave them a great advantage over other societies on the globe, preparing the way for European domination of much of the world.

The second aspect of the political evolution of early modern Europe was the creation, by the coalitions of the wars of the seventeenth century, of a system of international relations which acted as a government for the entire European community by the balance of power. No other form of government was possible since each of the states that emerged as sovereign preferred the military coercion of its neighbors to a law governing all. This European system of government spread as European domination spread; even today the United Nations can govern the world society only when a balance of power between the great states permits it.

A perhaps necessary concomitant to these political developments was the rise of western European capitalist economy. In the economic patterns of every society we find tension between the desires of individuals for freedom to follow their selfish interests and the demands of society for controls to organize economic life for the benefit of the larger community. Rigid control usually stifles changes in economic institutions while individual freedom leads to exploitation, greed, and even robbery. West European men managed to relax some of the controls that guilds, corporations, and royal governments placed upon individual initiative; this allowed the development of a commercial capitalism that could exploit the new markets of the world, making use of the maritime technology that built great ships and powered them effectively with huge sails. Toward the end of the period that we are writing about, the development of machines and new power greatly stimulated the growth of industrial capitalism. These economic developments were fundamental to the rise of European political and military power.

The rise of a new method for explaining the phenomena of nature was more than showing that, contrary to all common sense, the earth swings around the sun, or that the earth describes an ellipse rather than a circle in its rotation, or even that the entire system of planets and suns is held together by the mysterious force of gravity. More than any one discovery was the development of the scientific methods for establishing "truth." The question "How do you know?" has always been a most important one, but western Europeans were the first to establish a method of "knowing" that is self-correcting. Perhaps nothing in the intellectual history of man has had more influence upon the world we live in than the scientific revolution of the seventeenth century.

There are other factors in the history of these three hundred years that influence our era: the reformations of the church and the subsequent fragmentation of religious authority; the recovery and definitive editing of texts from the classical world, texts dealing with everything from moral behavior to the art of war; Baroque art, and the classical age of music.

No one will deny that the great revolutions in France and Russia are important for the modern world; but these revolutions did not create the modern world out of nothing; nor are they the sole influences in the present processes of our history. Early modern Europe forged political, economic, and intellectual processes that, for good or bad, shaped the nineteenth century, and still shape the twentieth.

SUGGESTED READING

M. S. Anderson, *The Eighteenth Century, 1715–1789* (1966) and R. J. White, *Europe in the Eighteenth Century* (1965) are good introductions. They can be compared with Max Beloff, *The Age of Absolutism* (1962). There are three volumes in the *Rise of Modern Europe* series: Penfield Roberts, *In Quest of Security, 1715–1740* (1963), Walter Dorn, *Competition for Empire 1740–1763* (1963) and Leo Gershoy, *From Despotism to Revolution 1763–1789* (1963). C. B. Behrens, *The Ancien Regime* (1967) and Albert Sorel, *Europe under the Old Regime* (1962), are still both useful books. There are several specialized studies: Franklin Ford, *The Robe and the Sword* (1953), R. R. Palmer, *Catholics and Unbelievers in Eighteenth-Century France* (1963), E. G. Barber, *The Bourgeoisie in Eighteenth Century France* (1955) tell us much about social structures. There are several interesting biographies. G. P. Gooch has written four: *Frederick the Great, Maria Theresa and Other Studies, Catherine the Great and Other Studies,* and *Louis XV* (1940–1956). Unfortunately only two are in paperback: *Maria Theresa* (1951) and *Catherine The Great* (1966). See also S. K. Padover, *The Revolutionary Emperor, Joseph the Second* (1967), G. S. Thompson, *Catherine the Great and the Expansion of Russia* (1962), E. A. Reitan, *George III—Tyrant or Constitutional Monarch?* (1964), and Charles G. Robertson, *Chatham and the British Empire* (1962).

HERMANN-MAURICE VON SAXE (1696–1750)

Hermann-Maurice was one of many illegitimate children of August II (the Strong) of Saxony-Poland. Even though his beautiful mother, Countess Aurora von Koenigsmark, did see that he was recognized and given opportunities to make his way in the world, a bastard son had to struggle to achieve place and fortune. Like many another young nobleman born in this era of conflict, he understood that a military career had more promise than any other. At twelve he was with Eugene's army besieging Tournay; the next year he was at Malplaquet (1709). Eugene had to admonish him with the remark that there was a difference between rashness and valor. In 1711 he joined his father in the war against the Swedes and was present at the siege of Stralsund. August II gave him a command and made him a count. In 1716 he fought in a Polish civil war; the next year he was with Eugene again in the Balkans. In 1719 he found himself in Paris studying mathematics and fortifications, and in 1720 the regent gave him a commission in the French army as *Maréchal de camp* (approximately equivalent to the rank of colonel). He was only twenty-four years old, but already he was a veteran of wars in all parts of Europe and a soldier with an established reputation.

His private life was turbulent. His mother arranged a marriage with a fabulously rich heiress (1714); two years later, he left her in Dresden because he could not put up with her objections to his infidelities. Like his father, Hermann-Maurice, a physically powerful man, was harassed by a voracious sexual appetite, and since he was handsome and personable, he encountered no difficulty satisfying it. In 1726 he was elected duke of Courland, but when he refused to marry Anna Ivanovna (niece of Peter the Great), he lost both his dukedom and the opportunity to mount the throne of Russia a few years later. Apparently these exploits did not interfere with his studies, for during these same years he became a competent military engineer and a knowledgeable tactician. He spent much time in the war ministry's archives studying the problems of logistics encountered in warfare in the Netherlands. His book on the art of war, *Mes Rêveries,* is a classic statement of the military problems of the period.

In 1734 he served brilliantly under Marshal Berwick (bastard son of James II), and Louis XV gave him a commission of lieutenant general. We next hear of his exploits in the opening years of the war over the Austrian succession. His capture of Prague (1741) and siege of Eger (1742) were the only bright spots in the record of the French army during those years. In 1743 he became Marshal of France in command of the armies in the Netherlands. It was there that he proved himself to be one of the great captains of the era. He was usually outnumbered by his enemies, but in battle after battle his sure touch gave him the advantage. By 1747–1748, he controlled the Netherlands for his king. It was his victories (Raucoux, 1746; Lawfeldt, 1747; and the successful capture of important fortresses) that created the myth that American and Indian colonies were won or lost on the battlefields of Flanders.

When peace came in 1748, Louis XV showed his gratitude to the soldier who could force his foes to return lost colonies in exchange for the Netherlands by giving him the chateau of Chambord for a life tenure. With the chateau he also included a cavalry squadron to guard and amuse the famous general. Today, visitors to Chambord see, in addition to the splendors of Francis I's palace, the

German-built porcelain stove and the cavalry barracks added to the chateau by its Saxon-born owner. Marshal Saxe died at fifty-four, physically worn out despite his great strength and vigorous constitution. He left several illegitimate children; one of the girls was the great-grandmother of George Sand. ■

WILLIAM PITT THE ELDER (1708–1778)

William Pitt was born to a family long associated with colonial administration and trade. His grandfather, Thomas Pitt, had been a merchant in India and Persia, an official in the British India Company, and a member of the House of Commons. Young William was educated at Eton and Oxford, made the grand tour of Europe, and then was elected to the House of Commons from a "rotten borough" (1735). He soon distinguished himself as one of the young patriots as well as a vigorous, if not always wise, critic of Walpole's government. His maiden speech managed to irritate the king so much that the monarch deprived Pitt of a commission in the cavalry which Pitt's family had purchased for him. After this debut, he spoke rarely, but when he did, it was as a critic, never as a supporter of the government. By the time Walpole's cabinet fell (1742), Pitt was known for his dislike of any policy that favored Hanover over England and for his espousal of the expanding colonial interests of the kingdom. When Newcastle came to power, Pitt became an official in the government of Ireland (1746) in spite of the king's objections to him. But when his rival, Henry Fox, became secretary of state under Grenville in 1755, Pitt was dismissed. He immediately became a critic of the regime that was miserably failing to support imperial interests in the opening days of the Seven Years' War. His attacks forced the resignation of the ministry, and despite the attitude of the king, Pitt came to power. England's fortunes were at a low ebb. The Anglo-Hanoverian army in Germany had disgraced the nation by its failure to support Frederick II. Thus England's position in the world was in hazard. At home, distrust of, and dissatisfaction with, the government was rampant.

Pitt was a man of action. He revitalized the fleet, reorganized the army, re-established credit. It was his efforts that saved Frederick the Great from destruction, for English money kept the Prussian army in the field. Frederick recognized his debt with the remark: "England has been a long time in labor and she has suffered much to produce Mister Pitt, but finally she has given birth to a man." Characteristically, Pitt placed his greatest emphasis upon the war beyond Europe, where he knew that England's destiny as a trading power must be found. In India, he supported Clive who drove out the French; he sent Wolfe to take Quebec; he ousted the French from the islands in the Caribbean. His money saved Frederick's Prussia from destruction and thereby determined much of the subsequent history of central Europe. Finally, as a result of his greatest efforts, English trade actually increased during wartime. Thus Pitt laid firm foundations for the first British empire. Pitt's plan was to bring Spain into the conflict and thus add much of Spanish America to England's empire, but the death of George II brought George III to the throne, and with him a Tory ministry anxious to end the war as quickly as possible. After his dismissal in 1761, Pitt contented himself with mere criticisms of the treaties of peace rather than vigorous opposition to George III's new government.

This moderation, in addition to recognition of his past services, led the king to elevate him to the peerage as Earl of Chatham and to invite him in 1766 to form a new government. When its composition was revealed, the nation was shocked. Pitt had chosen a collection of nonentities from all parties to help him govern England, and he proceeded to treat them as his creatures, imposing his will tyrannically upon all of them. In a short time, a pamphlet campaign denounced him vigorously: He had betrayed his role as "the Great Commoner" by accepting a title; he was a tyrant and a traitor. Since his new friends did not like him either, Pitt's second ministry ended in 1768. He remained in the House of Lords as a figure particularly critical of the regime when Lord North's tax policies provoked stiff opposition in the American colonies. "If you persist in your efforts to tax the Americans," he said, "a foreign war hangs over your heads suspended only by a thread." A few years later (1778), he had an attack of apoplexy during a speech in the House of Lords in which he was deploring the way the war was being fought in America. He died a few weeks later, and Parliament voted him a public funeral and a monument in Westminster. It also paid his debts. This imposing man with sharp eyes, an aquiline nose, and an acid tongue was one of the most important architects of England's eighteenth-century greatness. ■

INDEX